Eastern Africa Series

SPORTS AND MODERNITY IN
LATE IMPERIAL ETHIOPIA

Sports and Modernity in Late Imperial Ethiopia

KATRIN BROMBER

James Currey
is an imprint of
Boydell & Brewer Ltd
PO Box 9, Woodbridge
Suffolk IP12 3DF (GB)
www.jamescurrey.com
and of
Boydell & Brewer Inc.
668 Mt Hope Avenue, Rochester,
NY 14620-2731 (US)
www.boydellandbrewer.com

© Katrin Bromber 2022

The right of Katrin Bromber to be identified as
the author of this work has been asserted in accordance with
sections 77 and 78 of the Copyright, Designs and Patents Act 1988

All Rights Reserved. Except as permitted under current legislation
no part of this work may be photocopied, stored in a retrieval
system, published, performed in public, adapted, broadcast,
transmitted, recorded or reproduced in any form or by any means,
without the prior permission of the copyright owner

First published 2022
Paperback edition 2024

ISBN 978-1-84701-292-0 (James Currey hardback)
ISBN 978-1-84701-375-0 (James Currey paperback)

The publisher has no responsibility for the continued existence or
accuracy of URLs for external or third-party internet websites referred to in this
book, and does not guarantee that any content on such websites is,
or will remain, accurate or appropriate

British Library Cataloguing in Publication Data
A catalogue record for this book is available from the British Library

For Seyoum Mulugeta

Contents

List of Illustrations viii

Preface and Acknowledgements ix

List of Abbreviations xiii

Notes on Transliteration, Titles, Currency, and the Ethiopian Calendar xv

Introduction 1

1. The Emergence of Ethiopia's Modern Sports Scene (1900–1935) 35

2. Sports and Propaganda during the Fascist Occupation (1935–1941) 58

3. Muscular Reconstruction: Urban Leisure, Institutionalized Physical Education, and the Re-establishment of Boy Scouting (1940s–1960s) 89

4. Training Leaders and Athletes: The Ethiopian YMCA (1940s–1970s) 118

5. Sports' Material Infrastructure and the Production of Space (1910s–1970s) 154

6. Conclusion and Outlook 179

Bibliography 189

Index 213

Illustrations

1. Swimming pool at Haile Selassie I Secondary School	100
2. Table tennis at YMCA	123
3. Norris Lineweaver at YMCA Sahle Selassie Camp	144
4. Freestyle wrestling at the YMCA	150
5. Onni Niskanen and Per-Arne Thyberg at the Ethiopian Highland Rally, 1966	172

Full credit details are provided in the captions to the images in the text. The author and publisher are grateful to all the institutions and individuals for permission to reproduce the materials to which they hold copyright. Every effort has been made to trace the copyright holders; apologies are offered for any omission, and the publisher will be pleased to add any necessary acknowledgement in subsequent editions.

Preface and Acknowledgements

I began my research in summer 2009 with the aim of learning more about long-distance running and its historical development. However, the more I ventured into the history of sports in Ethiopia, the more it became obvious that running is only one of numerous athletic practices. I soon decided to bring this wealth of different sports to centre stage. For too long, the powerful global sports media complex has narrowed our perception of Ethiopian sports to the successful long-distance runners. Yet simply leafing through the sports pages of the *Ethiopian Herald* of the 1990s, I discovered a whole range of successful athletes in boxing, table tennis, and basketball as well as the formulation of a sports-for-all policy.

Going back to the 1980s brought my attention to a predecessor of this mass sports policy, the *Spartakiade*, modelled after such tournaments in socialist countries, as well as the systematic training of athletes and coaches in places such as Havana, Bratislava, Kiev, and Warsaw. At the Deutsche Hochschule für Körperkultur und Sport (German University for Sports and Physical Culture, DHfK) in Leipzig (German Democratic Republic), Ethiopian sports officials were trained to systematically identify sporting talent through the *Spartakiade* system. Beyond the identification of talent, the competitions and related programmes served to instil ideas about the 'fit citizen' into the minds of the athletes and, I would argue, society as a whole. However, citizenship training through sports was not particularly socialist, but an integral part of discourses and practices that served to mould the modern subject in very different social and geographical contexts: Western, colonial, post-colonial, working class, and bourgeois, to name but a few. I decided to go further back into twentieth-century history – into what I call the 'late imperial period' (c. 1920s–70s).

In this book, I look at the well-researched period under *Ras* Tafari, after his coronation *Ats'ē* Haile Selassie I, when existing reform processes in administration, education, and the military gained momentum. These changes, which responded to global developments, went hand in hand with early ideas about what a modern subject could mean in the Ethiopian context. From the perspective of sports, I inquire into the role of new athletic practices in its various forms, i.e. as leisure, as marker of a modern lifestyle, as propaganda tool, or as a way to mould youth into 'torchbearers of progress'. What kinds of sports were deemed suitable for whom and by whom? Which institutions at home and from abroad became involved in developing a modern sports scene? How did sports shape urban developments and vice versa? Did sports serve as a legitimation of power?

Thus, rather than looking at particular kinds of sports and their development over time, I chose to situate my research in the wider frame of social history. I thus link my book to relevant conceptual debates around sports, (Ethiopian) modernity, subject formation, and leisure (in Africa and the Middle East). In five chapters that cover a period from roughly the 1920s to the 1970s, I offer a chronology with changing perspectives that broadly revolve around issues of physical education (PE), sports in volunteer organizations, sports and propaganda, leisure and muscular entertainment, the materiality of sports in spaces, and the construction of national territory through, for example, motor racing or hiking.

This book is a typical product of academic work that emerged in conversation. In this case, this was with academics, former athletes, sports officials, and so many other people who opened my eyes to aspects that I would otherwise have not seen. There are too many to mention them all. When I first came to Ethiopia in June 2009, Mulugeta Hagos received me at the Department of Sport Studies, Addis Ababa University (AAU). I am grateful that you opened many doors and advised me on whom to approach in order to start my research. Amongst the people whom I met at the department, I would like to thank in particular Bezabih Wolde, who actively shared his knowledge with me. Yemane Gossaye Borena introduced me to Kotebe College, one of the most important PE teachers' training sites in Ethiopia. He facilitated access to the Sports Department of the Ministry of Education and openly shared documents on the history of sports teachers' education. Thank you so much for doing so. The numerous conversations with Shiferaw Agonafir helped me to understand the development of PE at schools and institutions of higher learning as well as the training of PE teachers. You were an important part of it. Edlawit Hirpa, Emnet Woubishet, and Tibebu Gorfu helped me to gather many details about stadium development in Addis Ababa. The same holds true for Abraham Tewelde, who introduced me to the history of Baloni Stadium in Mek'ele. Wolbert Smidt and Mel'aku Kidane facilitated my work on local wrestling practices in the rural areas around Mek'ele and shared their valuable insights into the historical development of the region. I warmly thank you for this and for your friendship. Ryan Bean, the enthusiastic archivist at the Kautz Family YMCA Archives (Minneapolis), greatly supported me in my work on the YMCA. The same is true for Norris Lineweaver, who shared his valuable memories about his time at the Addis Ababa YMCA in the 1960s. I am indebted to Bahru Zewde for his advice and comments on parts of this book. Fits'um Woldemariam Deginetu supported my archival work at the Institute of Ethiopian Studies (Addis Ababa University). Apart from helping me to research the sports news in the Amharic newspaper *Addīs Zemen*, he found every 'missing' journal or pamphlet, even during power cuts.

In the course of my research, I developed an intensive collaboration with Hanna Rubinkowska-Anioł and Ewa Sore-Work from the Department of African Languages and Cultures at the University of Warsaw. Working on the same period, Hanna and I thought intensively about Ethiopia's 'New Men' during Haile Selassie's rule. I am more than grateful for this. Hanna commented on chapters and provided me with source material from her institute's library. Ewa carefully checked the Amharic transliteration in the book manuscript. Thank you so much for doing this. I am very grateful to Peter Garretson and Matthew Carotenuto for their very valuable comments and suggestions.

This publication would never have seen the light of day without the institutional backing of the Leibniz-Zentrum Moderner Orient (ZMO, Berlin) and the generous financial support of the Bundesministerium für Bildung und Forschung (Federal Ministry of Education and Research) and the Leibniz Association. I am especially grateful to the director of ZMO, Ulrike Freitag, for her encouragement and support. Amongst the many colleagues who have commented on chapter drafts, special thanks go to Birgit Krawietz (Freie Universität Berlin) and the members of the ZMO research unit Progress: Ideas, Agents, and Symbols (2014–19) – Paolo Gaibazzi, Kyara Klausmann, Jakob Krais, Izabela Orlowska, Franziska Roy, Julian Tadesse, and Abdoulaye Sounaye. I am grateful to Rakiya El Matine and Svenja Becherer, who shared the workload of editing the manuscript with me, and to Andrew Tarrant for proofreading the English text.

Apart from the institutional and academic backing, I benefited greatly from my exceptional personal environment at home and abroad. First, I thank my husband, Markus Schraid, for his unconditional support. He and my daughters, Marie and Lena, never questioned that long absences from home are a vital part of my work. Thank you for your love and understanding. In Ethiopia, Constanze Prehl, Giuliano Cicoria, and Sigun and Werner Pohl warmly welcomed me into their families. I thank you so much for your friendship.

Conducting research on Ethiopia and especially its history is impossible without knowing Amharic. My highly esteemed teacher, Seyoum Mulugeta, took on the burden of introducing me to this language and, later, helped me translate the hundreds of documents and newspaper articles that form the major part of this book. Since Ato Seyoum belongs to the generation that is the focus of this publication, he also shared his memories and gave numerous detailed explanations. In long teaching hours and conversations, we developed a friendship and a deep appreciation for each other. Being more than grateful for this extraordinary experience, I dedicate this book to him.

Abbreviations

AA	Auswärtiges Amt
BMME	British Military Mission to Ethiopia
DHfK	Deutsche Hochschule für Sport und Körperkultur (German University for Sports and Physical Culture)
EC	Ethiopian Calendar
EISAA	Ethiopian Inter-School Athletic Association
ENA	Ethiopian National Archives (in footnotes)
FIFA	Fédération Internationale de Football Association
HSIU	Haile Selassie I University
IES	Institute of Ethiopian Studies
JATS	Jimma Agricultural Technical School
KCTE	Kotebe College of Teacher Education
KFYA	Kautz Family YMCA Archives
MoE	Ministry of Education and Fine Arts
PE	Physical Education
RNT TWU	Robert N. Thompson Collection, Trinity Western University, Canada
SOAS	School of Oriental and African Studies
UCAA	University College of Addis Ababa
UK	United Kingdom
UN	United Nations
UNESCO	United Nations Educational, Scientific and Cultural Organization
UNICEF	United Nations International Children's Emergency Fund

US	United States of America
USAID	United States Agency for International Development
YB	Year Book
YMCA	Young Men's Christian Association
YWCA	Young Women's Christian Association

Notes on Transliteration, Titles, Currency, and the Ethiopian Calendar

Ethiopia is a country with its own writing system, known for millennia, used for all the Semitic languages spoken within its territory, such as Amharic and Tigrinya. However, Ethiopic script transliteration remains a challenging issue. There is no single system best suited for all languages. Instead, each language has its own system for transliterating Ethiopian terms. Most appropriate for the English language is the BGN/PCGN 1967 System designed for use in Romanizing names written in the Ethiopic script approved jointly by the US Board on Geographic Names (BGN) as well as the Permanent Committee on Geographic Names (PCGN) for British Official Use. For this reason, all the geographical and proper names in this work transliterated directly from Amharic have been transliterated using this system. Nevertheless, Ethiopians and foreigners alike have been using various systems, which for years mixed and intertwined. Hence, some of the geographical terms and proper names have their own established forms that have not been changed in this work, including Addis Ababa, Haile Selassie, etc. Furthermore, works in Amharic mentioned by other authors are left in the form they are cited. Important to mention is the question of gemination – doubling of consonants – present in Amharic but not evident in its written form. In this work, it is marked only in some essential instances. The following honorary titles occur in the book: *Ats'ē* [king, emperor], *Le'ul Lij* [prince], *Ras* [head], the highest politico-military title below King, and *Dejazmach* [commander of the gate], the highest military title.

The currency of Ethiopia is Birr (1 Birr=100 santeem) but also known as the dollar. It was introduced in the early twentieth century. During the Italian occupation (1935–41) the currency was the Lira. In 1945, the Birr was re-introduced. The name Ethiopian dollar appeared on bank notes and in official correspondences. In the 1960s, 1 Eth$ equalled US$ 0.40. The Ethiopian calendar is a solar calendar that greatly differs from the Gregorian. It is seven to eight years 'later', depending on whether the actual date is before or after 1 January in the Gregorian calendar. The New Year (first meskerem) starts on 11 or 12 September. The Ethiopian calendar has twelve months of thirty days and a thirteenth month of five to six epagomenal days. In this book, date references in the Ethiopian calendar are marked with EC and accompanied by their Gregorian equivalent. In newspaper and journal articles, the Gregorian equivalent follows in brackets.

Introduction

'From now on, We give permission to all those who have a natural talent, to prepare, since We intend that Ethiopia should participate in world sports and athletic organizations.'[1]

When *Ats'ē* Haile Selassie I declared his ambitious aim in 1947, Ethiopia had already entered the world of modern sports. Physical education was about to have its own department within the Ministry of Education and Fine Arts (further referred to as Ministry of Education or MoE), which promoted school sports through inter-school competitions. Football was not only the most popular game amongst the male (urban) population, but an Ethiopian Football Federation had already organized a league. Ethiopia had founded its National Olympic Committee, officially recognized in 1954, and planned its participation in the world's most important sports event.[2] Thus, Ethiopia belonged to the first countries in sub-Saharan Africa to make the continent visible on the global athletic scene. In contrast to African athletes from colonial contexts, who represented Britain, France, or Portugal at major sporting events,[3] Ethiopians competed for Ethiopia.

With a few exceptions,[4] existing scholarship on modern sports in Ethiopia has focused on the present, narrowing the lens to long-

---

[1] Haile Selassie, Ye-Girmawī Niguse Negest K'edamawī Hayle Sillasēn yeliyu liyu ch'ewatawoch malaya (stadiyem) yemeseret dingay līyanoru yetenagerut k'al [Speech by His Majesty Emperor Haile Selassie on the occasion of laying the foundation stone at the place (Stadium), where various games will be shown], *Addīs Zemen*, 28 t'ik'imt 1940, 3 [8 November 1947].
[2] Founded in 1948, the Ethiopian Olympic Committee was officially recognized in 1954. It participated for the first time in the Olympic Summer Games in Melbourne (1956).
[3] Michelle Sikes, 'Sport History and Historiography', *Oxford Research Encyclopedia of African History* (2018), DOI: 10.1093/acrefore/9780190277734.013.232, p. 9.
[4] Tamirat Gebremariam and Benoît Gaudin, 'Sports and Physical Education in Ethiopia during the Italian Occupation, 1936–41', in Michael J. Gennaro and Saheed Aderinto (eds), *Sports in African History, Politics and Identity Formation* (New York, 2019), pp. 196–205; Bezabih Wolde and Gaudin Benoît, 'The Institutional Organization of Ethiopian Athletics', *Annales d' Ethiopie*, 23 (2007/8),

distance running and football. This largely distorted picture of Ethiopia's sports scene, past and present, ignores the diversity and history of modern athletic practices in the country. Thus, it is time to bring to the fore a much broader variety of disciplines and their social positions. This book specifically asks in which societal context modern sports emerged in Ethiopia. What role did it play in the period that scholarship on Ethiopian history has broadly described as Ethiopian modernity? I argue that sports as an everyday practice developed into a means to shape modern subjectivities, and explore the role of physical education in modern schools and volunteer organizations, especially the Young Men's Christian Association (YMCA) and the scouts movement in Ethiopia. This book shows the importance of sports in urbanization and the production of leisure spaces as part of Ethiopia's aim to transform into a modern empire. What do we see by focusing on the human body as a site where ideas of societal progress are inculcated? How did ideas and practices related to the 'fit Ethiopian' change due to the specific historical circumstances, i.e. the first reforms of the early decades of the twentieth century, the Italian Fascist occupation (1935–41), and the period between the liberation and the removal of the emperor from the throne in 1974? Who were the main drivers behind the introduction of these ideas and practices? What were the intended and unintended consequences of promoting a physical fitness that made Ethiopia part of a global modernity of the twentieth century?

This Introduction situates the book within the conceptual debates to which it contributes. I argue that the perspective on sports as an important mode of subject formation provides a fresh look at the centrality of the human body in Ethiopian modernity. Therefore, I support the shift from an overwhelming focus on intellectual practice to studies of the performance of modernity in changing rituals, dress codes, and representations of the human body in and through modern arts. My study thus connects with Timothy Mitchell's larger argument that modernity is determined by 'the way in which the modern is staged as representation'.[5] Furthermore, sports as a disciplinary tool, mode of self-fashioning, (useful) recreation, and as spectator leisure activity changed ideas

---

471; Katrin Bromber, '"Ethiopian" Wrestling between Sportization of National Heritage and Dynamic Youth Culture', *ITYOPIS: Northeast African Journal of Social Sciences and Humanities*, 2 (2013a), 23–40; Katrin Bromber, 'Muscularity, Heavy Athletics and Urban Leisure in Ethiopia, 1950s–1970s', *The International Journal of the History of Sport*, 30:16 (2013b), 1915–28; Katrin Bromber, 'Improving the Physical Self: Sport, Body Politics, and Ethiopian Modernity, ca. 1920–1974', *Northeast African Studies*, 13:1 (2013c), 71–99; Katrin Bromber, 'The Stadium and the City: Sports Infrastructure in Late Imperial Ethiopia and Beyond', *Cadernos de Estudos Africanos*, 32:1 (2017), 53–72.
5   Timothy Mitchell, 'The Stage of Modernity', in Timothy Mitchell (ed.), *Questions of Modernity: Contradictions of Modernity*, vol. 11 (Minneapolis, 2000), p. 16.

about and practices for constructing a healthy national body by moulding what I refer to as Ethiopia's 'New Men', that is, those who would be most involved in projects of progress. Despite the attempt to remain in control through patronage, sponsorship, and symbolic power, the individuals and institutions I look at varied or even thwarted ideas of Haile Selassie's healthy, educated, and loyal subjects. Thus, the study of athletic practices, the institutions that promoted sports, and the sports-related places and facilities in the urban landscape makes it possible to probe the argument that modernization under Haile Selassie was not superficial, but went deeper.

Starting from the assumption that modernity was global and that coloniality was an integral part of that modernity,[6] I argue for discussing sports in Ethiopia within existing academic debates on sports and leisure in Africa, the Middle East, and beyond. Especially in the first half of the twentieth century, long-standing connections to the Middle East and North Africa led to a self-perception as well as an external contextualization of the empire as Middle Eastern. Haggai Erlich's substantial work on the history of Ethiopia's relations to the Middle East, Egypt, and Saudi Arabia provides substantial evidence in this respect.[7] In the early 1960s, reports of the Israel Oriental Society still listed Ethiopia amongst the 'Non-Arab Countries in the Middle East', together with Turkey, Cyprus, and Iran.[8] This happened when Egyptian and Ethiopian football officials, who represented two nations of antagonistic camps within Cold War political order, competed for the establishment of the Confédération africaine de football headquarters in Cairo or Addis Ababa.[9] At the same time, the location of an all-African YMCA training centre in Addis Ababa was rejected by the North American International Committee with the argument that Ethiopia was not 'sufficiently African'.[10]

These, very practical examples echo African studies and 'orientalist' scholarship that describes Ethiopia as a 'paradox'; i.e. located in

---

[6] Here I follow Elizabeth Wolde Giorgis' argumentation for Ethiopia, which she based on Walter Mignolo's works. Elizabeth Wolde Giorgis, *Modernist Art in Ethiopia* (Athens OH, 2019).

[7] Haggai Erlich, *Ethiopia and the Middle East* (Boulder, London, 1994); Haggai Erlich, *The Cross and the River: Ethiopia, Egypt, and the Nile* (Boulder, Denver, London, 2002); Haggai Erlich, *Saudi Arabia and Ethiopia: Islam, Christianity and Politics Entwined* (Boulder, London, 2007).

[8] See for example Yitzhak Oron (ed.), *Middle East Record,* 1:1, for The Israel Oriental Society, Jerusalem (London, 1960), 306–7.

[9] Peter Alegi, *African Soccerscapes: How a Continent Changed the World's Game* (London, 2010), p. 66. Whereas Egypt under Gamal Abdel Nasser became the main figure of Pan-Arab socialism, Haile Selassie was an anti-communist.

[10] Joel Nystrom to Marvin Ludwig, 3 April 1963, KFYA, Y.USA.9-2-37, YMCA International Work in Ethiopia Box 6, correspondence 1963.

Africa but not Africa.[11] The whole discussion completely disregards with the multi-relatedness of Ethiopia to the Middle East, to Africa, and to diverse global networks during the historical period discussed in this book. Looking at material from early physical education and Boy Scouting, for example, establishes evidence for a strong connection to the Middle East, i.e. Egypt and Lebanon. With the re-establishment of the Boy Scout Association of Ethiopia in the late 1940s, not only do we see a growing North American influence but also the integration of the Ethiopian movement into East African structures which were managed by the regional headquarters in Nairobi. Thus, any meaningful discussion on sports and modernity in late imperial Ethiopia has to account for these shifts by including relevant studies on the Middle East, existing scholarship on sports in Africa as well as research on global networks such as America's 'moral empire',[12] e.g. the YMCA. Together they provide valuable insights into the extent to which modern sports in late imperial Ethiopia provides a lens through which to study urban life, the control of time, space, and bodies, modes of resistance, and practices of inclusion and exclusion.

Conceptualizing Social Transformation

Ethiopian Modernity

In his seminal essay on 'Modernity', Frederick Cooper critically discussed the value of the term as a conceptual category. He argued that neither approaches that centre on modernity's singularity with European roots, nor the use of the term in the plural, help much in terms of conceptual clarity. Instead, he invites us to pay closer attention to who uses the term, in what way, and for what ends.[13] For the Ethiopian context, I have looked into the term's use in two arenas. First, the way in which academic scholarship has applied the term 'modernity' and discussed its value for nineteenth- and twentieth-century developments in Ethiopia. Second, I consider the usage of the term within the period under research; an approach that involves a methodological problem. The available sources often cover only the voices and ideas of a few, mostly elitist authors, and say little about any wider under-

---

[11] For a reflection on the debate see, Jon D. Carlson, 'Ethiopia and the Middle East: The Red Sea Trade, Prester John, and Christians in the Muslim World', in Jon D. Carlson (ed.), *Myths, State Expansion, and the Birth of Globalization* (New York, 2012), pp. 115–43.

[12] With America's 'moral Empire' I refer to Ian Tyrrel's seminal work *Reforming the World: The Creation of America's Moral Empire* (Princeton NJ, 2010).

[13] Frederick Cooper, 'Modernity', in Frederick Cooper (ed.), *Colonialism in Question: Theory, Knowledge, History* (Berkeley, Los Angeles, London, 2005), p. 115.

standing of the term or the ideas related to it. In order to tackle this problem up-front, the art historian Elizabeth Wolde Giorgis rightly argues in her analysis of the discourse on modernity in the Amharic journal *Berhanena Selam* that intellectuals 'embraced the anxieties and resentments of the watching public to domesticate it' to wider narratives about modernity and the modernizing projects associated with it.[14] Such an approach not only emphasizes the dialogic nature of knowledge production, but also gives true relevance to the agency of Ethiopians beyond elite circles.

Scholarly Debates on Zemenawīnet

How has scholarship discussed Ethiopian modernity? As an historical period, Ethiopian modernity was broadly conceived as a teleological process of stages, ranging largely from the second half of the nineteenth century to the mid-1970s. This is most obvious in Tibebu Teshale's work on Ethiopian modernity, which described *Ats'ē* Tewodros II (1818–68) as the 'initiator', *Ats'ē* Yohannes IV (1837–89) as 'elaborator', and *Ats'ē* Menelik II (1844–1913) as the 'consolidator' in a state-building process that was successfully completed by *Ras* Tafari, later *Ats'ē* Haile Selassie I (1892–1975), with a centralized sovereign state.[15] The focus lies on the formative decades between 1916 and 1974. Tibebu thus situates Ethiopian modernity within a grand narrative of an uninterrupted past, which critical scholarship has questioned from various angles such as art history, literature, and philosophy over the past four decades.

As early as 1984, the historian Bahru Zewde criticised most of his colleagues for using the unclear yet loaded term 'modern' or its derivatives 'modernity' and 'modernization' for this period without defining them.[16] He further argued that what had been labelled as 'modern' was in fact absolutist. The various reforms under the last emperor, including modern institutions, schools, and media all aimed at executing better control, strengthening and legitimizing Haile Selassie's power without changing the principals of the state. Haile Selassie saw himself as an absolutist monarch and a gift from God, and modernity became part of an imperial ideology. On the thirty-first anniversary of his coronation, he explicitly claimed his active role by stating that he was the one who 'turned Ethiopia's face in the direction of progress and modernity'.[17] Looking at Ethiopian modernity from the perspec-

---

[14] Elizabeth Wolde Giorgis, *Modernist Art in Ethiopia*, p. 55.
[15] Tibebu Teshale, *The Making of Modern Ethiopia: 1896–1974* (Trenton NJ, 1995), p. 31.
[16] Bahru Zewde, 'Economic Origins of the Absolutist State in Ethiopia (1916–1935)', in Bahru Zewde (ed.), *Society, State and History: Selected Essays* (Addis Ababa, 2008), p. 98.
[17] Haile Selassie, 'Modern Ethiopianism, 2 November 1961', in The Impe-

tive of the state-cum-monarchy, it was nothing radically new. Rather, modernity relocates established ideological models within the *telos* of Western modernization.[18]

The modernizing vanguard, intellectuals and others, received the appropriate training in a centralized educational system in Ethiopia or abroad. Instead of describing these measures as a deliberately planned process, historians foreground the role of Ethiopians and non-Ethiopians who generated important debates about the meaning and practice of modernization before and after the Italian Fascist occupation.[19] Their understanding of Ethiopian modernity links up to African scholarship that described modernity as a non-linear, variation-centred process of social transformation with multiple centres that includes a multitude of agents with converging, co-existing, or contradicting ideas, ambitions, and resources of power.[20]

Modernity in Ethiopia, as discourse and practice, rests – as Sara Marzagora argues – on a 'Grand Narrative' or 'Great Tradition'[21] of an uninterrupted history that had changed by the late nineteenth century in response to global processes of nation-state building. It 'incorporated a new territorial kind of identity, a new configuration of the relationships between national core and national periphery, a new epic of national independence and a new teleology of state-driven modernisation'.[22] In her study of the first three generations of twentieth-century intellectuals, Sara Marzagora investigates their writings in Amharic with regard to a local concept of modernity – *zemenawīnet*.[23] Instead of Western categories, it builds a theoretical framework based on Amharic terminology, most notably *limat* (growth, development) and *keshefa* (failure). Marzagora identified four specific meanings of *zemenawīnet*.

---

rial Ethiopian Ministry of Information (ed.), *Selected Speeches of His Imperial Majesty Haile Selassie First, 1918 to 1967* (Addis Ababa, 1967), p. 458.
[18] Sara Marzagora, 'Alterity, Coloniality and Modernity in Ethiopian Political Thought: The First Three Generations of 20th Century Amharic-Language Intellectuals' (Unpublished Ph.D. dissertation, SOAS, University of London, 2016), p. 109.
[19] Especially see, Messay Kebede, *Survival and Modernization: Ethiopia's Enigmatic Present* (Trenton NJ, 1999); Bahru Zewde, *Pioneers of Change in Ethiopia: The Reformist Intellectuals of the Early Twentieth Century* (Oxford, 2002); Marzagora, 'Alterity, Coloniality and Modernity'.
[20] James Ferguson, 'Global Disconnect: Abjection and the Aftermath of Modernism', in Peter Geschiere, Birgit Meyer, and Peter Pels (eds), *Readings in Modernity in Africa* (Oxford, 2008), pp. 8–16.
[21] Sara Marzagora, 'History in Twentieth-Century Ethiopia: The "Great Tradition" and the Counter-Histories of National Failure', *Journal of African History*, 58:3 (2017), 425–44.
[22] Marzagora, 'Alterity, Coloniality and Modernity', pp. 77–8.
[23] *Zemenawīnet* is a clipped compound of *zemenawī* (modern, up-to date, contemporary) and the abstract suffix *-net* (-ism).

First, its association with political and administrative institutions, such as modern administration, currency, the banking system, as well as borders, treaties, and diplomatic relations that established Ethiopia as a sovereign state on an international level.[24] Second, it meant the acquisition of modern technological developments in the industrial sector, infrastructure, medical, and military sectors, without losing the country's cultural and religious specificities.[25] The third meaning concerns the required knowledge necessary to bring about development (*limat*). Primarily framed in a utilitarian sense, it distinguished between the kinds of knowledge useful for development, which was scientifically grounded, and those kinds of knowledge that were not scientific enough to serve development. Thus, politicians often criticised knowledge in a general sense as being useless for progress.[26]

In contrast to the positive attitude surrounding *zemenawīnet*'s first three meanings, the fourth, which concerned modern lifestyles, aroused much debate. On the one hand, these lifestyles included the knowledge of Western languages and cultures acquired through travel for educational purposes. On the other hand, these modern lifestyles were associated with the flipside of modernity, pointing at (what was considered as) immoral behaviour, the waste of resources, and degenerative trends in society. Highly gendered accusations portrayed modern women as sinners and modern men as disoriented. The city was the place where one could both observe and live. Thus, *zemenawīnet* also meant *ketemawīnet* (urban-ness).[27] This holds true for the topic of this book. Urban areas are the ideal site to exhibit one's individually fit body dressed in modern clothes, one's interest in the consumption of football matches or in becoming an athletic champion. Urban sports and educational infrastructure are areas where the state attempted to manage its population (or at least sections of it) in order to produce a healthy and strong national body. The city with its avenues, open squares, and stadiums provided the stages where sports could potentially serve as a propaganda tool.

The various interpretations of the modern (athletic) body resulted in a broad spectrum of practices navigating a social field shaped by optimistic modernization and socio-political persistence. The unfulfilled expectations and unexpected changes that the road to the future included were at the heart of scholarly multi-disciplinary discussions held in Addis Ababa in 2010/11 that shed fresh light on the study of Ethiopian modernity and modernism. Addressing the question 'What

---

[24] Marzagora, 'Alterity, Coloniality and Modernity', p. 103.
[25] Ibid., pp. 103–4.
[26] Ibid., pp. 104–7.
[27] Ibid., pp. 108–9.

is *Zemenawīnet?*',²⁸ scholars from various fields took seriously Elizabeth Wolde Giorgis's call to meaningfully discuss the inter-related or co-existing social-political and cultural phenomena that include the 'non-modern (mythical)' and the 'modern (objectivist)'.²⁹ In temporal terms, the debate largely shifted the period of Ethiopian modernity – starting with the times of global social optimism in the 1920s and extending to the 1990s. In terms of definition, the philosopher Andreas Eshete argued from a universalist perspective and defined modernity as 'the realization of human freedom' for all human beings at the same time and, thus, a 'a shared destiny, and a shared public culture'.³⁰ Such an approach contrasts sharply with any scholarly argument that would credit Haile Selassie's with having been 'modern'. Despite acknowledging the fact that the 'Pioneers of Change'³¹ had already articulated and advocated ideas of modernity in the first half of the twentieth century and that Ethiopian leaders introduced modern administration, technologies, and educational systems, Andreas Eshete attributes the role of modernity's midwife in Ethiopia to the Ethiopian Student Movement of the 1960s and 1970s. The ambivalence, violence, and despair of these decades paired with the hope, optimism, and demands for a better (socialist) future that permeated society. This combination of factors left significant traces in some of the most important literary productions in Amharic of these years, as Tewodros Gebre has convincingly demonstrated.³²

Modernity's ambivalence also reveals itself in urban development and architecture, especially in the capital Addis Ababa. Recent literature on these issues shows how places with pioneering architectural buildings became signifiers of a modern national space that excluded large parts of the urban population.³³ These material representations testify to the insufficient mediation between modernization as tech-

---

28   Following a lecture series titled 'What is "Zemenawinet"? Perspectives on Ethiopian Modernity' at the University of Addis Ababa in 2010/11, Elizabeth Wolde Giorgis edited the volume, *What is 'Zemenawinet'? Perspectives on Ethiopian Modernity* (Friedrich-Ebert-Stiftung: Addis Ababa, 2013) and the special issue on the same set of problems in *Northeast African Studies* 13:1 (2013).
29   Elizabeth Wolde Giorgis, 'Charting Out Ethiopian Modernity and Modernism', *Callaloo,* 33:1 (2010), 82.
30   Andreas Eshete, 'Modernity: Its Title to Uniqueness and its Advent in Ethiopia', *Northeast African Studies,* 13:1 (2013), 7.
31   Bahru Zewde coined this name for the early modernizers whom he described in his book *Pioneers of Change in Ethiopia: The Reformist Intellectuals of the Early Twentieth Century* (Oxford, 2002).
32   Tewodros Gebre, 'Period, History, and the Literary Art: Historicizing Amharic Novels', *Northeast African Studies,* 13:1 (2013), 19–51.
33   Ayala Levin, 'Haile Selassie's Imperial Modernity: Expatriate Architects and the Shaping of Addis Ababa', *Journal of the Society of Architectural Historians,* 75:4 (December 2016), 449.

nological progress and modernity as socio-political project. More than anything else, they represent the negotiations between Haile Selassie and expatriate architects over the presentation of the capital as a modern Africa/Ethiopia, resting on an uninterrupted continuity with the past. However, a look at the multiple uses of parts of these buildings reveals examples where modernization and modernity meet. The lobby was not only the place to meet business partners or people who were allowed regular access. It was also the venue for table tennis tournaments at weekends and boxing bouts in the evening.[34] Consideration of the use of buildings and open spaces for athletic purposes speaks to the politics of urbanization and ways of inhabiting the city, as well as problems of spatial justice.[35] In terms of architecture and urban development, studies of *zemenawīnet* analyse the production of space on the 'lived', 'perceived', and 'conceived' levels as well as their intersections.[36]

Studies of *zemenawīnet* emphasize the role of gender and, especially, women in shaping modern Ethiopia. This trend of research is not restricted to recent studies on cultural and artistic productions such as theatre, dance, and music,[37] but includes political agency as well. The exceptional role of female agents in the re-establishment of the Ethiopian scouts movement after liberation from Fascist occupation is but one example.[38] Such studies balance the overpowering male narrative and address female experiences with the major socio-political changes in Ethiopian history.[39] A true study of the role of gender should, however, not take the category of 'man' for granted. In her critique of studies on African males, Luise White argues that men were presented as monolithic and

---

[34] I elaborate on spatial issues of modern sports in Chapter 5, *Sports' Material Infrastructure and the Production of Space (1910s–1970s)*.
[35] Bezunesh Tamru and Amina Saïd Chiré, 'Citadinités dans les villes de la Corne de l'Afrique', *Annales d'Èthiopie*, 32 (2018/19), 15.
[36] Here, I refer to Henri Lefebvre's seminal work, *The Production of Space*, trans. Donald Nicholson-Smith (Oxford, 1991) and its application by Shimelis Bonsa, 'The City as Nation: Imagining and Practicing Addis Ababa as a Modern and National Space', *Northeast African Studies*, 13:1 (2013), 167–213.
[37] See for example Aboneh Ashagrie, 'The Role of Women on the Ethiopian Stage', *Journal of African Cultural Studies*, 24:1 (2012), 1–8, and chapter 5 in Grit Köppen, *Performative Künste in Äthiopien: Internationale Kulturbeziehungen und postkoloniale Artikulationen* (Bielefeld, 2017), pp. 101–38.
[38] Girl patrols had been formed in the early 1940s at Princess Zenebe Work School soon after liberation under the leadership of the school's headmistress, Mignon Innes Ford.
[39] Elizabeth Wolde Giorgis, 'The Aureal, the Visual, and Female Agency in the Mušo', *Northeast African Studies*, 13:1 (2013), 101–19; Wendy Laura Belcher, 'Sisters Debating the Jesuits: The Role of African Women in Defeating Portuguese Proto-Colonialism in Seventeenth-Century Abyssinia', *Northeast African Studies*, 13:1 (2013), 121–66.

homogeneous.[40] Instead, they should ask in which contexts specific masculinities are produced, and overlap with or contradict other ideas about and practices to form maleness. Such an approach opens the lens wide in order to understand how powerful ideas such as Muscular Christianity, which was spread in Ethiopia through, for example, the YMCA, the Boy Scout movement, modern educational institutions, and the reformed armed forces, intersected or co-existed with local concepts of masculinity and chivalry.[41] In this respect, the perspective on the human body and its clothing offers new perspectives on how new masculinities and femininities were shaped, experienced, and perceived.[42]

The most important argument that studies of *zemenawīnet* make is a clear articulation and systematic approach to analysing Ethiopian singularity within broader frameworks of uneven and combined development as well as coloniality as an inherent feature of Ethiopian modernity. Ethiopia retained its relatively autonomous status by responding to the colonial expansion of the nineteenth century through the acquisition of vast territories, securing boundaries, and navigating a complex international political terrain. From the mid-twentieth onwards, dynastic centralization under Haile Selassie targeted the formation of an internationally recognized nation-state guided by a divine monarchical ruler. As Fuad Makki has convincingly argued, the attempt to conjoin divine monarchy and nationalism, which rest on mutually exclusive principles of sovereignty, produced the deep socio-economic contradictions that led to the overthrow of the monarchy in 1974.[43]

Studies on modernity and coloniality address the epistemic legacy of globally circulating projects of linear progress, technical modernization, and their mediated forms in colonial contexts that shaped ideas, experiences, and practices of Ethiopian singularity and modernity. In the realm of sports, the systematic exclusion of local athletic practices from modern institutions, their relegation to tradition (and backwardness), and their absence in narratives on modernity is one feature that

[40] Luise White, 'Separating the Men from the Boys: Constructions of Gender, Sexuality, and Terrorism in Central Kenya, 1939–1959', *The International Journal of African Historical Studies,* 13:1 (1990), 1–25.
[41] For an elaborate conceptual and methodological discussion about overlapping, intersecting, and co-existing masculinities from an African studies' perspective see Stephan F. Miescher and Lisa A. Lindsay, 'Introduction: Men and Masculinities in Modern African History', in Stephan F. Miescher and Lisa A. Lindsay (eds), *Men and Masculinities in Modern African History* (Portsmouth NH, 2003), pp. 1–29.
[42] Katrin Bromber, 'Muscles, Dresses, and Conflicting Ideas of Progress: Ethiopia in the 1960s and 1970s', in Josep Martí (ed.), *African Realities: Body, Culture and Social Tensions* (Newcastle upon Tyne, 2014), pp. 171–90.
[43] Fouad Makki, 'Empire and Modernity: Dynastic Centralization and Official Nationalism in Late Imperial Ethiopia', *Cambridge Review of International Affairs,* 24:2 (2011), 266.

Ethiopia shares with other colonial nation-states. The power of colonial-cum-racist epistemic notions about blackness materialized, for example, in discussions about the skin colour of potential YMCA fraternal secretaries from North America to Ethiopia, who shaped sports and leisure programmes.[44] Furthermore, when Ethiopian YMCA physical education secretaries visited the United States in April 1953, they experienced racial segregation in hotels and other facilities.[45] In the early 1960s, debates on whether Ethiopians are African enough to host an African YMCA secretaries' training centre in Addis Ababa resonate with the Ethiopian exceptionality conceived in 'orientalist' scholarship.[46] These examples link up to larger arguments around the function of Ethiopia as an exceptional identity: first as a challenge to Western racism and, second, as an antidote against a Pan-Africanism that prioritised continental over regional belonging.[47]

Finally, yet importantly, *zemenawīnet* studies attribute due relevance to the spiritual and religious, which shaped both narratives and practices of modernity in Ethiopia. Various agents, ranging from the emperor to physical education teachers from Ethiopia or abroad, recurrently emphasized the sacredness of the human body as a temple. Apart from notions of bodily sacredness in Islam or Orthodox Christianity, the YMCA's vision of a liberal 'Protestant Modernity'[48] most forcefully promoted sports as well as urban social hygiene in post-liberation Ethiopia. They demanded daily care in the form of physical exercises, a balanced diet, and personal hygiene as well as abstinence from harmful substances (alcohol, nicotine, drugs) or prostitution, and general control of the sinful human body. Furthermore, practices such as preaching before the start of competitions were as common as placing a holy book under the goal posts before a football match.[49]

---

[44] Correspondence between General Secretary Merlin Bishop and Lenning Sweet (International Committee of North American YMCAs), on the question of whether an additional secretary from the US should be 'white' or a 'Negro', 21 September 1954, KFYA, Y.USA.9-2-37, YMCA International Work in Ethiopia Box 1, correspondence 1954.

[45] This incident was widely reported and generated an extensive correspondence between New York and Addis Ababa. KFYA, Y.USA.9-2-37, YMCA International Work in Ethiopia Box 1, correspondence 1953.

[46] Joel Nystrom to Marvin Ludwig, 3 April 1963, KFYA, Y.USA.9-2-37, YMCA International Work in Ethiopia box 6, Correspondence 1963.

[47] Marzagora, 'Alterity, Coloniality and Modernity', p. 78.

[48] Harald Fischer-Tiné, Stefan Huebner, and Ian Tyrrell, 'The Rise and Growth of a Global "Moral Empire": The YMCA and YWCA during the Late Nineteenth and Early Twentieth Centuries', in Harald Fischer-Tiné, Stefan Huebner, and Ian Tyrrell (eds), *Spreading Protestant Modernity: Global Perspectives on the Social Work of the YMCA and YWCA, 1889–1970* (Honolulu, 2020), p. 2.

[49] Sintayehu Tola, 'The History of St. George Sport Club' (Unpublished BA thesis, Addis Ababa University, 1986), p. 11. The manuscript is archived at the

What is *Zemenawīnet*? It is a lively academic debate that gives voice to a multitude of ideas, experiences, practices, agents, and materialities. Studies of *zemenawīnet* address the socio-economic and cultural contexts as well as the political ideas that conditioned them. They look at the long-term consequences and give reasons to productively question established periodizations of Ethiopian history.[50] They critically engage with ideas of Ethiopian singularity by systematically integrating aspects of coloniality into the study of modernity in Ethiopia. They attempt to speak about modernity with Amharic terminology.

Modernity's Socio-Political Vocabulary

What kind of vocabulary existed that came close to notions of the modern, modernity, modernization, or societal progress? According to the political scientist Paulos Milkias, the term *zemenawī-silt'anē* (modern civilization) had already been introduced by *Ats'ē* Tewodros II in the mid-nineteenth century, but was not generally used before Haile Selassie's rule. It broadly meant modern institutions, modern education, and modern thinking, which included an anti-clerical connotation.[51] Unfortunately, the author did not reveal the context in which the term was used. Did he mean the intellectual circles or does his observation include the multitude of people of different social, educational, and ethnic backgrounds who were part of the various reforms from the 1920s onwards? Hence, can we assume a relative stability of audience and context in which *zemenawī-silt'anē* as a formal expression of a political concept emerged? If the term transcended the intellectual circles of the Shoa Amhara nobility, we can further assume that it varied according to other visions of modernity, such as Islamic or lowland culture.

In her analysis of the journal *Berhanena Selam*, Elizabeth Wolde Giorgis argued that *silt'anē* [seltane] (civilization) was used in the sense of bringing about progress and development through the eradication of ignorance.[52] She separates this term of the intellectual elite from other existing terminology. In a more informal way, *Zebanay* referred to the

---

Institute of Ethiopian Studies Library (further ref. IES) under the reference number 796 SEN.
[50] Elleni Centime Zeleke's book on the after-life of the theoretical, programmatic, and practical ideas of the Ethiopian Student Movement provides an impressive account of their impact on current Ethiopian politics: *Ethiopia in Theory: Revolution and Knowledge Production, 1964–2016* (Leiden, 2019).
[51] Paulos Milkias, *Haile Selassie, Western Education and Political Revolution in Ethiopia* (London, Amherst NY, 2006), pp. 53–5.
[52] In this respect, she refers to Kidane Wold's etymology of *silt'anē* as 'distance from ignorance'. Kidane Wold Kiflē, *Mets'ahafe sewasiw wegis wemezgebe k'alat hadīs* (Addis Ababa, 1956), p. 10, cited in Elizabeth Wolde Giorgis, *Modernist Art in Ethiopia*, p. 41.

parading of 'arrogance in clothes and tastes'.[53] Arada, the name of the prominent Addis Ababa neighbourhood, developed into a metaphor for an urban sophisticated style. By engaging with the anxieties of the common people, intellectuals embraced feelings of contingency – the world is about to change, but it is not entirely sure in which direction – as an argument for the measures taken or projected to bring about *silt'anē*. By explicitly addressing the problem of people's backwardness as blocking the road to modernity, contributors to the journal made clear that modernity is only attainable with the inclusion of the people.[54] Further elaborating on the intellectual discourse in this journal, Elizabeth Wolde Giorgis states that, for the intellectuals and artists of the 1920s and 1930s, *silt'anē* and divine monarchy complemented each other.[55]

The brutality of the Italian occupation did not interrupt discourses on civilization and modernity. It reconfigured them in line with the colonial project and disseminated them through modern media: print, radio, and film.[56] Amharic newspapers and journals published during this period transformed existing notions of social and technological progress by imposing a colonial modernity modelled after Fascist modernity in Italy. They were potentially able to tap into discourses and practices around (Western) ideas of modernity that had gained ground amongst sections of the urban population in Ethiopia. Arguably, prominent Ethiopian intellectuals who worked for the Italian propaganda machine, partly by force, guaranteed discursive continuity. Amongst them was the prize-winning writer Kebede Mikael, who worked as broadcaster at the Italia East Africa Radio Station during the occupation, and later thought and published extensively about civilization. The famous novelist Afewerk' Gebre Īyesus and the journalist Welde-Gīyorgīs Welde-Yohannis both wrote for propaganda newspapers. In contrast to *Berhanena Selam*, these print media highlighted the colonized athletic body as the signifier of civilizational progress, quite similar to propaganda about the regenerated Italian body. The monthly magazine *YeRoma Birhan* referred to sports as '*yesilt'anē temarī bēt*' (school of civilization).[57] It described competitions as a chance to 'see'

---

[53] Elizabeth Wolde Giorgis, *Modernist Art in Ethiopia*, p. 41.
[54] Ibid., p. 58.
[55] Ibid., p. 51.
[56] Meseret Chekol Reta, *The Quest for Press Freedom: One Hundred Years of History of the Media in Ethiopia* (Lanham, 2013), p. 64; Asfaw Geremew, *Ye' ethiopia radio ketelant esk zare. 1923–1992 EC* [Ethiopian radio from yesterday until today, 1930/31–1999/2000] (Addis Ababa, 1992 EC (1999/2000)), pp. 8–9; John Gartley, 'Broadcasting', in Siegbert Uhlig (ed.), *Encyclopaedia Aethiopica*, 1 (Wiesbaden, 2003), pp. 29–31, at pp. 29–30. The weekly *Ye-K'ēsar Mengist Mel'iktenya* (The Messenger of Caesar's Government) occasionally reported on film shows held at market places.
[57] 'Yesport dirijitina yehaymanot timhirt' [Sports organization and religious

civilization[58] and the Fascist greeting used by athletes during ceremonies as *besilt'anē akwahwan tet'egtew ye-Roma selamta* (the civilized Roman salute).[59] The discourse on colonial modernity continued and intensified during the Fascist period and, for the first time, included physical fitness as an important element.

After the liberation, discourses on *silt'anē* continued in intellectual circles as well as in the public media. In his book *Ethiopia and Western Civilisation*, Kebede Mikael argued for a 'greater' or 'true' civilisation, by combining Ethiopian 'spiritual civilisation' with Western 'material civilisation'.[60] *Limat* (growth, development) and *keshefa* (failure) were, thus, the dynamic elements framed by an eternally valid morality (that included strict observance of hierarchies).

In his speech on the thirty-first anniversary of his coronation, Haile Selassie himself spoke of 'Modern Ethiopianism'.[61] Listing achievements, such as the Revised Constitution of 1955 and the establishment of important legal codes, he emphasized the national character of the necessary socio-economic advancement. Looking at the symbolism of power during Haile Selassie's coronation in 1930, the historian Hanna Rubinkowska-Anioł analysed ritual, architecture, and iconography to show the complicated message the emperor wanted to deliver, i.e. to point to Ethiopia's grand history and at himself and Ethiopia being modern. She analysed how much the ritual of coronation changed over the centuries, what it meant to make a change, and what it meant to follow tradition.[62]

The quotation that I used to open this Introduction is but one example that supports the argument that Haile Selassie saw himself as the 'One Who Gives', including in the realm of sports. His appearance at all major sporting events, as well as the inclusion of athletic performances in official ceremonies such as the visit of the Swedish crown prince Gustav Adolf in 1935 and the Silver Jubilee of Haile Selassie's coronation in 1955, suggests that the latter was fully aware of the power of sports as a propaganda instrument. In 1930, horse races were offered to the guests of the coronation ceremony as one of the entertainments.

---

education], *YeRoma Birhan,* 1:5, 22 t'ik'imt 1932 [28 October 1939].
[58] 'Tillik' t'ik'im yalew ch'ewata' [The great benefit of sports], *YeRoma Birhan*, 1:5, 22 t'ik'imt 1932 [28 October 1939].
[59] 'Meskerem 20 k'en beAddīs Abeba siletederegew liyu liyu ch'ewata' [On the various competitions held on 20 meskerem], *YeRoma Birhan*, 1:5, 22 t'ik'imt 1932 [28 October 1939].
[60] Kebede Mikael, 'Ītyop'yana mi'irabawī silt'anē' – *Ethiopia and Western Civilisation – L'Éthiopie et la civilisation occidentale* (Addis Abeba, 1948/49), pp. 123–4.
[61] Haile Selassie, 'Modern Ethiopianism', 458.
[62] Hanna Rubinkowska-Anioł, *Etiopia pomiędzy tradycją a nowoczesnością: Symbolika koronacji Cesarza Etiopii Hajle Syllasje I* [Ethiopia between tradition and modernity: Symbolism of the emperor of Ethiopia during Haile Selassie I's coronation] (Warszawa, 2016).

On the one hand, horse racing is the sport of kings and emperors and, thus, grounded in tradition. On the other hand, the entertainment aspect shows how Haile Selassie changed in terms of perceiving sports as something attractive to his guests while at the same time proving himself to be 'modern'. Such a top-down approach, however, misses the fact that sports also produces self-consciousness amongst the most malleable part of society – the youth. Thus, looking at modern sports is but one gateway to asking how far Haile Selassie's modern measures were not only superficial, but also induced social and cultural transformation, as I argue throughout this book.

Zemenawī also simply meant popular or contemporary. *Zemenawī muzīk'a* (modern or contemporary music) for example became the name of a popular music style that was based on traditional Ethiopian music.[63] Ts'egayē Debalk'e, composer, lecturer at the National Yared School of Music in Addis Ababa and critic, attempted to broaden the style beyond popular music into classics.[64] Ethiopian traditional dancing types that developed along with the music were called *zemanawī* too. The music and dance styles of 'Swinging Addis' have by now become legendary.[65] *Zemenawī* also included hairstyles such as the *gofere* (the Afro) or plaited hair (also for men), dress, including mini-skirt and jeans, and the consumption practices of modern foods, such as licking ice-cream in public.[66] In contrast to these styles, sports was conceived of as modern per se and did not need *zemenawī* as an additional qualification.

'Modern' included a wide range of ideas, practices, and styles, while never expressing a uniform perception of what it exactly was. Modern related to ruling elites and revolutionary youth, artists and stylish city-dwellers – all those who attempted to embrace the contingent forces of societal progress and perceived themselves at various times as the 'New Men' of Ethiopia. Sports provides a useful lens for viewing how parts of the population became targets for the planned formation of a vanguard.

---

[63] Described from a contemporary perspective by Ashenafi Kebede, 'Zemenawi Muzika: Modern Trends in Traditional Secular Music of Ethiopia', *The Black Perspective in Music*, 4 (1976), 289–302.
[64] Cynthia Tse Kimberlin, 'Säggaye Däbalqe', in Siegbert Uhlig (ed.), *Enyclopaedia Aethiopica*, 4 (Wiesbaden, 2010), pp. 456–7.
[65] Francis Falceto, *Abyssinie Swing: A Pictorial History of Modern Ethiopian Music* (Addis Ababa, 2001).
[66] In contrast to other African states that had just gained their independence and sanctioned the dissemination of Western dress, music, or behaviour, Ethiopia did not officially prohibit these styles. To the contrary, the emperor as well as high-ranking officials incorporated these trends into their symbolic repertoire of being modern. For further discussion see Bromber, 'Muscles, Dresses, and Conflicting Ideas of Progress', 179–85.

Forming Ethiopia's 'New Men'

The term 'New Man' is usually associated with the 'Socialist Man', the 'Fascist Man', or the 'Superman' of the first decades of the twentieth century. In my book I demonstrate that Ethiopia is but one example for countering arguments that the concept had fallen out of use by the second half of the twentieth century. This rather Eurocentric discussion ignores the fact that large-scale social engineering and the creation of the right type of human being not only persisted, but also acquired new urgency, in various nation-building projects in the global South, especially in the era of decolonization. Being 'new' also meant to be at the forefront of societal progress and, thus, to be exposed to selection according to age and gender, but also class or religious background. The criteria varied by historical context as well as the concrete understanding of how society functions.

In the first three decades of the twentieth century, Ethiopia's 'New Men' were the intellectual elite with local and, most importantly, foreign training who were to bring about the modernization of the empire. The Young Ethiopians who formed the second generation of modern intellectuals certainly fall into this category.[67] However, an exclusive focus on them is to overlook the many non-elite segments of the population who participated as rank-and-file in the reformed armed forces, as pupils in modern schools, or as young enthusiasts of newly introduced modern kinds of sports. They not only faced new temporal and spatial regimes, but also new body regimes relating to hygiene and physical fitness.

Arguably, the diverse everyday measures in modern institutions and beyond, which aimed at the mental, spiritual, and bodily regeneration of a purportedly backward society, were observed, discussed, copied, and interpreted in a number of ways by various actors. In a critical engagement with Michel Foucault's pioneering work *Discipline and Punish* (including his own works on governmentality),[68] it becomes clear that subject formation is never only a one-way street of subjection. It also creates multiple forms of response (including resistance), which result in unexpected subjectivities and identities and not a uniform, modern *habitus*. Following Pierre Bourdieu's argument about the incorporation of society into the human body and the relative stability of a culturally specific *habitus*,[69] the various types of Ethiopian 'New Men' blended with existing ones.

---

[67] For academic and non-academic perceptions of the Young Ethiopians see Marzagora, 'Alterity, Coloniality and Modernity', pp. 45–54.
[68] Michel Foucault, *Discipline and Punish: The Birth of the Prison* (New York, 1977).
[69] See especially to Pierre Bourdieu, *Distinction: A Social Critique of the Judgement of Taste* (London, 1984).

Thus, any discourse on or concrete practice surrounding the modern subject following the occupation tapped into existing discourses and practices relating to modernization and civilization. The Fascist propaganda in Amharic newspapers, which circulated during the occupation period (1935–41), transformed them in their own interests and conceptualized the *Etiope Nuovo* as a civilized, yet colonized subject.

In post-liberation Ethiopia, the 'New Man' seems to have been understood in two ways. First, as a mass man trained in schools and volunteer organizations to achieve superior physical and mental attributes fitting of the 'New Era' (*addīs zemen*) that the emperor had declared after his return from exile (1941). Second, the 'New Man' was understood as a potential leader who accepted social hierarchies along the lines of established ideas of loyalty. Existing potential leadership, i.e. the second generation of educated elites known as Young Ethiopians, had already been critical of Haile Selassie's politics and were often barred from upward social mobility. Thus, it is no wonder that YMCA General Secretary Merlin Bishop attributed the alleged lack of local leadership to the fact that the Ethiopian government did not encourage and allow local leadership to develop.[70]

Since the 'New Man' was to demonstrate particular, if often ill-defined, spiritual/ideological, mental/attitudinal, and bodily characteristics, concrete projects typically targeted this triangle in combination. The red triangle in the emblem of the YMCA, which commenced work in Ethiopia in the late 1940s, explicitly symbolizes this attitude to developing the 'Whole Man'. In Ethiopia, as elsewhere, practical attempts to create the necessary conditions for the 'New Man' to emerge became institutionalized, influential, and in high demand. The post-liberation period saw the establishment of volunteer organizations, which had already proved their effectiveness in forming a vanguard – a force that was already tamed and, thus, itself a potential taming force for all kinds of deviation from the 'right path to progress'. Furthermore, these organizations became a site for instilling responsibility, notions of care for lesser privileged members of society, and humanitarian work in times of crises. Volunteer organizations such as the YMCA, the scout movement or the Ethiopian Red Cross Society promoted a moral masculinity beyond the individual.

Modern educational institutions, volunteer organizations, and places of urban leisure formed social spaces around specific athletic practices.[71] None of these institutions provided space for so-called traditional sports. Team sports included volleyball, football, and basketball, but

---

[70] Merlin Bishop to Floyd A. Wilson, YMCA Bangkok (Thailand), 6 October 1953, 3, KFYA, Y.USA.9-2-37, YMCA International Work in Ethiopia Box 1.
[71] Pierre Bourdieu, 'Program for a Sociology of Sport', *Sociology of Sport Journal*, 5 (1988), 154.

never *genna* (a form of hockey). Boxing, judo, karate, and freestyle wrestling proliferated at the YMCA, completely side-lining any local forms of wrestling or combined martial arts. Arguably, these latter were too strongly associated with the rural context to function as appropriate practices in the formation of modern subjectivities.

Ideas about the 'New Man', which despite appearances included women and especially children, often produced idealized personality types that could be created by way of a deliberate and planned social process. Thus, concrete values for personal development were associated with specific athletic practices. In the eyes of YMCA sports secretaries, gymnastics would 'help to discipline the physical condition of the body'[72] and jumping on the trampoline let 'the mind and the body work harmoniously'.[73] Volleyball, which seems to have been as important as basketball, not only supported in the young men the development of 'precision, teamwork and physical skill', but also allowed them to become 'the complete man' and, above all, 'a good citizen in his community'.[74] For Boy Scouts, swimming and hiking were primarily framed in terms of survival and not in terms of leisure.

Perceived on a spectrum between opportunity and problem, youth constituted an ideal target for social experimentation. Concrete practices in Ethiopia ranged from correction and prevention to preparing youth as leaders and 'torchbearers of progress'. On the one hand, we see the establishment of institutions such as the Training School and Remand Home for Boys[75] (established in 1958) and the YMCA-led Operation Better Boys, an independent youth work project launched in Addis Ababa in 1967.[76] They targeted 'problematic' youth in order to mould them into 'well adjusted, satisfied, contributing and responsible citizen[s]'.[77] Football became a way to attract young boys, but also a means to teach them team spirit and fair play. Gymnastics targeted the disciplined use of individual body parts. On the other hand, sports clubs connected to foreign communities or institutions

[72] 'Sewinetin lemegrat kemīyazut yemegelebabet timhirtoch t'ik'ītochu', YMCA Annual Report 1970, p. 5.
[73] The report says '*wedelay ... aydelem wede ch'erek'a! ...gin haylin kesewinet k'ilt'ifina gar lemastebaber*' [Up! Not to the moon, but to help the mind and the body work harmoniously], YMCA Annual Report 1969, p. 6.
[74] YMCA Annual Report 1967, p. 13.
[75] Modelled after correction homes in Britain, the institution was established to separate juvenile delinquents from adult prisoners – Zenebu Kefelew, 'The Role of the Training School & Remand Home in Correcting Juvenile Delinquents in Ethiopia' (Unpublished senior paper, School of Social Work, Haile Selassie I University, 1973), p. 20.
[76] For 'Operation Better Boys', see, Katrin Bromber, 'Make Them Better Citizens: YMCA Training in Late Imperial Ethiopia (1950s–1970s)', *Annales d'Ethiopie*, 32 (2018/19), 35–9.
[77] Kefelew, 'The Role of the Training School & Remand Home', 20.

of higher learning as well as sports facilities with very limited access such as hotels, provided spaces of social distinction with disciplines such as lawn tennis, swimming, and bowling. Due to its great popularity in the 1960s, bodybuilding also became a social marker. It required expensive equipment and specialized knowledge. Young men from a wide social spectrum became very innovative in constructing weight sets and interpreting bodybuilding as sport as well as a source of income via profitable athletic shows.[78] Thus, we see what Pierre Bourdieu described as dispersion and transformation of a sport through 'social diversification of the practitioners'.[79]

Officials of different ranks, and especially the emperor, expected that volunteer organizations mould individual bodies and minds into a community of multipliers, i.e. people who are trained to pass on knowledge, who are loyal to the existing political order. On a global level, volunteer organizations were instrumental in bringing about the shift in the conception of the 'New Man' from the uniform element in an organicist societal structure to the multiplier. In the sports sector, athletic heroes emerged, of course, since sports functions within the binary of victory and defeat. However, their sporting success was, at least on a discursive level, only valid within a moral framework of 'fair play', observation of rules, and 'self-control'. Apart from training body and mind, sports became as a means to instil moral and social values.

Restricting the 'New Man' to youth and young adults, who did not necessarily belong to the echelons of power, would miss a decisive point, however. Rulers had to become 'New Men', too. The 'New Emperor' was understood as a modern head of state, although still with divine qualities, who was accompanied by the First Lady, Empress Menen. Haile Selassie's practice of and explicit appreciation of yoga as bodily and spiritual regeneration served a man of his physique much better than riding, tennis, or other sports marking social distinction.[80] The change in the image of the emperor as an important part of Ethiopia's modernization played out in the sphere of symbolism and propaganda. It comes, then, as no surprise that newspapers and journals such as *Addīs Zemen* or *Menen* also presented Haile Selassie as sportsman – playing *genna* or table tennis.[81] The emperor's appearance at sports finals, his personal interest in physical education, and the invitation of the victorious

---

[78] Bromber, 'Muscularity, Heavy Athletics and Urban Leisure', 1922–24.
[79] Bourdieu, 'Program for a Sociology of Sport', 155.
[80] On the importance of yoga for Haile Selassie see, *Important Utterances of H.I.M. Emperor Haile Selassie I, 1963–1972* (Addis Ababa, 1972), p. 553. For sports as a means of social distinction, see Pierre Bourdieu, *Distinction*, p. 217.
[81] The front-page of *Menen,* December 1961, displays the emperor as a traditional ruler and sportsman playing *genna*. In contrast, *Addīs Zemen* 1963 [1970/71] published an image of the sophisticated ruler in a table tennis match against his son Asfa Wossen in front of a Chinese visitor.

Ethiopian national football team to the palace after the Africa Cup of Nations in 1962[82] are what the sports sociologist Karl-Heinrich Bette refers to as the semiotic configuration of presidents or prime ministers in the sporting setting.[83] As an active football player, *Ras* Mengesha Seyoum (last governor of Tigray) not only emphasized his love for modern sports, but also his role as a modern ruler of a province. Arguably, the inclusion of a conceptualization of a disciplined and healthy body of 'the' modern Ethiopian elite was an important part of subject formation strategies in Ethiopia. The education of Prince Makonnen, the emperor's favourite son, by French naval officer Henri Gigli included a variety of modern sports, most notably boxing. Although boxing had changed its social meaning from working-class to a gentleman's sport in Europe, it was still considered a ruffian's sport in 1950s Addis Ababa.[84] This example speaks well to Pierre Bourdieu's observation that 'different classes do not agree on the profits expected from sport'.[85] In this way, what should have served as symbolic capital for promoting the modern ruling class undermined its legitimizing purpose.

Citizens in the Making

Can we understand these attempts at getting the Ethiopian 'New Man' into shape as part of a wider process of citizenship training, as pamphlets, programmes, and newspaper articles of that time suggest? And if so, did the youth – the target of these social engineering practices – understand themselves as 'citizens in the making' or as 'modern'? Was there a suitable political vocabulary in place and did all those affected by the practice potentially derived from it understand the terms in the same way? Most probably not, I would argue. The fact that not 'until the drafting of Ethiopia's aborted 1974 constitution did the concept of "citizen" for most of the population become relevant',[86] making it difficult for the YMCA leadership, for example, to find the right Amharic terminology for advertising its Future Citizen School.[87] The term *zēga*, which later 'came to be applied to anyone within the boundaries of the modern

---

[82] In 1962, Ethiopia won the third African Cup of Nations.
[83] Karl-Heinrich Bette, *Sportsoziologie* (Bielefeld, 2010), p. 8.
[84] The legendary bodybuilder Girma Cheru spoke about this general perception in an interview with Wendimu Negash Desta, 'Girma Cheru – gʷolmasaw sportenya I' [Girma Cheru – a fully accomplished athlete], *Yekatīt*, hidar 1974 [November 1981], p. 32.
[85] Bourdieu, *Distinction*, p. 211.
[86] Edmond J. Keller, 'Constitutionalism, Citizenship and Political Transition in Ethiopia: Historic and Contemporary Processes', in Francis Mading Deng (ed.), *Self-Determination and National Unity: A Challenge for Africa* (Trenton NJ, 2010), p. 58.
[87] The YMCA Future Citizen School programme started in the 1950s and linked the concept of citizen to (mass) education.

state, under the domination of the nation',[88] carried historical baggage, which made its use for 'citizen' – understood as the bearers of rights and duties – almost impossible. Based on historical sources such as eighteenth-century land charters and administrative manuals for religious institutions, Habtamu Mengistie Tegegne very convincingly argues that despite variations 'it is clear that *zēginet* was understood primarily as a form of servitude and that the *zēgoch* represented a class of highly impoverished people with a lack of social rights'.[89] Thus, these terms might not have been suitable to denote 'citizenship' and 'citizens' in the modern sense. The YMCA leadership, for example, resorted to expressions that avoided *zēga*, instead using 'Programme Given to Children' (*lehits'anat yemīset' program*) or 'School for Good Developers' (*yemelkam tadagīwoch timhirt bēt*). The literal translation of 'Future Citizen School' (*yewedefīt zēgawoch timhirt bēt*) did not appear before the early 1970s.[90]

Similarly, the foundational documents of the Boy Scout Association of the 1950s, as well as pamphlets that explained the aims of the organization, translated the English 'loyal citizen' into 'loyal subject' (*tamany tegezh*). Arguably, this translation is owed not only to the absence of a suitable political vocabulary but also because Haile Selassie preferred loyal subjects to citizens as bearers of rights and duties.

The *Journal of the Agricultural Technical School in Jimma* drew the most explicit link between sports and citizenship training. It said that in

> the schools where the pupils are boarders they spend their leisure time by co-operating to organize different kinds of games. So, it is what pupils do in their spare time that really prepares them to take their places in society as citizens when they complete their studies.[91]

Given the fact, that the Agricultural Technical School in Jimma received support from the Point Four Program of the United States, which also included American staff members, it is legitimate to ask whether such ideas and related athletic practices were introduced from abroad. Perhaps it was so in this specific case, in which American staff members helped to produce a journal. In general, local/Ethiopian questions of citizenship, which had lingered in the background since the 1930s, required answers and concrete practices of crafting citizens in a changing post-Second World War context shaped by emerging Cold War politics and anti-colonial movements on a global scale.

---

[88] Donald L. Donham and Wendy James (eds), *The Southern Marches of Imperial Ethiopia: Essays in History and Social Anthropology* (Athens OH, 2002), p. 43.
[89] Habtamu Mengiste Tegegne, 'Rethinking Property and Society in Gondärine Ethiopia', *African Studies Review*, 52:3 (2009), 95.
[90] For a more detailed discussion see, Bromber, 'Make Them Better Citizens', 24, 32.
[91] 'Value of Sports', *Year Book of the Jimma Agricultural Technical School*, 2:1 (1958), IES YB JATS, p. 6.

Sports as Leisure: Contributions to Current Debates

'What does the average Ethiopian do in his leisure time?'[92] In an attempt to answer this question, Tereffe Asrat – author of the article 'The Excitement Game of Leisure', which appeared in the monthly magazine *Addis Reporter* in April 1969 – does not mention sports at all. He instead talks about allegedly 'trivial activities' such as visiting friends and relatives, enjoying *t'ej* (honey wine) and *t'ella* (local beer), and having conversations about the weather, crops, and health issues as characterizing the rural population. In the cities, he continues, people grapple with loneliness and boredom by going to hotel bars, nightclubs, and brothels or to crowded areas such as pools or stadiums. 'This routine of leisure', he argues, 'is not a source of happiness but of despair. Thus, leisure amongst our leisure class is not really leisure: it is drudgery.'[93]

In Tereffe's opinion, leisure was for a certain stratum of the urban (male) population, the 'leisure class', which had the means for conspicuous consumption. His critical tone is reminiscent of Thorstein Veblen's essay in which he relates consumerism to social class.[94] The 'leisure class' was also distinct because of the time available for consumption, since leisure was 'the freedom from the duties and labours of ... work'.[95] At the time of Tereffe's publication, academic debates about work and leisure as related spheres of life had just started in the journal *Past and Present*.[96] Calling leisure 'drudgery' calls to mind Georg Simmel's works on the restlessness of modern subjectivities, as attempts by young male urban workers to escape loneliness. Furthermore, Tereffe's article on Ethiopia in the 1960s addresses some of the issues that later became important in conceptualizing leisure in Africa. It contextualizes what Paul Tiyambe Zeleza calls the four variables that condition leisure, namely participation, place, provision, and politics.[97] They inform questions of time and place, of rural and urban experiences, of acceptability and morality, of gender and mentality and, last but not least, consumption[98] by an emerging 'leisure class'.

---

[92] Tereffe Asrat, 'The Excitement Game of Leisure', *Addis Reporter* (21 April 1969), p. 17.
[93] Ibid.
[94] Thorstein Veblen, *The Theory of the Leisure Class: An Economic Study in the Evolution of Institutions* (New York, 1899).
[95] Tereffe, 'The Excitement Game of Leisure', 17.
[96] Keith Thomas, 'Work and Leisure in Pre-Industrial Societies', *Past and Present,* 29 (1962), 50–62; E.P. Thompson, 'Time, Work-Discipline and Industrial Capitalism', *Past and Present,* 38 (1967), 57–97.
[97] Paul Tiyambe Zeleza, 'The Creation and Consumption of Leisure: Theoretical and Methodological Considerations', in Paul Tiyambe Zeleza and Cassandra Rachel Veney (eds), *Leisure in Urban Africa* (Trenton NJ, Asmara, 2003), vii.
[98] On the nexus between sports, leisure, and consumption, see Susan Baller

The growing body of studies on cinema, dance, sports, and music in African (colonial) nation-states as well as the existing conceptual literature on leisure in Africa have questioned Eurocentric notions of leisure in a number of ways. In his critical approach to the study of leisure in Africa, Charles Ambler reminds us of the following aspects. First, that understandings of the concept differ according to race, class, gender, or ethnicity. Second, that people attempt to resist the imposition of specific forms of leisure, e.g. as welfare or useful recreation, and to keep control over their spare time. Third, that industrial development and colonialism 'created the conditions that inspired new ideas about leisure', as well as expectations that Africans associated with them.[99] In the following, I show where exactly the book contributes to this larger debate on leisure in Africa and beyond.

Time, Gender, Class, and Age

Although debates on leisure in Africa are situated within the post-Victor Turner distinction between work and leisure as separate spheres of action (i.e. the work-time vs. free-time binary), time matters. In her study on colonial Brazzaville, Phyllis Martin[100] argues that conceptions of time in the rural areas around the capital did not know a 'work-free' day in the Weberian sense, but only days with less demanding work – especially for women. These conceptions then travelled to urban areas with the migrating labour force. Quite similar to their experiences in the countryside, men embraced the new leisure activities, whereas women remained in their productive and reproductive roles.

Although this observation can to a large degree also be substantiated for Ethiopian urban centres, women become visible in athletic events from the post-liberation period onwards. Images at the Institute of Ethiopian Studies (IES) in Addis Ababa and the Surafiel Photo Studio in Mek'ele show female volleyball and tetherball teams as well as women's bicycle races of the early 1960s. Schoolgirls participated in mixed teams in the various athletic performances in Haile Selassie I Stadium. The *Ethiopia Observer* illustrated an article on the opportunities gained by ensuring gender equality in the revised version of the Ethiopian constitution of 1955 with a photograph of a female athlete.[101] Whether the short sports dress was an issue is still a matter of debate.

---

and Scarlett Cornelissen, 'Introduction: Sport, Leisure and Consumption in Africa', *The International Journal of the History of Sport,* 30:16 (2013), 1867.
[99] Charles Ambler, 'Writing African Leisure History', in Paul Tiyambe Zeleza and Cassandra Rachel Veney (eds), *Leisure in Urban Africa* (Trenton NJ, Asmara, 2003), pp. 3–4.
[100] Phyllis Martin, *Leisure and Society in Colonial Brazzaville* (New York, 2002).
[101] 'The Ethiopian Women', *Ethiopia Observer: Journal of Independent Opinion, Economics, History and the Arts,* 3:3 (1957), 76.

Most probably, it was less problematic than wearing the mini-skirt that simultaneously became a symbol of the modern woman and a marker of social decadence in Ethiopia, as elsewhere.[102] Although urban women faced considerable moral and temporal constraints, had far less access to educational facilities and sports clubs and, thus, physical education, they became visible as a vanguard that carved out athletic possibilities.

These positive examples, however, cannot hide the fact that modern sports in late imperial Ethiopia was primarily male. As in other colonial contexts, such as neighbouring Kenya, sports served as the litmus test for the 'right type' of man. In line with late Victorian ideals of manliness, playing by the rules and putting the team before the individual testified 'character built on the common good ... control of his sentiments ... [as well as] his aggressions'.[103]

If one purpose of sports is to bring the body into muscular shape, then muscular bodies become part of an ideal. From the mid-nineteenth century onwards, bodybuilding spread in waves on a global scale. Muscles became signifiers of successful combat against diverse forms of (male) weakness, effeminacy, and degeneracy in the first half of the twentieth century. They belonged to the symbolic repertoire that established semiotic links to a global modernity.[104] Independence struggle and post-colonial self-esteem without the image of the muscular male body? No way! Represented in media, posters, and live performances, muscles mattered. I argue that this global trend spread in Ethiopia from the mid-twentieth century onwards and became visible with the growing media landscape of the post-liberation period. The covers of annual publications such as the *Journal of the Inter-School Athletic Association*, *Armed Forces Sports Day*, and *University Sports Day* displayed scantily clad muscular male bodies – usually brandishing a spear to underline the aspect of defence. Speeches and media articles recurrently emphasized that every young man could develop a strong body through exercise, abstaining from 'substances' such as alcohol and nicotine as well as from any form of immoral behaviour. Discipline and self-control were the keys to bodily transformation towards modern civilization (*zemenawī-silt'anē*) – a concept that includes a cognate of the linguistic base for 'become trained' (*selet'ene*).

Mental and physical discipline was nothing new, but deeply rooted and highly diversified in the Ethiopian Empire. In wrestling, for example, I argue against Donald Levine's description of the Amhara

[102] On the mini-skirt, see Bromber, 'Muscles, Dresses, and Conflicting Ideas of Progress', 179–85.
[103] Joanna Lewis, *Empire State-Building: War & Welfare in Kenya 1925–52* (Oxford, Nairobi, Athens OH, 2000), p. 209.
[104] Especially see Wilson Chacko Jacob, *Working Out Egypt: Effendi Masculinity and Subject Formation in Colonial Modernity, 1870–1940* (Durham NC, London, 2011).

masculinity ideal as 'aggressivity unbound'.¹⁰⁵ His interpretation of *gobezinnet* (bravery, male strength, chivalry) exclusively in terms of 'aggressive capacity' completely ignores the regulating features and the strict supervision by elders and the community as a whole in the upbringing of young boys.¹⁰⁶ From the inter-war period onwards, the notion of acceptable or even desired masculinity began to be transformed. Amongst other local and foreign agents of modernity, Hakīm Werk'neh, who had received education in British institutions at the turn of the century, transmitted nineteenth-century ideas of Muscular Christianity through secular schools.¹⁰⁷ Arriving in Ethiopia in late 1947, the YMCA, or more precisely, the North American version of it, stood at the forefront of muscling-in initiatives. It combined inward-looking character development and outward-looking religiosity with the idea of Muscular Christianity.¹⁰⁸ Incorporating sports as a morally positive activity became a powerful strategy for the creation of an athletic lifestyle. Bodybuilding and weight training were the most popular sports at the YMCA, which provided the teams and infrastructure for the display of male muscular beauty in public shows as well as in the media (print and, from 1964 onwards, television). Despite the fact that these uncovered bodies in muscular pose contrasted sharply with the bodies of the male majority and, what is more, with ideals of the covered human body in Orthodox Christianity, ideas of male muscular beauty spread beyond the YMCA in the 1960s. Apart from physical fitness shows on TV hosted by the famous bodybuilder Girma Cheru, they resulted in the establishment of the Ethiopian Weightlifting and Bodybuilding Federation (1972), which still exists today at a time when Ethiopia is experiencing a new phase of male muscular beauty.

With regard to class, sources suggest that modern sports in Ethiopia was largely the pastime of the male educated elite or those serving

---

¹⁰⁵ Donald Levine, 'The Masculinity Ethic and the Spirit of Warriorhood in Ethiopian and Japanese Cultures', *International Journal of Ethiopian Studies*, 2:1/2 (Summer/Fall 2005–2006), 164.
¹⁰⁶ Bromber, 'Ethiopian Wrestling', 27.
¹⁰⁷ Peter P. Garretson, *A Victorian Gentleman & Ethiopian Nationalist: The Life & Times of Hakim Wärqenäh, Dr. Charles Martin* (Woodbridge, 2012), p. 127.
¹⁰⁸ Clifford Putney defined Muscular Christianity 'as a Christian commitment to health and manliness': *Muscular Christianity: Manhood and Sports in Protestant America, 1880–1920* (Cambridge MA, London, 2003), p. 2. Looking at protestant circles in the US, he argues that the idea declined after the Second World War. This observation cannot be substantiated for Ethiopia and, arguably, not for other parts of the global South either, discussed for instance in Harald Fischer-Tiné, Stefan Huebner, and Ian Tyrrell (eds), *Spreading Protestant Modernity: Global Perspectives on the Social Work of the YMCA and YWCA, 1889–1970* (Honolulu, 2020). The authors provide a general discussion of Muscular Christianity as part of the 'Protestant Modernization Project' in their introduction to the volume, pp. 8–10.

in the armed forces. This observation especially holds true for those sports that required expensive equipment. Studies on sports in Africa of the 1970s already demanded scholars investigate which kinds of sports were pursued by which class. Thus, Ali A. Mazrui derives the success of African and Afro-American athletes in athletics (boxing, wrestling, or running) from the fact that these sports were labour-intensive and not capital-intensive as with horse riding or lawn tennis.[109] However, class boundaries become blurred at times. In my book, I demonstrate how the YMCA opened its doors to youth from underprivileged strata and, thus, spread ideas about modern sports to young people from the poor sections of (urban) society. The part on the early Boy Scout movement in Ethiopia in Chapter 3 argues that the selection of orphans as pupils of the so-called 'Boy Scout School' explicitly served to break the hereditary privileges of Ethiopian elite families in military contexts. Football was appropriated by all strata of the urban population, including the provincial governor of Tigray. Furthermore, I argue that the existing data on leisure activities in the productive sector in Ethiopia under Haile Selassie's rule indicate links between labour unions, sports clubs, and politics[110] – which we can clearly see later for the socialist period – started before 1974.

A study on modern sports that focuses exclusively on youth misses half of the story, however. Thus, I include the changing lives of instructors, coaches, PE teachers, and sports officials within the athletic complex. The biography of Yidnek'achew Tesemma (1921–87), the father of Ethiopian football, is but one telling example of how an athlete became a sports official within three successive regimes (Fascist, imperial/Haile Selassie, and socialist). His career shows remarkable continuity across historical periods. Others, such as 'father of Ethiopian bodybuilding' Girma Cheru, split their time between working as a PE teacher, exercise to achieve their personal athletic ambitions, and coaching. In such cases, the boundary between leisure and work becomes blurred.

Sports, Leisure, and Pleasure

In their seminal article on leisure in African history, Emmanuel Akyeampong and Charles Ambler stress the fluidity of the concept and call for a thorough examination of how activities are conceptualized as leisure and by whom.[111] Ethiopian institutions of higher learning, where sports was

---

[109] Ali A. Mazrui, 'Boxer Muhammad Ali and Soldier Idi Amin as International Political Symbols: The Bioeconomics of Sport and War', *Comparative Studies in Society and History,* 19:2 (1977), 205.

[110] Lisa A. Lindsay, 'Trade Unions and Football Clubs: Gender and the "Modern" Public Sphere in Colonial Southwest Nigeria', in Paul Tiyambe Zeleza and Cassandra Rachel Veney (eds), *Leisure in Urban Africa* (Trenton NJ, Asmara, 2003), pp. 105–24.

[111] Emmanuel Akyeampong and Charles Ambler, 'Leisure in African History:

a compulsory subject; volunteer organizations and correction homes, where sports served as a means of character training; and hotels such as the Addis Ababa Hilton, which formed female sports teams for the sake of gender equality, all most likely resorted to a discourse on 'rational' recreation rather than to notions of 'fun'. In contrast, recent scholarship on Africa explicitly foregrounds leisure as pleasure and fun and, thus, 'off-limits topics'. They enable us to gain a fresh look at everyday life in African settings, i.e. 'ordinary and extraordinary aspects of lived experiences and daily practices that provide valuable insights into broader social issues'.[112] Sports in youth clubs, which aimed at the correction of problematic youth, provided space for camaraderie and friendship.[113]

Including the growing body of memoir literature, as well as blogs and online photo archives, I argue that modern sports was not only a tool for correction through useful recreation but also a source of fun in urban Ethiopia during the 1950s to 1970s.[114] A look at travelogues, ethnographic works, and general descriptions of Ethiopia from the 1930s that cover the subject of games, sports, and leisure, already stress both aspects, i.e. seriousness and fun.[115] Incidentally, during my numerous research visits to Ethiopia from 2009 to 2018, I found the theme of sports and leisure a fantastic door-opener to conversations about everyday experiences in the past, simply because it is associated with youth and fun.

Sports, Technological Development, and the Production of Space

Studies on the development of cinema culture and the spread of modern media, as well as the installation of electricity in African cities, highlight the nexus between technological development and leisure.[116] My book contributes to studies which use sports as a gateway to research

---

An Introduction', *The International Journal of African Historical Studies*, 35:1 (2002), 6.
[112] Oluwakemi M. Balogun and Melissa Graboyes, 'Every Day Life in Africa: The Importance of Leisure and Fun', in Oluwakemi M. Balogun, Lisa Gilman, Melissa Graboyes, and Habib Iddrisu (eds), *Africa Every Day: Fun, Leisure, and Expressive Culture on the Continent* (Athens OH, 2019), p. 1.
[113] Michael J. Gennaro, '"We are Building the New Nigeria": Lagos, Boy's Clubs, and Leisure, 1945–60', in Oluwakemi M. Balogun, Lisa Gilman, Melissa Graboyes, and Habib Iddrisu (eds), *Africa Every Day: Fun, Leisure, and Expressive Culture on the Continent* (Athens OH, 2019), pp. 155–64.
[114] For sports especially see Fik'ru Kĭdane, *YePĭyassa lij* [Child from Piazza] (Addis Ababa, 2009) and Michel B. Lentakis, *Ethiopia: A View from Within* (London, 2005).
[115] Most notably, Marcel Griaule, *Jeux et divertissements abyssins* (Paris, 1935); Ladislas Farago, *Abyssinia on the Eve* (London, 1935); Adrien Zervos, *L'empire d'Ethiopie: le miroir de l'Ethiopie moderne 1906–1935* (Athènes, 1936).
[116] Laura Fair, *Pastimes and Politics: Culture, Community, and Identity in Post-Abolition Urban Zanzibar, 1890–1945* (Athens OH, 2007).

this relationship. Apart from motor races and stadiums with loudspeakers and floodlights, technical equipment used in competitions, such as the stopwatch and measuring tape, and other normal tools for technical disciplines, have transformed the perception of sports. Films about 'the best ways to throw the javelin shot ... and good methods for running, high jumping, broad jumping and playing tennis' were screened in public.[117] Newspaper articles provided information about medical apparatuses used to measure the biotechnical data of Olympic champion Abebe Bikila and other athletes.[118] Radio broadcasts made football games accessible to thousands of Ethiopian fans. Those who could not afford a ticket to enter the stadium used electricity poles to watch the game. Thus, technological development transformed sports as an athletic practice as well as its consumption.

I further argue that the appropriation of modern sports not only resulted in the proliferation of new body techniques but also in the spread of suitable spaces in the urban fabric such as playing fields, gymnasiums, and stadiums. They became spaces of highly regulated inward and outward mobility, however. Membership fees limited access to facilities of the YMCA and sports clubs. Enrolment in schools and university colleges opened possibilities to participate in athletics classes. Employment at hotels or in the public sector provided the means and the institutional structure for inclusion in welfare measures such as sports teams.

Looking at motor races, which became popular in Ethiopia from the mid-1950s, I demonstrate how they changed perceptions of spaces and produced, in the case of the Ethiopian Highland Rally, a new conception of 'the' Ethiopian Highlands. Its advertisement as 'Africa's toughest car race'[119] changed ideas about the Highlands from a lovely tourist destination to a demanding space for man and machine. Furthermore, races going as far as the Eritrean capital Asmara were not only a form

---

[117] On 18 February 1959, the USIS presented an outdoor film on sports in front of the municipal hall in Jimma. The audience mainly consisted of the students from the Jimma Agricultural Technical School, which was supported by the Point Four Program. Carl Kurth, coach at Trinity College in Connecticut and interim sports master through an exchange programme, commented on the film: *Year Book of the Jimma Agricultural Technical School* 1959, 4, IES 371.805 JIM AGR.

[118] 'Ye-Abebe Bīkīla t'ēninet' [The examination of Abebe Bikila], *Addīs Zemen*, 24 nehasē 1960 [30 August 1968], 3.

[119] 'Ethiopia: Cars Start Gruelling Three Thousand Mile Rally. Despite World Petrol Shortage. 1973', British Pathé, www.britishpathe.com/video/VLVACVOBOHRQ371LZQB7IS89NBKKA-ETHIOPIA-CARS-START-GRUELLING-THREE-THOUSAND-MILE-RALLY-DESPITE/query/MILE [accessed 15 September 2021].

of leisure for motor sports enthusiasts, but also a strategy to constitute imperial territory that included Eritrea as a province.

The production of imperial space also occurred via largely identical choreographies of regional competitions organized by the Inter-School Athletic Association. I argue that they became replicas of the final sports meet in Haile Selassie I Stadium in Addis Ababa with its emphasis on the loyal, fit, educated youth. On the representational level, stadiums turned into political spaces. However, stadiums are also venues that reveal the impossibility of absolute regulation when observing the consumption side of sports. Football fans and other sports enthusiasts found numerous ways to watch from outside the stadium depending on the natural surroundings, the structure of the stadium (walled or open) and the availability of electricity poles, billboards, or roofs. As meeting points, stadiums potentially turned into spaces of sports, fandom, and economic transactions, with all sorts of legal and illegal activities going on in and around their premises. I argue that these spaces of order through spatial regulation could easily turn into spaces of disorder and limited control. Reconstructions of stadiums for various occasions served not only to enlarge their capacity but also to regain control.

Sports and Propaganda

If leisure is, potentially, a form of social control, it also serves propaganda aims – i.e. to advertise and inculcate specific values or a particular 'idea of man'.[120] In twentieth-century Ethiopia, this idea was by no means uniform but highly diversified according to socio-economic, regional, ethnic, and religious contexts. I argue that sports as an element of propaganda appeared in relation to changing ideas of the Ethiopian 'New Man' – as the modern subject and potential citizen of the emperor, the modern colonial subject during the Italian Fascist occupation, or as the Socialist Man after 1974.

From the 1920s onwards, a growing number of official print, radio and, from 1964, television media regularly covered sports events, athletes' biographies, and the construction of sports infrastructure. School yearbooks and YMCA annual reports documented and advertised sports as an important tool for shaping a well-rounded or balanced (male) personality. Mass events such as athletic performances during state visits as well as the presentation of Boy Scout manoeuvres to foreign journalists served to advertise Ethiopia's road to modernity from the 1930s onwards. In an adaptation of Italian Fascist propaganda to the colonial context, sports made up one-third of the news in the Amharic press published during the

---

[120] Instead of formulating a general propaganda definition, Thymian Bussemer (communication studies) emphasizes historical and geographical specificities and suggests looking for constants within the discursive system, especially the 'idea of man': *Propaganda: Konzepte und Theorien* (Wiesbaden, 2005), p. 16.

occupation. It advertised a colonial modernity that brought cycling races to urban centres, regulations for existing horse races, and sports facilities to segregated 'native' areas. I argue that the sports pages showed in text and visuals that the Ethiopian 'New Man' under occupation was an athlete or enthusiastic sports fan who showed loyalty to the occupiers in uniform and collaborating *Rases*.

Print media of the post-liberation period portrayed sports as a means to strengthen defence and to form the youth into a fit vanguard carrying the flag of progress throughout the empire. In contrast to other statesmen of the time such as Stalin or Mao Tse-tung, Haile Selassie never appeared as the sportsman in order to display political virility, but rather as the guiding, benevolent ruler who rewards the champions. In this position, we can also see him conveying the trophies in beauty contests and other leisure events. I argue that these occasions became part of a symbolic repertoire that served to present him as a modern head of state.

Structure of the Book

By contextualizing sports in daily practices and institutions outside the armed forces, athletic clubs, and Olympic ambitions, this book looks at physical education, sports as leisure, in urban development, as propaganda, and through volunteer organizations. By shifting the focus to these aspects, the chapters of the book reveal more than one possible chronology. The chronologically separate chapters overlap and present continuities in a number of ways. They cast light on long-term developments such as physical education, the changing spatial configuration of urban leisure or the transformation of the Boy Scout movement from a paramilitary body to a volunteer organization.

I start with sports as an urban leisure practice from 1900 to the mid-1930s, i.e. before the invasion of the Italian occupying army. Chapter 1 focuses on the promotion of sports through urbanization via infrastructure development and economic growth, through the emergence of modern education schools, and through an element of military reform that targeted the youngest educated stratum of the population, i.e. the establishment of the Boy Scout Association. I argue in favour of applying a broad lens that studies sports not only at modern educational institutions, but also as a form of associational leisure activity that gained ground on a global scale. I show how sports as useful recreation emerged due to increasing infrastructure developments such as railway construction and the related influx of migrant labour. Institutionalization in foreign politics that resulted in the opening of foreign legations also played a role, leading for example to transformations in horse racing culture. Accounts from personnel from the Middle East as well as teachers from European countries and the US add to the understanding of the introduction and development of physical education in Ethiopia. The ideas they brought suited local forms of physical fitness with military backgrounds. These were most prominent in the combination of schooling and Boy Scouting, charged with the task of training the much needed cadets for a modern Ethiopian army.

In Chapter 2, I analyse the role of sports in propaganda during the Italian Fascist occupation, focusing on two Amharic newspapers: *Ye-K'ēsar Mengist Mel'iktenya* (The Messenger of Ceasar's Government) and *YeRoma Birhan* (The Light of Rome). In contrast to studies on sports in Africa, past and present, which analyse the sports pages in newspapers that were less affected by censorship, although still political,[121] I demonstrate how sports reporting served as a political instrument for creating consensus on Fascist ideas and practices. Apart from being the means of distributing propaganda experiences, with sports as the creator of consensus, I suggest that some of the ideas around Italian regeneration met the very specific context of an existing local attempt at modernization. Thus, sports became part of the newspapers' rhetoric of a (Fascist) 'civilizing' mission. The 'civilized' product should not only be an athlete, but also a person that understood the consumption of matches and races as a form of useful entertainment. Apart from introducing codified rules (especially in football) and related temporal and spatial regimes, the Italian Fascist administration also implemented segregation along racial and religious lines. Sports reporting legitimized and actively supported this policy by normalizing it.

Covering the time span between the mid-1940s and the late 1960s, Chapter 3 looks at the role of sports in education and leisure. I start with a section on modern sports as urban leisure and argue that the Ethiopian 'New Man' of the post-liberation period was by no means only the educated, disciplined, and physically fit subject, but also a personality that belonged to an emerging 'leisure class'. Although this part draws heavily on memoirs by male writers, it offers more than football narratives. The 1940s was the decade when sports as physical education was introduced at all levels of the educational system, which prompted the demand for qualified physical education teachers. Their training and acceptance were by no means easy, as the chapter will show. Enthusiasts from the Department of Physical Education and Boy Scouting (MoE), headmasters, and PE teachers built a sports-related network, the Ethiopian Inter-School Athletic Association (EISAA), which organized a refined system of competitions from the provincial to the national level. In the final section, I deal with the re-established Boy Scouts

---

[121] Michelle Sikes, 'Print Media and the History of Women's Sport in Africa: The Kenyan Case of Barriers to International Achievement', *History in Africa*, 43 (2016), 323–45.

as part of the Ethiopian and Eritrean educational systems. I argue that the Ethiopian movement shifted away from its emphasis on national defence. Instead, it promoted a broader, demilitarized form of civic engagement and fitness through adventure and hiking.

The history of modern sports and youth training would remain incomplete without a chapter on the YMCA. Thus, Chapter 4 specifically considers the multiple functions of sports within the Ethiopian Young Men's Christian Association. Commencing its work in the late 1940s, the Ethiopian YMCA's organized activities ranged from sports as useful recreation to the creation of successful athletes and national teams. I discuss the role of the Ethiopian, Egyptian, and North American secretaries in the promotion of sports and physical education. With regard to sports facilities and programmes that mushroomed at the various YMCA branches in the empire, I explicitly discuss the question of who had access and, thus, an athletic chance. This became all the more important when the YMCA hosted the national federations in table tennis, boxing, volleyball, and basketball that competed on the national and international level. This chapter shows how, from the mid-1950s onwards, the YMCA became a hot spot for shaping the 'muscular Ethiopian' and stood at the forefront of establishing bodybuilding and weightlifting in the country. Looking at the development of sports through the Ethiopian YMCA offers an excellent opportunity to question established chronologies that formulate the revolution in 1974 as a radical break. At various points in the chapter, I demonstrate that the focus on leadership training, helping specifically the underprivileged sections of the population and investing in the development of athletic success, guaranteed the YMCA's comparatively smooth transition into the socialist societal context and the institutional frame of the Sports Commission in 1978.

Where did Ethiopians, and those who made Ethiopia their home, engage in sports? Which kinds of infrastructure existed and for whom? What functions did places like stadiums, hotel lobbies, or motor racing circuits fulfil beyond sports proper? In Chapter 5, I discuss socio-spatial aspects of sports and expand upon arguments about this issue made in earlier chapters. I start with educational institutions, by highlighting how creative teachers and pupils tackled the shortage of athletic facilities and equipment up-front. Institutions of higher learning, where sports continued as a compulsory activity, had to provide the necessary facilities for their students, which also served as advertisements targeting prospective international staff. In Ethiopia as elsewhere, stadiums are always more than places for doing sports. They are spaces for political ritual. Looking at early stadium construction and usage, I demonstrate how opening ceremonies, athletic performance, and the presentation of trophies by politicians produced social spaces that served both sports as a physical activity in competition and sports as a spectacle for political power. I continue the chapter by looking at how places of entertainment, locations for tourism, and work-related buildings included sports. In the capital especially, cinemas and theatres served as venues for boxing bouts and bodybuilding shows. Sports facilities became part of modern hotels. Lobbies of public buildings in municipalities hosted table tennis matches. I finish the chapter with an account of motor races that gained popularity in a number of Ethiopian urban centres from the mid-1950s. I argue that motor races such as the Ethiopian Highland Rally symbolized technological and urban progress through a sport that included the most important symbol of modern life, including on an individual level – the motor car. The race's international reputation as a great challenge for man and machine because of the demanding terrain was yet another way to put Ethiopia on the global sports map.

Writing this book after more than ten years of research, I had to make choices. As a result, a number of gateways remain to be explored and the wealth of material that I came across should be developed further. In the conclusion of my book, I share my ideas about how research on the social history of sports in Ethiopia could be continued.

Sources

This book is based on a multitude of written, oral, and visual historical sources. Archival documents include official correspondence, pamphlets, posters, newspapers, and journal articles in Amharic, Tigrinya, English, German, and French, as well as historical photographs. They are located in the following archives, libraries, and private collections: The Institute of Ethiopian Studies (Addis Ababa); the Ethiopian National Archive (Addis Ababa); the Archive and Library of the Ministry of Education (Addis Ababa); the Library of the Kotebe College for Teacher Training (Addis Ababa); the Library and Archive of the Ethiopian Sports Commission (Addis Ababa); the Library of the Centre Français des Études Éthiopiennes (Addis Ababa); the Kautz Family YMCA Archives, University of Minnesota (Minneapolis, USA); the Norma Marion Alloway Library, Trinity Western University (Langley, Canada); The National Archives (London, UK); the Political Archive of the Federal Foreign Office (Berlin, Germany); and Surafiel Photo Studio – private collection (Mek'ele, Ethiopia). I would have loved to look at police reports of the time, which might potentially bring local voices about the appropriation of modern athletic practices more to the fore, but this was beyond the scope of this book.

I conducted oral interviews with former sports officials who had previously worked for the Ethiopian Olympic Committee, former PE teachers, coaches, and athletes, as well as former officials and members of the Ethiopian YMCA and Boy Scout Association. Between 2009 and 2012, I interviewed the heads and technical directors of the following national sports federations: cultural sports, boxing, athletics, cycling, football, karate, volleyball, bodybuilding, and weightlifting. In 2016 and 2017, officials and members of the Armenian, Greek, Italian, and Yemeni communities generously shared their memories, documents, and photos with me. Concerning the topic of sporting grounds and stadiums, further interviews were organized with officials in Addis Ababa and Mek'ele. Apart from semi-structured interviews based on approved questionnaires, numerous informal conversations transpired regarding sports and leisure activities during the 1960s and 1970s. These correspondences included e-mails and letters. I also used historical materials – especially films and photographs – that are freely available on the internet, as well as published memoirs in Amharic and English.

The purpose of this book, as outlined above, has been specifically to examine the societal context in which modern sports emerged in Ethiopia. In developing that focus, there were areas that I decided the book would not and could not cover. Readers who are specifically searching for information on topics such as the Ethiopian army sports clubs or the development of institutional structures such as the National Olympic Committee will be disappointed. This is also true for those who are interested in specific sports' histories, such as football or long-distance running, or extended biographies of famous athletes such as Abebe Bikila or sports officials like Yidnek'achew Tesemma.[122] They are not absent, but I only deal with organizing bodies and famous people when they appear in the contexts that I develop in the chapters outlined above. Thus, when I talk about 'muscling-in' at the Ethiopian YMCA, I cannot do so without describing the development of the Ethiopian Bodybuilding and Weightlifting Federation. In the same chapter, Abebe Bikila does not appear as a marathon champion, but as a member of the YMCA Physical Education Committee. There, he instructed boys and young men on how they might better develop their physical prowess and helped them to see other opportunities in recreation. Such an approach, I would argue, contributes to the enrichment of personal and institutional biographies because it shows formerly neglected fields of agency.

---

[122] For biographical data on Yidnek'achew Tesemma especially see, Tadele Yidnek'achew Tesemma, *Yidnek'achew Tesemma, meskerem 1-1914 – nehasē 13-1979. Be'alemna besport 'alem* [Yidnek'achew Tesemma, 11 September 1921 to 19 August 1981: In the world and in the sports world] (Addis Ababa, 1989 EC, 1996/7).

1
The Emergence of Ethiopia's Modern Sports Scene (1900–1935)

In 1924, when *Ras* Tafari travelled through Europe, he gained firsthand experience of modern sports and the 'Olympic spirit' at the eighth Olympic Games in Paris. He enquired of Pierre de Coubertin (President of the International Olympic Committee), in a private conversation, about the possibility and requirements for participating next time. *Ras* Tafari then formally applied to the IOC for Ethiopia's participation in the ninth Olympic Games in Amsterdam, 1928. The newly appointed Belgian president of the organization, Henri Baillet-Latour, refused this on the grounds that Ethiopia as well as other African countries would have neither the ability nor the facilities to participate in or to host Olympic Games.[1]

Nevertheless, the application clearly shows that Ethiopia's 'chief modernizer' had understood the potential of modern sports as a key to worldwide recognition. Although the modern Ethiopian (male) body was not a topic in *Berhanena Selam* – the journal that usually discussed modernizing the empire – various bodily practices performed on different social scales brought corporeal modernity into educational institutions and diverse places of leisure.[2]

This chapter scrutinises the introduction of modern sports through modern institutions and changing perceptions of leisure. It focuses on its promotion through urbanization via infrastructural development and economic growth, through the establishment of modern schools, and through an element of military reform that targeted the youngest educated stratum of the population. Arguably, developments in Ethiopia resonate what the historian Michelle Sikes described in her general statement for colonial Africa during the first half of the twentieth century:

---

[1] Yidnek'achew Asefu, *Yaltenegerelet yehager balewileta, – Bek'ele Alemu 'Gant'* [The man whose service for his country was not talked about – Bek'ele Alemu 'Gant'] (Addis Ababa, 2004 EC/2011/12), p. 16; Tamirat Gebremariam and Benoît Gaudin, 'Sports and Physical Education in Ethiopia during the Italian Occupation, 1936–41', in Michael J. Gennaro and Saheed Aderinto (eds), *Sports in African History, Politics and Identity Formation* (New York, 2019), p. 197.

[2] I am grateful to Fits'um Woldemariam Deginetu for checking all issues for contributions about physical fitness.

'Forces unleashed by colonial capitalism fused with local conditions [and shaped] the contours of African athletic development [and] sports such as cricket, rugby, tennis, hockey, athletics, boxing, and gymnastics were all in circulation', with football assuming the lead.[3]

Although there are practically no sources that allow any sound statement on the introduction of modern sports through the reformed armed forces, there are assumptions about the role of these institutions. However, Tamirat Gebremariam and Benoît Gaudin may not be wrong in basing their thoughts about the early promotion of athletics in the Ethiopian army on existing research on sports in colonial armies elsewhere in Africa.[4] Despite the fact that foreign advisors, students from noble families who had experienced physical education abroad, or members of the foreign communities in Ethiopia, pushed modern sports and related ideas about disciplining youth through useful recreation and entertainment, initiatives were by no means restricted to them. In order to be successful on a broader scale, modern sports practices had to tap into existing ones, such as local wrestling, boxing, *genna*, or local chess. Included in the agrarian cycles, festivities, and rituals, their competitive nature testifies that *Sportgeist* was nothing particularly European.[5] In contrast to colonial contexts in Africa and elsewhere, many 'folk games, martial traditions, and regional cultures that did not match European interests were diluted and gradually disappeared',[6] local sports practices in Ethiopia continued and fulfilled their various social functions. What can be established is that they were rarely reported on in media that discussed Ethiopia's modernization, such as *Berhanena Selam*, *Ethiopian Herald*, or *Addīs Zemen*.

Research in *yebahil sport* (cultural sports) or *nebbar sport* (traditional sports), started in the 1930s by the French ethnographer Marcel Griaule,[7] describes wrestling as a widespread and highly diversified practice in Tigray, Wello, Gojjam, Begemder, and Shoa. From the late 1970s onwards, surveys pursued throughout Ethiopia revealed an even higher diversity as physical practice often linked to specific social functions such as religious festivals or life cycle events.[8] Wrestling's historical political impor-

---

[3] Michelle Sikes, 'Sport History and Historiography', *Oxford Research Encyclopedia of African History* (2018), https://doi.org/10.1093/acrefore/9780190277734.013.232, p. 7.
[4] Tamirat and Gaudin, 'Sports and Physical Education in Ethiopia', p. 198.
[5] Peter Alegi, *African Soccerscapes: How a Continent Changed the World's Game* (London, 2010), p. 1.
[6] Sikes, 'Sport History and Historiography', p. 3.
[7] Marcel Griaule, *Jeux et divertissements abyssins* (Paris, 1935), p. 58.
[8] Tefere Mekonnen, *Nebbar sport* [Traditional sports], MS. Library of the Ethiopian Sports Commission (Addis Ababa, 1973 EC, 1981/2); Tibebu Gorfu, *Yebahil sport mazewterīya sifrawoch standerd menesha t'inat* [Pilot study on the standardization of places for doing everyday cultural sports] Addis Ababa,

tance is often stressed by relating it to *Ats'ē* Tewodros II (1818–68). The story goes that he invited British settlers to try the strength of some of his men and rewarded the winner with the full complement of arms and armour – as befits a warrior – as well as mules, oxen, and sheep. Tewodros himself is said to have acted as the referee in these matches.[9] In contrast to Kenya,[10] where colonial and post-colonial governments, marginalized local wrestling practices to an extent that local rules seem hardly to be revived, Ethiopia provides a different example. Despite not being considered 'modern', its strong relevance for local communities even prevented Olympic and freestyle wrestling to get firm ground in Ethiopia outside the so-called foreign communities. Local forms of horse riding competitions *feres shert* and *gugs*, which Richard Pankhurst described as 'mock cavalry warfare',[11] remained an important athletic practice primarily but not exclusively, for the Ethiopian elite. As we will see in this chapter, they were part of the prince's education and past-time, and provided links to 'modern' horse races as well as polo. *Genna*, a form of hockey, is especially associated with Christmas. In Ethiopia, legend has it that the shepherds played the game when they heard from the angels that Christ was born.[12] It is one of the rare athletic scenes in popular orthodox religious paintings. In contrast to wrestling and horse riding, the local form of chess called *shent'erej* was increasingly side-lined and almost non-existent by the 1960s.[13]

Since the development of modern sports was largely an urban phenomenon, this chapter starts with some reflections about the nexus between urbanization, changing industrial patterns, and sports. In this respect, Ethiopia did not differ from developments elsewhere. In contrast to contexts where colonial governments and foreign companies attempted to have exclusive control over these processes, all industrial, urban, and infrastructural projects in Ethiopia had to be negotiated with

---

uncatalogued MS., Library of the Ethiopian Sports Commission (1993 EC, 2000/1); Be'ītyop'iya bahilawī sport fēdērēshin, *Bahilawī sportochachin sir'at iniwek'achew* [Ethiopian Cultural Sports Federation, Let us know our cultural sports correctly] uncatalogued MS., Library of the Ethiopian Sports Commission (Addis Ababa, 1992 EC, 1999/2000).
[9] Be'ītyop'iya bahilawī sport fēdērēshin, *Bahilawī sportochachinin*, p. 31.
[10] Matthew Carotenuto, 'Grappling with the Past: Wrestling and Performative Identity in Kenya', *The International Journal of the History of Sport*, 30:16 (2013), 1889–1902.
[11] Richard Pankhurst, 'The Horsemen of Old-Time Ethiopia', *Ethiopia Observer*, 8:1 (1970), 7.
[12] J. Gordon Melton (ed.), *Religious Celebrations: An Encyclopedia of Holidays, Festivals, Solemn Observances, and Spiritual Commemorations*, vol. 1 (Santa Barbara, 2011), p. 289.
[13] Richard Pankhurst, 'History and Principles of Ethiopian Chess', *Journal of Ethiopian Studies*, 9:2 (1971), 170.

Ethiopian officials, often including the emperor.[14] Under *Ats'ē* Menelik II (1889–1913), Ethiopia opened up more widely through trade and, most importantly, infrastructural developments such as the railways. Similar to what Peter Alegi observed for the history of football in Africa, the spread of modern sports in Ethiopia was pushed by the railway line running from Djibuti to Dire Dawa and later to Addis Ababa.[15] Construction heavily relied on foreign vocational expertise. Growing foreign communities brought with them specific ideas about useful education and recreation. The chapter thus continues with a discussion of the development of modern sports through the establishment of modern schools. Although the physical fitness of the modern Ethiopian subject was never much discussed by the modernizing elite, it is the very fact that physical education was taught at modern schools quite early that suggests their role in larger attempts to form it. Arguably, the modernizers did not only think about modern kinds of physical fitness in terms of 'sound mind in sound body' metaphors. It was in some cases also very concretely linked to producing cadets for the reformed armed forces. Thus, the third part of the chapter will consider physical fitness via early Boy Scout activities as preparation for a military career.

Urbanization, Labour, and Leisure

Due to the scarcity of sources that specifically deal with the emergence and development of modern sports in Ethiopia during the first half of the twentieth century, detours or indirect ways of approaching the subject are necessary. One gateway is to link sports to economic development, which brought about the emergence or growth of settlements into towns. Villages at the crossroads of important trade routes such as Dessie or Nekemte became commercial centres with large markets. Existing towns such as Harar reconfigured and expanded their translocal relations due to a shift in power relations after the conquest by *Ats'ē* Menelik II in 1887. Apart from the newly built political centre of Addis Ababa, other urban centres came into being because of important infrastructural developments. Gambela in Western Ethiopia, for example, emerged as a modern, planned inland port town in connection with the establishment of a shipping route between Western Ethiopia and Anglo-Egyptian Sudan. The other prominent example is Dire Dawa, also a planned town, which became the most important place along

---

[14] Hasib Ydlibi's biography provides an excellent account about the difficulties that foreigners faced when attempted to set up a business during the reign of Menelik II (May Ydlibi, *With Ethiopian Rulers: A Biography of Hasib Yidlibi*, edited by Bahru Zewde (Addis Ababa, 2006)).

[15] Alegi, *African Soccerscapes*, pp. 1–2.

the Djibouti – Addis Ababa Railway. In relation to the development of modern sports, this industrial boomtown provides several cases examined more closely in this chapter.

Urban development through reconfigured economic as well as political ties resulted not only in the growth of the urban population as such, but also a growing influx of foreigners from South Asia, the Middle East, and Europe. Greek, Armenian, and South Asian business people shared in and competed over the local trade and regional monopoly. French and British personnel assumed leading roles in the implementation of infrastructure projects. Foreign diplomatic missions opened in the capital and consular offices in other towns such as Harar, or Gore – a major commercial centre near Gambela.[16] Emerging workshops and small factories ensured growing demand for new material goods. Commercial and communication networks established by post offices and branches of the Bank of Abyssinia facilitated financial transactions and the exchange of information. Hotels and restaurants opened to cater to the needs of foreign migrants and people who had made Ethiopia their new home. They offered possibilities to spend time on games as a way to interact, channel homesickness, or simply kill time. Later, when families joined the workers, their children needed education; the majority did not have the financial means to send their children to schools in Sudan, Egypt, or even further away. Thus, schools opened in various towns, with teaching conducted in European languages as well as in Arabic and Amharic. They met the growing demand for modern schooling, including physical education, as early as under *Ats'ē* Menelik II and later *Ras* Tafari/Haile Selassie – a topic that deserves separate space in this chapter.

Arguably, such economic, political, and educational developments, which already began in the late nineteenth century and gained momentum after the First World War, gradually changed perceptions of time including leisure and spare time. New urban entertainment produced spaces for sports-related activities for foreign workers, but also the local nobility. In various localities, hotels offered the opportunity to meet to play billiards.[17] *Le'ul Lij* Īyasu, for example, who followed Menelik II on the throne, frequented the Taitu Hotel (built in 1907) in Addis Ababa to enjoy the game. He is reported to have been an excellent billiards player.[18] In his memoirs *Ras* Imru Haile Selassie pointed out that 'Lij Īyasu sometimes made him [*Dejazmach* Teferī] go to a hotel, where he would per-

---

[16] Richard Pankhurst, *The History of Ethiopian Towns from the Mid-Nineteenth Century to 1935* (Stuttgart, 1985), pp. 240, 264.
[17] Herbert Vivian, *Abyssinia: Through the Lion-Land to the Court of the Lion of Judah* (London, 1901), p. 113, cited in Pankhurst, *The History of Ethiopian Towns*, p. 261.
[18] Built in 1907, the hotel was also known as Etegue Hotel, and, during the Italian occupation, Hotel Imperiale.

suade him so that they played *kerenbola* [billiards]'.[19] Narratives also hint at *Le'ul Lij* Īyasu using the game to humiliate *Dejazmach* Teferī and other people.[20] Other such places, like the Hotel de France with its Club de l'Union, which served as a 'bar, dancing hall, cinema, casino, and club',[21] might not have been the place for noble Ethiopians to enjoy billiards: in the 1920s, it was particularly attended by the French community.

Furthermore, if Dire Dawa was practically a 'French town',[22] we might assume that workers from the railway workshops played *boule* or one of its varieties, as people do in this town even today. In Djibouti – the starting point of the railway – *baguette* and *boule* are 'combined traces' of how French immigrants tried to idle 'away a few empty hours in the afternoon'.[23] In Dire Dawa, these people might also have been Greek workers who had received French citizenship while building the Suez Canal. They came and settled in large numbers in Dire Dawa and soon outnumbered the French.[24] Most probably, they knew *pétanque* – a *boule* variety that was widely spread all over the Mediterranean.

In Addis Ababa, the zone around St. George's Cathedral, in Mehal Arada and Seratenya Sefer (Workers' Quarter) became the main Greek residential area. The name of the latter indicates that its inhabitants built the new Ethiopian capital in the first decades of the twentieth century. Apart from mentioning billiards in various hotels, sources are silent about their (sporting) leisure activities. However, the football narrative explicitly links the Greek community of Addis Ababa to the advent of modern sports in Ethiopia. There seems to be general agreement that members of the foreign communities, who numbered approximately 14,500 in the Empire and 6,000 in Addis Ababa, introduced the game.[25] In the 1930s, the Greek community formed football teams in

---

[19] Ras Imru Haile Selassie, *Kayehut kemastawisew* [Of what I saw and remember] (Addis Ababa, 2002 EC, 2009/2010), p. 30. I am grateful to Ewa Wolk-Sore for identifying and translating the source.

[20] Michel B. Lentakis, *Ethiopia: A View from Within*, p. 41. In his biography of Haile Selassie, his nephew Asfa-Wossen Asserate recalls a story when the last emperor proved to be the best pool billiard player of the imperial family, indicating that the sport was one of his ways to relax. Asfa-Wossen Asserate, *Der letzte Kaiser von Afrika: Triumph und Tragödie des Haile Selassie* (Berlin, 2014), p. 15.

[21] Milena Batistoni and Gian Paolo Chiari, *Old Tracks in the New Flower: A Historical Guide to Addis Ababa* (Addis Ababa, 2004), p. 49.

[22] Arnold Henry Savage Landor, *Across the Widest Africa: An Account of the Country and the People of Eastern, Central and Western Africa as Seen During a Twelve Months' Journey from Djibuti to Cape Verde*, vol. 1 (London, 1907), pp. 16–18.

[23] Muddle Suzanne Lilius, 'Multiple Loyalty: Complex Identities in the Horn of Africa', in Muddle Suzanne Lilius (ed.), *Variations on the Theme of Somaliness* (Turku, 1998), p. 250.

[24] Lentakis, *Ethiopia: A View from Within*, p. 21.

[25] Sintayehu Tola, 'The History of St. George Sport Club' (Unpublished BA

Dire Dawa and Addis Ababa. In the capital, the precursor of Olympiacos – the Hellenic Athletic Association (formally established in 1943) – emerged. As early as the 1920s, children of the Greek community who had attended English schools in Egypt and Sudan created a team after their return to the Ethiopian capital. During the Italian occupation, which will be the topic of the next chapter, the Greek team took part in competitions organized by the Fascist Sports Bureau. When the Greek players defeated the Italian team 3–0 and 'Ethiopian fans burst into cheers, denouncing the Italian occupiers',[26] the Fascist administration banned all athletic activities of the Hellenic Athletic Association.

From 1924 onwards, four teams from the capital – Ararat (Armenian), Juventus (Italian), Olympiacos (Greek), and Indian Team (South Asian) – had a reserved place to play at the Jan Mēda racing grounds.[27] When a French Navy team from Djibouti played against an Ethiopian team in Addis Ababa in 1935, the home team consisted of players from these communities. There might be many reasons for the absence of Ethiopians on the 'Ethiopian' team. Local enthusiasts and players existed in the capital, but the acceptance of the sport amongst the population was very low. 'In some areas where good playing fields exist[ed], the owners of the land did not permit them to play in it. Whenever the players were found playing in such fields, they were whipped and sometimes imprisoned by Arada Zebenya (city police)'.[28] If possible, they used existing facilities such as Jan Mēda, Medfenya Gibī, Filwoha, T'alyan Sefer, and Shola Sefer in Addis Ababa, or school compounds. However, training facilities were rare, the equipment bad, and teams did not yet 'formally' exist. However, even before the Italian occupation, Ethiopian teams began to play, often representing the local quarters. When the Italian Fascists occupied the capital, four local football teams competed regularly. They proved of great propagandistic value during the Italian occupation, which is the topic of the next chapter.

In Addis Ababa, Armenian sports clubs also pursued other goals than simply spending leisure time, investing in hard training. The Armenian Sporting Association for Ethiopian-Armenian Youth, founded in 1928, excelled in football with its Ararat team. Another Armenian sports club, the Arax Union (est. 1930), was strong in football, too, but also trained thirty athletes in boxing, wrestling, and cycling. Both clubs aimed at the 'développement physique et moral de la jeunesse arméni-

---

thesis, Addis Ababa University, 1986), p. 5.
[26] 'History of Olympiacos', no date, typescript provided by the Greek Club in October 2017, 3.
[27] Tamirat and Gaudin, 'Sports and Physical Education in Ethiopia', p. 198; Solomon Addis Getahun, 'A History of Sport in Ethiopia', in Svein Ege, Harald Aspen, Birhanu Teferra, and Shiferaw Bekele (eds), *Proceedings of the 16th International Conference of Ethiopian Studies* (Trondheim, 2009), p. 114.
[28] Sintayehu Tola, 'The History of St. George Sport Club', 11.

enne de la Capitale'.[29] Later, well-known Armenian families, such as the Behesnilians, Djerrahians, and Pojharians had tennis courts in their private compounds where they hosted invitation-only matches on Saturdays.[30] As elsewhere, tennis became a marker of distinction. However, the real sign that Armenians were recognized as amongst the influential people in town was Khosroff Boghossian's role in horse racing, which brought him the title *Chevalier de l'étoile d'Ethiopie*.[31]

Equestrian sports are well studied for Ethiopia.[32] They provide an excellent lens to examine how far an established practice served one purpose, but developed in two different directions. Horse riding and racing were not only very popular in various parts of the empire, but they also served to distinguish the rider through chivalry, displayed through racing (*feres shert'*) or chasing with shield and lace (*gugs*). The relation between owner/jockey and his horse found expression in gallant titles (mostly reserved for nobles and emperors), which consisted of the word *Abba* (father) plus the name of his horse. Just to mention one very prominent example: Haile Selassie's father, *Ras* Makonnen, carried the gallant title Abba Kagnew. Much later, in the 1950s, this name re-appeared as the official name of the first stadium in the provincial capital of Mek'ele (Tigray), until the downfall of the empire in 1974. Although horsemanship, chivalry, and thus equestrian sports, were primarily performed and narrated as men's business, women were successful on horseback, too; amongst them Weyzero Tsehaywork Darghie, the granddaughter of King Sahle Selassie (who had ruled the Province of Shoa from 1813 to 1847), and close relative of *Ats'ē* Menelik II.[33] It would of course be interesting to know if she carried a gallant title, too.

Whereas traditional horse racing and chasing continued throughout the empire, the capital saw the transformation of the Jan Mēda racing grounds into a modern race track[34] to merge the needs of both the local nobility and the foreign communities residing in the capital. Created in 1903, Menelik II granted the open field to the Imperial Club.[35] Apart

[29] These clubs aimed at the 'physical and moral development of the Armenian youth of the capital'. Vivian, *Abyssinia*, p. 499.
[30] Interview with Vartkes Nalbandian, President of the Armenian Community in Ethiopia (Addis Ababa, 27 February 2014).
[31] Adrien Zervos, *L'empire d'Ethiopie: le miroir de l'Ethiopie moderne 1906–1935* (Athènes, 1936), p. 140.
[32] Richard Pankhurst, 'The Horse-Men of Old Time Ethiopia', *Ethiopia Observer*, 13:1 (1970), 2–7; Ethiopian Equestrian Association, *Ethiopian Riders and Their Horses* (Addis Ababa, 2005).
[33] Ethiopian Equestrian Association, *Ethiopian Riders*, p. 52.
[34] Later, Jan Mēda became Ethiopia's first airport. I am grateful to Peter Garretson for this information.
[35] Charles F. Rey, *Unconquered Abyssinia* (London, 1923), p. 147, cited in Milena Batistoni and Gian Paolo Chiari, *Old Tracks in the New Flower: A Historical Guide to Addis Ababa* (Addis Ababa, 2004), p. 146.

from horse races of distances between 150 and 1,200 metres, Jan Mēda hosted football games, polo matches at a specially prepared segment of Jan Mēda race track, and included a tennis court. A pamphlet published on the centenary of the British legation in Addis Ababa (2003) mentions that Sir John Harrington, who had commenced work as an agent in Ethiopia in 1898 and became the first head of the diplomatic mission (1903–09), introduced polo in the capital.[36] Resembling the local sport *gugs*, the game was already popular amongst the Ethiopian elite.

In his memoirs, *Ras* Imru Haile Selassie points out that *Le'ul Lij* Īyasu, who followed *Ats'ē* Menelik II on the throne, preferred to play *gugs* on the field at the back of the palace or to go out for a ride rather than to concentrate on his work. In contrast, 'Dejazmach Teferī was not so keen on physical exercises, so his character differed considerably in that respect from that of Lij Īyasu'.[37] Hakīm Werk'neh (1865–52), also known as Dr. Charles Martin, who belonged to the first generation of Ethiopian modernizers, repeatedly mentions in his diary that he played polo in Addis Ababa with members of foreign legations as well as local notables, amongst them *Le'ul Lij* Īyasu.[38] Furthermore, Hakīm Werk'neh built a house that 'was slowly rising to overlook Īyasu's playground for his favourite game, *gugs*, perhaps best described as an Ethiopian form of polo'.[39] Meetings with the heir to the throne after a game at Hakīm Werk'neh's home became frequent and sports might have opened a gateway to gain the political influence Werk'neh needed.[40] When Ladislas Farago visited the capital nearly three decades later, he realized that the European communities did not support polo that well. Allegedly, the climate or the altitude prevented them from actively participating. Thus, the British legation used to send their Indian guards to play in their place.[41] In order to promote the game, a polo committee was formed in 1933. It consisted of members of the British, French, Armenian, and Indian communities in the capital.[42] By 1935, Addis Ababa had 'two teams which, to one who knows little about polo, look very proficient'.[43]

[36] *The British Embassy Centenary Spectacular Programme*, cited in Ethiopian Equestrian Association, *Ethiopian Riders*, p. 102.
[37] Imru Haile Selassie, *Kayehut kemastawisew*, p. 30.
[38] Peter P. Garretson, *A Victorian Gentleman & Ethiopian Nationalist. The Life & Times of Hakim Wärqenäh, Dr. Charles Martin* (Woodbridge, 2012), pp. 52, 84, 87, 90.
[39] Ibid., p. 89.
[40] Having been brought up in India and Britain within an educative framework of Victorian morals and manliness, Hakīm Werk'neh's 'direct way' and his perception as foreigner made access to power difficult for him in Ethiopia.
[41] Ladislas Farago, *Abyssinia on the Eve* (London, 1935), p. 51.
[42] Zervos mentions L.D. Gurman Singh and A.L.D. Hardit Singh: *L'empire d'Ethiopie*, p. 140.
[43] Carleton S. Coon, *Measuring Ethiopia and Flight into Arabia* (Boston MA, 1935), pp. 72, 73, 284.

As a sport of kings and emperors, horse races were ideal events to display power through segregation in the form of separate boxes for the imperial family, the nobility, and the foreign communities as well as regulations about who was allowed to race. Historical photographs suggest the presence of a tent-like grandstand and a wooden structure (the imperial pavilion). The spatial configuration of the racing grounds often turned the place of sports and leisure into spaces of international politics. Post-First World War, post-Treaty of Versailles races were clear cases in point. When Wilhelm Haas, the German Attaché, won the most important race in 1921 and the German Ambassador Fritz Max Weiss received the trophy from the regent's hand in front of all ambassadors to Ethiopia, it contributed to the restoration of Germany's place amongst the European powers – at least on the racing grounds.[44]

Adrien Zervos, who described Ethiopia's socio-economic situation of the early 1930s, also portrayed the country as an emerging tourist destination, providing sportsmen with ample facilities for horse riding and chasing.[45] Even the fashionable 'discover the country by bike' theme was already present. Kaj Hansen, a Danish engineer working in L'union Miniére d'Ethiopie, cycled through Benishangul and further up to Khartoum.[46]

Although Italy had long-standing economic and cultural relations with Ethiopia, the first substantial group of Italians settled as a consequence of the Battle of Adwa (1896). After their defeat in Adwa, Italian prisoners of war served in noble households in Addis Ababa. Others, mostly skilled labourers, worked at construction sites in the new capital. Sebastiano Castagna, for example, designed St. George's Cathedral and the Bank of Abyssinia. The latter was built by the Italian construction firm Vaudetta in 1907.[47] The establishment of diplomatic relations between Ethiopia and Italy through the statesmanship of Count Friderico Ciccodicola in 1898 facilitated the recruitment of workers from Italy who participated in the construction of the Addis Ababa – Addis Alem road from 1902 onwards.[48] The T'alyan Sefer [Italian Quarter] grew around the telegraph office connecting Addis Ababa and Asmara. Italians – including many of those defeated at Adwa – began to settle there.[49] The social life of these workers and specialists and their families included sports. Men's past times such as wrestling and boxing

---

[44] Peter Junge and Silke Sybold, *Bilder aus Äthiopien: Malerei und Fotografie 1900–1935* (Bremen, 2002), p. 8.
[45] Zervos, *L'empire d'Ethiopie*, p. 103.
[46] Ibid., p. 102; Mouchegh Yerevanian, *The Ethiopian-Armenian Community from 1941 to 1975* (Glendale CA, 1996), p. 56.
[47] Batistoni and Chiari, *Old Tracks in the New Flower*, p. 70.
[48] Bahru Zewde, *A History of Modern Ethiopia, 1855–1991*, 2nd edn (Oxford, 2001), p. 150; Batistoni and Chiari, *Old Tracks in the New Flower*, pp. 23, 74.
[49] Lincoln de Castro, *Nella terra dei negus* (Milano, 1915), p. 231.

were especially popular. By the 1930s, the Italian community had formed their own football team (Juventus).

So far, this chapter has described the emergence of modern sports, largely, as 'European'-style leisure or leisure of the European and, in part South Asian, communities that had made Ethiopia their home. Taking historical entanglements seriously, we can assume that there were encounters between these communities and Ethiopians who resided in the urban centres, even if these encounters took the form of exclusion. Boxing might serve as an example. There seems to be overall agreement on Italian communities in Asmara and Addis Ababa having practised boxing in its modern form in the early 1930s.[50] The Armenian boxers of the Arax Union mentioned earlier also belonged to Addis Ababa's boxing scene. Bek'ele Alemu 'Gant', one of Ethiopia's later boxing champions, argues that other foreign communities also practised the sport.[51] Although none of the clubs allowed Eritreans or Ethiopians to participate, Africans saw the sport. They started to engage in boxing according to what they observed, and began to compete amongst themselves. In doing so, they could draw on existing local varieties of what came near to boxing bouts. The French ethnographer Marcel Griaule described a kind of mixed martial art as entertainment in the rural areas of Abyssinia, i.e. Tigray, Wollo, Gojjam, Begemder, and Shoa, that included fist fighting.[52]

On a more institutionalized level, boxing might have been trained in the armed forces, which underwent a substantial reform with the help of foreign personnel. Even Prince Makonnen, the emperor's favourite son, exercised and allegedly excelled in boxing during his private education supervised by the French naval officer Henri Gigli.[53] Furthermore, the experience of boxing includes Ethiopians who studied in Europe or the US. Yosēf and Bīnyam Werk'neh, for example, participated in boxing bouts while studying engineering at Loughborough College in Leicestershire, England, from the late 1920s up to the mid-1930s. There, they also excelled in cricket, hockey, and rugby – showing 'an uncommon appetite for sports'.[54] It remains to be studied to what extent the returning students of noble Ethiopian families made modern sports a marker of elites that had literally incorporated a Western model of education. It might be doubtful if football, associated with the working class, really served this purpose, as Tamirat

[50] Gezahhegne Beyene, 'Emergence and Development of Boxing in Ethiopia' (Unpublished BE thesis, Kotebe College of Teacher Education, 1998), pp. 6, 36.
[51] Yidnek'achew Asefu, *Yaltenegerelet yehager*, p. 29.
[52] Marcel Griaule, *Jeux et divertissements abyssins* (Paris, 1935), p. 58.
[53] Farago, *Abyssinia on the Eve*, p. 96.
[54] Bahru Zewde, *Pioneers of Change in Ethiopia: The Reformist Intellectuals of the Early Twentieth Century* (Oxford, 2002), p. 86.

Gebremariam and Benoît Gaudin suggested.[55] What the story about educated 'returnees' indicates, however, is the role of modern educational institutions in the spread of modern sports.

The Establishment of Physical Education in Modern Schools

It seems to be a universal claim that education is 'the' key to progress. According to developmentalist narratives, formal education opens up possibilities, prepares one for them and thereby pays off the initial investment. By the turn of the twentieth century, *Ats'ē* Menelik II and parts of the intellectual elite had recognized that the elaborate education offered by the Ethiopian Orthodox Church or Islamic centres of learning such as Harar did not meet the challenges of modern times.

Historiographies and official histories seem to agree that modern education in the form of modern schools began in 1908. This statement somehow contrasts the extensive research on the long-standing missionary education (reaching back into the seventeenth century) and its role in modernization in Ethiopia.[56] Furthermore, educational reform was not a planned top-down process until the formal establishment of the Ministry of Public Instruction and Fine Arts in 1930. Under *Ats'ē* Menelik II, education belonged to the Ministry of Religion. For *Le'ul Lij* Īyasu, education was of minor significance and a standardized educational policy was lacking.[57] With regard to *Ras* Tafari, Fritz Max Weiss, the German Chargé d'Affairs and later minister, comments that despite his [the Regent's] interest in schools, 'they are left alone. A clear educational aim does not exist. Pedagogical experience is lacking'.[58]

Just how far schools promoted modern physical education is an open question. However, the topic is linked to more fundamental thoughts about the role of religious institutions such as the Ethiopian Orthodox Church in promoting physical education, even if indirectly. Sports activities were, and still are, a part of the daily routine of religious instruction. In 2012, during field research in the Hawzien wereda,

---

55 Tamirat and Gaudin, 'Sports and Physical Education', p. 197.
56 For the earliest discussion see Donald Crummey, 'The Politics of Modernization: Protestant and Catholic Missionaries in Ethiopia', in Getatchew Haile, Aasulv Land, and Samuel Rubenson (eds), *The Missionary Factor in Ethiopia* (Frankfurt/ M., 1998), pp. 85–99. For a recent debate see Fantahun Ayele, 'Missionary Education: An Engine for Modernization or a Vehicle towards Conversion?' *African Journal of History and Culture*, 9:7 (2017), 56–63.
57 Bahru, *Pioneers of Change*, p. 33.
58 '*Trotz des großen Interesses, das der Thronfolger an den Schulen zu nehmen scheint, bleiben sie sich selbst ueberlassen. Ein fest umrissenes Bildungsziel existiert nicht. Es fehlt an pädagogischer Erfahrung*'. Errichtung einer deutschen Schule in Addis-Abeba, Auswärtiges Amt (henceforth AA) R 77868.

Resedebrī Gebreanenia Gebremedhin, a 78-year-old inhabitant of Mariam P'ap'aseti village, revealed that in the religious school in Chala (near Hawzien) the students practised wrestling during school breaks. One of the priests acted as referee (*danya*). Resedebrī Gebreanenia, who himself gives religious instruction to a small group of boys, continued this practice.[59]

More importantly, the orthodox clergy influenced decisions about where foreign teachers for the first modern schools should come from. Haggai Erlich,[60] who extensively studied Ethiopia's relations with the Middle East, argued that modern education in Ethiopia was largely brought about by teaching personnel from Egypt. One of the main reasons for this choice was the opposition of the Ethiopian Orthodox clergy and the heads of the political establishment to employing European teachers. As a compromise, the head of the Ethiopian Orthodox Church, the Egyptian Copt Matewos, requested Coptic teachers from Cairo – teachers who were the product and part of a modernized education system in Egypt. They came to Ethiopia from a vibrant environment where the human (male) body had become the prime target for producing a new social body that was modern and physically fit.[61]

During 1906–07, ten teachers from Egypt arrived in Ethiopia and were assigned to schools in Addis Ababa, Harar, Ankober, and Dessie. Under the direction of Egyptian headmaster Hanna Salib Bey, some of them became the main educating force in the Menelik II Imperial School that opened in 1908.[62] The curriculum not only included a large variety of languages, maths, and science, but also included physical education right from the beginning. However, it is possible to doubt the popularity of the subject, since physical exercises also belonged to the catalogue of punitive measures.[63] Although the role of the Egyptian teachers diminished with the growing influx of European personnel, it was the Egyptian expatriate Michel Wassef who planned and supervised the implementation of physical education at all school levels in the years immediately following the Italian Fascist occu-

[59] Interview with Alemnesh Gessesew and Resedebrī Gebreanenia Gebremedhin, Mariam P'ap'aseti Village, 18 July 2012.
[60] Haggai Erlich, 'The Egyptian Teachers of Ethiopia – Identities and Education along the Nile', in Walter Raunig and Asfa-Wossen Asserate (eds), *Äthiopien zwischen Orient und Okzident: Wissenschaftliche Tagung der Gesellschaft Orbis Aethiopicus, Köln*, 9. –11.10.1998 (Münster, 2004), pp. 117–38.
[61] For an excellent study on the subject, see Wilson Chacko Jacob, *Working out Egypt: Effendi Masculinity and Subject Formation in Colonial Modernity, 1870–1940* (Durham NC, London, 2011).
[62] Richard Pankhurst, *Economic History of Ethiopia, 1800–1935* (Addis Ababa, 1986), p. 676.
[63] For the introduction of sports at Menelik II School, see Bahru, *Pioneers of Change*, p. 24.

pation (1935–41).[64] The Egyptian engagement decreased and finally ended during the Nasserite period.

Ideas about sports and physical education also travelled with returning Ethiopian students, who had received education at prestigious colleges Egypt and Lebanon.[65] From 1918 onwards, Victoria College, which was modelled along the lines of English Public Schools and founded in Alexandria in 1901, admitted Ethiopian pupils on a yearly basis.[66] Right from the start sports was important. The first headmaster was not only expected to have a university degree, but an 'active interest in cricket, football and other games'.[67] The 'Eton of the Middle East' as the school was called, also offered hockey and, from 1914 onwards, boxing, fencing, and riding. In the 1920s and 1930s, sailing, lawn tennis, table tennis, cross-country runs, and 'bathing' was added.[68] Apart from the facilities on the school compound, school teams were allowed to use the playing fields of the Alexandria Cricket Club.[69] On his visit to Victoria College while travelling to Europe in 1924, Ras Tafari struck up cordial relations between himself as the future emperor and the college's headmaster Ralph Reed.[70] Arguably, the visit confirmed already existing ideas to establish the Tafari Makonnen School after his return to Ethiopia.[71]

Despite its early beginnings, the designation of physical education as a compulsory subject did not come about until the late 1920s. Unfortunately, there are no data that make it possible to know whether physical education was taught at the numerous schools that existed in towns such as Harar, Dire Dawa, Dessie, Gore, Nekemte or Gambela.[72] However, there is information about the institutions of higher learning in the capital. There, Tafari Makonnen School (later re-named Entoto Vocational and Technical School) taught sports from 1925 onwards. Its first superintendent, Hakīm Werk'neh, who was educated in India, sought to inculcate the students with the kind of Muscular Christianity that was characteristic of nineteenth-century Victorian preparatory

[64] Here I refer to Michael Wassef, about whom I will speak extensively in Chapter 4: *Training Leaders and Athletes: The Ethiopian YMCA (1940s–70s)*.
[65] Bahru, *Pioneers of Change*, p. 81.
[66] Sahar Hamouda, 'The Reed Phenomenon', in Sahar Hamouda and Clement Collins (eds), *Victoria College: A History Revealed* (Cairo, New York, 2002), p. 73.
[67] Advertisement for position of headmaster in *The Times*, 15 April 1901, cited in Sahar Hamouda, 'A School is Born', in Hamouda and Collins (eds), *Victoria College*, p. 21.
[68] Hamouda, 'The Reed Phenomenon', p. 99.
[69] Hamouda, 'A School is Born', pp. 39, 40.
[70] Hamouda, 'The Reed Phenomenon', p. 73.
[71] Haggai Erlich, 'Ethiopia and Egypt – Ras Tafari in Cairo, 1924', *Aethiopica*, 1 (1998), 71.
[72] Detailed for the pre-occupation period in Pankhurst, *The History of Ethiopian Towns* and Zervos, *L'empire d'Éthiopie*.

schools of Britain and spread throughout the British empire. According to Peter Garretson it was Muscular Christianity, which signals 'a significant departure from the ethos of the Menilek School and a major contribution that Wärqenäh brought to modern Ethiopian education'.[73] Furthermore, pictures of the school for freed slaves, orphans, and children of poor people – which was established and financed through Hakīm Werk'neh's *Fik'irina Agelgilot Mahber* [Love and Service Association] near the Filwoha Hot Springs – also suggest an emphasis on physical education.[74]

Empress Menen School for girls and the Kokebe Tsibah Haile Selassie I School started physical education in 1931. The Swedish Evangelical Mission had eight schools in the empire and all of them taught gymnastics. This also applies to the Seventh Day Adventists' boys' schools in Addis Ababa and Addis Alem.[75] An image from 1928, which is located in the Institute of Ethiopian Studies (IES), shows a class at 'Swedish drill' – as gymnastics was called – outside a school compound in Addis Ababa.

Furthermore, the community schools in Addis Ababa and Dire Dawa promoted modern and local forms of physical exercises. A photograph taken in 1907 shows French staff members of the Alliance Française School in the capital monitoring the game of *genna* (local lawn hockey) on their compound.[76] The already mentioned school for the children of manumitted slaves, orphans, and children of poor families in Filwoha, Addis Ababa, taught a mixture of gymnastics and drill.[77] In November 1926 the minister of the German legation mentions *Turnen* (gymnastics) at two Armenian schools and at the Greek Community School.[78] During his visit to the empire, Ladislas Farago saw a gymnastics display, physical exercises, tug-of-war, and a football match at Tafari Makonnen School.[79] According to Adrien Zervos, there were schools from other communities, such as the Gujarati/Indian and Italian communities. He also mentions such private initiatives as, for example, the Ecole Américaine, which was established in 1934 by three (Afro-)

---

[73] Garretson, *Victorian Gentleman & Ethiopian Nationalist*, p. 127.
[74] Anonymous, *Das ist Abessinien* (Leipzig, 1935), p. 35.
[75] Lakew Yiglit'u, 'Ye-Ītyop'ya sport wididir' [Ethiopian sports competition], *Ethiopian Interschool Sports Competition Magazine* (1988), 28, cited in Negussie Alemu, 'Addis Ababa Inter School Sports Competition: Past, Present and Future Perspective' (Unpublished BE thesis, Kotebe College of Teacher Education, 2001), p. 11; Pankhurst, *Economic History of Ethiopia*, pp. 676–82.
[76] Fasil Giorgis and Denis Gérard, *Addis Ababa 1886–1941: The City and its Architectural Heritage* (Addis Ababa, 2007), p. 286.
[77] Anonymous, *Das ist Abessinien*, p. 35.
[78] Uebersicht ueber den gegenwaertigen Stand des Schulwesens in Addis-Abeba, AA R 77868.
[79] Farago, *Abyssinia on the Eve*, p. 170.

American women.⁸⁰ We might assume that no physical exercise was taught at these schools, since Zervos explicitly mentions this subject for other schools in his text.

Pictures published in travel reports and photographs located at the visual archive of the IES, Addis Ababa University, show three kinds of activities at these institutions: drill, football, and gymnastics. However, if leisure is the place where newly introduced physical activities met established forms of physical recreation, there might have been other activities or even mixed styles. Again, wrestling or, more likely, mixed martial arts – which the French ethnographer Marcel Griaule described in his book on games and entertainment in Tigray, Wollo, Gojjam, Begemder, and Shoa – might have had a place on the school compound, too.⁸¹ Arguably, such combat sports were even desired for those who joined or, better, were drafted into the emerging scout movement.

Climbing, Running, and Fighting: Physical Fitness as Pre-military Training in Early Boy Scouting

Physical exercises, whether taught at schools for discipline, or practised as leisure for letting off steam, also serve to create a physically fit and mentally alert militarized body at an early age. With the reform of the armed forces well under way, the establishment of Boy Scouting in Ethiopia specifically served the aim of preparing boys to become soldiers.

Scouting started in Ethiopia in the late 1910s, when the movement spread from Great Britain and the United States throughout the globe. In his study on the Boy Scout Movement in British colonial territories in Africa, Timothy Parsons convincingly argues that it was the adaptability of the movement's basic ideas and practices to local contexts and values that made Boy Scouting so successful.⁸² In his memoirs, Haile Selassie emphasized that the first scout patrols were formed under his guidance at a time when he was still *Ras* Tafari and Governor of Harar in 1919.⁸³ The centenary celebrations in February 2019 with the theme '100 Years of Volunteerism and Active Citizenship' confirm this historical awareness within the current movement in Ethiopia.⁸⁴ The purpose of creating the Boy Scouts in Ethiopia was,

80 Zervos *L'empire d'Ethiopie*, p. 226.
81 Griaule, *Jeux et divertissements abyssins*, p. 58.
82 Timothy Parsons, *Race, Resistance, and the Boy Scout Movement in British Colonial Africa* (Athens OH, 2004), p. 25.
83 Haile Selassie I, *My Life and Ethiopia's Progress, 1892–1937*, trans. and annotated Edward Ullendorff (New York, London, 1976), p. 12.
84 Africa Scout Region, 'Scouting in Ethiopia Turns 100', SCOUTS. Creating

in the first instance, neither to produce active citizens nor people who take responsibility and rely on their own judgement.[85] The movement, and its early institution in Addis Ababa, was a means of transforming boys from the earliest age possible into soldiers and cadets.

Apart from its mention in Haile Selassie's memoirs, nothing is yet known about how many boys joined the movement in 1919 and what they actually did. Instead, it was most probably the Greek community that took the (scouting) lead in Ethiopia. With the first attempts to introduce Baden-Powell's principles in 1908, the establishment in Greece in 1910, and the official recognition of *Soma Hellinon Proskopon* (Greek Boy Scouts Association) by a Royal Decree of 12 May 1912, the movement not only had more than two decades of experience, it also quickly spread to the Greek diaspora. Although largely absent from official histories on the Egyptian movement or studies of physical culture and citizenship in Egypt,[86] the Greek community played an active role in the establishment of scouting in places such as Alexandria as early as 1913.[87]

Seeking employment in the construction and business sectors, many Greeks had migrated to Ethiopia from Egypt. Some kept ties with North Africa and even sent their children to Greek schools in Egypt. There, they had a high chance of gaining experience in scouting. Upon return, they might become active within the Greek scouts division in Ethiopia, which was part of *Soma Hellinon Proskopon*. Apart from Addis Ababa, Greek scouts were active in the town of Dire Dawa. Telios Bollolakos,[88] the influential the Greek consul in this town, and owner of the Hotel Continental, founded educational facilities including a Com-

---

a Better World, 12 February 2019, www.scout.org/ethiopia100 [accessed 15 September 2021].

[85] Eduard Vallory, 'Status Quo Keeper or Social Change Promoter? The Double Side of World Scouting's Citizenship Education', in Nelson R. Block and Tammy M. Proctor (eds), *Scouting Frontiers: Youth and the Scout Movement's First Century* (Newcastle upon Tyne, 2009), p. 216.

[86] Again, Egypt is a well-researched example. Jacob, *Working out Egypt*, pp. 92–124.

[87] Almost simultaneously with the official recognition of scouting in Greece, the first group of Greek scouts was founded in Alexandria, Egypt, at the initiative of the gymnastics professor Antonios Kokkinos. Around mid-1912, the group was organized within the Athletic Club of Fans of Alexandria, and the following year Anthony Benakis proceeded to formally establish the Greek Boy Scouts in Egypt (Irene Chryshoheri, 'The Greeks of Alexandria', www.google.com/search?client=firefox-b-d&q=Alexandria+Greek+Boy+Scouts [accessed 15 September 2021].

[88] Also referred to as Bollobakos in John Anestis Ghantakis, 'The Greeks of Ethiopia, 1889–1970' (Unpublished Ph. D. dissertation, Boston University Graduate School, 1979), p. 76.

mercial School, which also had Boy Scout patrols.[89] According to its 1912 charter, the Scouts of Greece aimed at 'moral and physical development' as well as the 'production of good citizens and soldiers'.[90] Whereas citizenship was not yet an issue in Ethiopia, the demand for modern soldiers existed.

Early scouting might also have played a role in Tafari Makonnen School. Amongst its teachers was Mr Aron Jackson who taught sports and scouting. He was one of the African-American teachers whom Hakīm Werk'neh (first superintendent of the school after 1925) had brought from the Unites States.[91] Furthermore, twelve graduates from Tafari Makonnen School continued their studies in Beirut (Lebanon) from 1926 onwards. Six went to the American College of Beirut and six to the French Mission Laïque, where scouting was part and parcel of the extracurricular educational programme.[92] Children from prominent Ethiopian families, who studied at Victoria College in Alexandria (Egypt) during the 1920s, were involved in scouting activities, which had started at the school already in 1912.[93] It is not unlikely that Ethiopian graduates from Victoria College later supported the Boy Scout movement in Ethiopia. This suggests that early scouting, together with the already mentioned experiences Greek students from Ethiopia enjoyed at Egyptian schools, might be a special field worth study as part of the development of sports and physical culture in Ethiopia in connection with similar developments in the Middle East. This argument is further strengthened when looking at the main figures who built up the so-called 'Boy Scout School' in Addis Ababa.

Various sources mention the Boy Scout School, established in Gulele (the north-western outskirts of Addis Ababa).[94] The language of instruction was French as in most of the schools, well-fitting the language of

---

[89] Zervos, *L'empire d'Ethiopie*, p. 361; Ghantakis, *The Greeks of Ethiopia*, p. 127 even speaks of a 'school for Greek boy scouts'.

[90] Dora Giannaki, 'Youth Work in Greece: An Historical Overview', *The History of Youth Work in Europe*, 4 (2014), 95.

[91] Tadäsä Betul Kebrät, *Azaj Hakim Wärqenäh Eshätu* [Chief Hakīm Werk'neh Eshetu] (Addis Ababa, 2009 EC, 2016/7), p. 161, cited in Garretson, *Victorian Gentleman & Ethiopian Nationalist*, p. 189.

[92] Garretson, *Victorian Gentleman & Ethiopian Nationalist*, p. 131.

[93] Sahar Hamouda, 'A School is Born', p. 47. See picture of 'Victoria College scout troop (1921–22)', in Hamouda and Collins (eds), *Victoria College*, p. 147. So it was Victoria College that started scouting in Egypt and not Prince 'Umar Tusun who formed Egyptian scout patrols in Alexandria in 1914. For reference see Jamal Khashba, *Harakat al-Kashshafa fi 78 'Am* (Cairo, 1992), p. 115, cited in Aaron Jakes, Extracurricular Nationalism: Youth Culture in the Age of Egypt's Parliamentary Monarchy (Unpublished MA thesis, University of Oxford, 2005), p. 47.

[94] Pankhurst, *Economic History of Ethiopia*, pp. 682, 714.

command in the reformed armed forces.[95] Apart from reading, writing, natural sciences, and mathematics, Boy Scout activities were part of the curriculum.[96] It is not entirely clear if this was a separate school or a part of the School of the Redeemer for Orphans (later Medhane Alem School), which opened in Gulele in 1931. Haile Mariam Guezmou became the director of the school, which employed six Ethiopian teachers plus Frederick Kamal (sometimes spelled Frédérick Kamel), from Lebanon. While some sources mention him as the founding director of the Boy Scout School,[97] others speak of an 'Abyssinian schoolmaster'.[98] Making it part of his *History of the Ethiopian Army*, Richard Pankhurst comments that '[a] certain limited amount of training was also given on the eve of the war at the Boy Scout School which was founded in 1934 and directed first by a Lebanese, Frederick Kamal, and later by an Ethiopian assisted by a locally born Greek'.[99] Nonetheless, since Boy Scouting was well established in the Middle East, and especially in Lebanon, Frederick Kamal was the perfect man for potential knowledge transfer.

Haile Selassie, who had a personal interest in the Boy Scout movement, donated a large tract of land adjacent to the School of the Redeemer for Orphans. He also provided the money for constructing the necessary buildings. Christo Moraitis, an influential member of the quite large Greek community in Addis Ababa, seems to have run this place, which accommodated 375 boys. In his memoirs, his brother John Moraitis remembers that 'Christo was a founding member of the Ethiopian boy scouts and its chief organiser. In later years he would receive a gold medal from Crown Prince Gustav Adolphus of Sweden for his work'.[100]

Since Haile Selassie considered scouting a part of modern youth training, it increasingly served as an advertisement for Ethiopia's path to modernization. Thus, it could happen that, when foreign journalists came to the empire, the emperor personally directed them to visit scouting activities in the capital. One of them was the Hungarian journalist Ladislas Farago, who visited Ethiopia in 1935.

---

[95] Richard Pankhurst, *An Introduction to the History of the Ethiopian Army* (Addis Ababa, 1967), p. 26.
[96] It later became Medhane Alem School. Befek'ade Sillasē Fantaye, *Sile boy iskawt agelgilot ach'ch'ir meglech'a* [On the Boy Scout service: A short explanation] (Addis Ababa, 1947 EC, 1954/5), p. 3; Zervos, *L'empire d'Ethiopie*, p. 231.
[97] Richard Pankhurst, 'Educational Developments of the 1930s' www.linkethiopia.org/blog/article/educational-developments-of-the-1930s [accessed 15 September 2021]; Zervos, *L'empire d'Ethiopie*, pp. 225, 230.
[98] Farago, *Abyssinia on the Eve*, p. 138.
[99] Pankhurst, *History of the Ethiopian Army*, p. 28.
[100] Elizabeth Germany, *Ethiopia My Home: The Story of John Moraitis* (Addis Ababa, 2001), p. 14. Interestingly, Christo convinced John to become active as a Boy Scout, when he was studying at the English secular school in Cyprus in the early 1920s.

> Haile Selassie had arranged my afternoon programme. I was going to see the Boy Scouts of Abyssinia. A barracks for 300 boys has been arranged far out of the town at the castle of the exiled Ras Hailu. In one way the Abyssinian Boy Scout movement is different from any others; the members are not voluntary and the organisation is not half serious, half sporting, but it forms the youngest section of the Abyssinian Army. They live together, training on the broad parade grounds and learning tactics in the surrounding countryside.[101]

Adrien Zervos, who looked specifically at the modernizing elements of the empire, confirmed the impression that the Boy Scout Associaion was a 'formation prèmilitaire des jeunes Ethiopiens'.[102] Farago emphasized that the emperor had two reasons why he created and actively supported the movement. The first resembled very much Robert Baden-Powell's objectives for creating the Boy Scouts. Namely, to create a reliable messenger service. The second reason was a more delicate one, namely to form a highly qualified and modern officer corps. In order to do so, Haile Selassie had to break the aristocratic privilege of becoming a general by birth, instead instilling a soldiering attitude by training. Thus, it does not come as a surprise that he made his favourite son, Prince Makonnen, Chief Scout. Prince Makonnen, whom Farago described as a distinguished sportsman, received his education from the retired French naval officer Commandant Henri Gigli.[103] The emperor promoted his son Makonnen to the rank of an honorary officer and gave him command of the Boy Scouts.

Haile Selassie himself selected the pupils whom he wanted to become officers. Outdoor training in the form of manoeuvres, which the journalist described in detail, were intended to turn children from the age of five years into soldiers. Later, the most promising of these children went to the newly established Haile Selassie I Military Training Centre at Holeta (also known as Guennet Military School), which was staffed by Swedish officers and opened in January 1935. Ladislas Farago commented on this transition

> In the officer's school in Oletta [sic], a new generation of commanders is growing up. Only a short time ago, these boys were all members of the well-organised Boy Scout Movement that the Emperor founded in autumn of 1934. Swedish officers are now in charge of the education of these children who are destined to be officers in the Abyssinian army in six months' time. I had a talk with the director of this military kindergarten, Captain Tamm.[104]

Scouting in Ethiopia was pursuing a clearly militaristic path at a time when the Baden-Powell movement had already taken the road to paci-

---

[101] Farago, *Abyssinia on the Eve*, p. 137.
[102] Zervos, *L'empire d'Ethiopie*, p. 232.
[103] Farago, *Abyssinia on the Eve*, p. 96.
[104] Ibid., p. 137; Farago refers to Captain Viking Tamm.

fism. In contrast to Martin Crotty's argument that scouting only flirted with militarism, in the Ethiopian case, scouting was absorbed into it.[105] However, Ethiopia was not alone in this. In Israel, for example, scouting had shifted from a civilian enterprise to 'paramilitary and colonising schemes'.[106] Scouting in the Middle East in general, and in Lebanon in particular, had become militaristic youth training and part of the nationalist project.[107] Therefore, Frederick Kamal's knowledge might have perfectly matched Ethiopian requirements. On 25 September 1934, during an official ceremony at the school, the Lebanese teacher had the honour of addressing the audience and presenting the Ethiopian flag to the emperor, his sons, and other high-ranking members of the society

In its next issue, the government newspaper *Berhanena Selam* published an extensive account that gives an idea of the kind of subjects who should emerge from the training at the school. In his address to the emperor, director Haile Mariam Guezmou emphasized the importance of instilling a heroic attitude into the children, which rests on the heroic history of the Ethiopian people. The new quality, however, is to combine heroism with modern military training and modern symbols such as an oath to God, the emperor and the nation (symbolized by the flag). Arguably, the Boy Scouts formed a bridge between existing warrior traditions and the formation of a new (militarized) civic identity. By being selected to become the future Ethiopian soldiers, the boys would have the chance and honour to achieve the level of European children. Specifically addressing Chief Scout Prince Makonnen, the director gave assurances that his school does its utmost to prepare the young scouts to be attentive and ready to 'secure the borders, to shame our enemies, to make Ethiopia a proud by keeping its freedom, and, as our forefathers did, to observe the orders of the Emperor'.[108] Thus, notions of patriotism, heroism, and sacrifice as well as opportunity and responsibility were found in Ethiopia as elsewhere.

Amongst the emperor's ideas to transform Ethiopia into a modern imperial (nation) state with a high degree of centralized power (also

---

[105] Martin Crotty, 'Scouts Down Under: Scouting, Militarism and "Manliness" in Australia, 1908–1920', in Nelson R. Block and Tammy M. Proctor (eds), *Scouting Frontiers: Youth and the Scout Movement's First Century* (Newcastle upon Tyne, 2009), p. 74.
[106] Eitan Bar-Yosef, 'Fighting Pioneer Youth: Zionist Scouting and Baden-Powell's Legacy', in Block and Proctor, *Scouting Frontiers*, p. 44.
[107] Esther Möller, *Orte der Zivilisierungsmission: Französische Schulen im Libanon 1909–1943* (Göttingen, 2013), pp. 115–17; Jennifer Dueck, 'A Muslim Jamboree: Scouting and Youth Culture in Lebanon under the French Mandate', *French Historical Studies*, 30:3 (2007), 485–516.
[108] 'Sile īt'yop'ya boy eskawt temarīwoch sendek' alama mek'ebel beʽal akebaber'," [The Ethiopian Boy Scouts receive the flag with honours], *Berhanena selam,* 21 meskerem 1927 [1 October 1934].

guaranteed by a reformed army), pre-military training in the Boy Scout School seemed to be of great importance. Orphaned children who had nobody else to turn to took an oath to work and even sacrifice their lives for emperor and country. Discipline through drill, physical fitness training, and manoeuvres was to prepare their bodies for this task. During his visit to the school in 1934, Ladislas Farago observed a manoeuvre. His description of it tells us something about physical fitness, too. The journalist mentions running in the first place, but was most impressed by the climbing of thin trees.

> The trees were quite young and not more than three inches thick, but the boys climbed them like monkeys, and almost before we knew that they had begun to climb, a small figure was at the top of each tree. They knew how to distribute their weight without bending the trunks one way or another, and every tree stood as straight as a candle under the weight of no less than five stone.[109]

Apart from that, the author observed fist fighting which was, as already mentioned, part of existing mixed martial arts and, in the form of modern boxing, even a specialty of the Chief Scout. However, it is difficult to say if this was part of the training or a performance of 'unbound aggressiveness', which is always part of the war (game).

Throughout the book, I explore the ways that the development of modern sports in Ethiopia from the early twentieth century until the late 1970s is linked to urban development, emerging ideas of (useful) recreation, and institutions that specifically targeted the human body as a site to mould the modern Ethiopian personality. In this chapter, I have argued in favour of applying a broad lens that does not only study sports at modern educational institutions, but also as a form of associational leisure activity that had gained ground on a global scale. Members of the so-called foreign communities who had made Ethiopia their home, primarily settled in urban centres, organized themselves into sports clubs or tapped into existing local structures of good standing, such as racing clubs. By including the Ethiopian Boy Scout movement, which was during its formative years understood as a pre-military education, this book gives due importance to the physically fit and educated young male as the desired soldier. Haile Selassie was well aware of the fact that physical fitness and modern sports were markers of belonging to the community of modern states. Becoming a member of the League of Nations was important, but so was participating in the Olympic Games.

The Italian invasion of Ethiopia in 1935, and subsequent Fascist occupation until 1941, brought scouting to an abrupt end. It is not clear to what extent pupils trained in the Boy Scout School actually served in

---

[109] Farago, *Abyssinia on the Eve*, p. 189.

the Ethiopian army, as the emperor later emphasized.[110] Since the students of this school were prepared to enter Holeta military college, the current scout movement in Ethiopia remembers them as having formed 'the nucleus of the Black Lion Contingent of the Ethiopian Army'.[111] Although such a statement is overstating the importance of the Boy Scouts in this context, and completely ignores the role of Ethiopian graduates of military training institutions and academies such as the *École Spéciale Militaire de* Saint-Cyr in France,[112] there is a kernel of truth in it.

During the occupation, the Fascist regime closed most of the existing modern schools or used them for other purposes, and forced many non-Italian teachers to leave Ethiopia. Although Tafari Makonnen School continued, only Italian children were admitted. Children of the Ethiopian nobility were indoctrinated rather than educated. In terms of physical education and sports as leisure, the loss of schools meant 'the loss, to Ethiopians, of sports equipment and sport fields'.[113] Instead of Boy Scouting, they established the Fascist Youth Brigade and Training School for Boys as well as paramilitary units of the Fascist youth movement, The Wolves of Ethiopia. Their uniformed appearance resembled that of the Boy Scouts to such an extent that it became difficult to re-launch the movement after the liberation. With regard to the foreign communities, the regime issued a law that European nationals would only be permitted to educate their children at schools *Tipo Italiano*.[114]

As the next chapter will show, modern sports became a propaganda tool in the hands of the occupiers and their collaborators. Fascist newspapers in Amharic, as well as existing and newly established venues, provided ideal opportunities to perform strength, technical skills, and uniformed bodies to the suppressed Ethiopians living in the urban quarters segregated for them. Sports, as a political tool, became an outlet to display colonial-cum-Fascist modernity. Trophy ceremonies served as ideal instruments to instil the symbolism of the loyalty to the Fascist regime expected from collaborators, athletes, and the urban population. However, competitions also produced unwanted effects, such as boosting local pride via local heroes.

---

[110] Haile Selassie I, 'Address to the Boy Scout Movement on 6 June 1959', in The Imperial Ethiopian Ministry of Information (ed.), *Selected Speeches of His Imperial Majesty Haile Selassie First, 1918 to 1967* (Addis Ababa, 1967), p. 648.
[111] 'The Scout & Guide Spirit Flame', International Scout and Guide Fellowship, Amitié Internationale Scoute et Guide, 3 July 2008, www.isgf.org/index.php/en/publications/284-the-effects-of-the-spirit-flame [accessed 15 September 2021].
[112] Pankhurst, *History of the Ethiopian Army*, pp. 25–6.
[113] Tamirat and Gaudin, 'Sports and Physical Education in Ethiopia', p. 201.
[114] Schulgesetz für Italienisch-Ostafrika, 26 July 1937, Georg-Haccius-Schule, AA RAV 89.

2
Sports and Propaganda during the Fascist Occupation (1935–1941)

Despite all the Ethiopian attempts to prevent Italian military aggression, especially through Haile Selassie's speech to the League of Nations with its emphasis on collective security,[1] the Italian army invaded Ethiopia on 3 October 1935. Within seven months, the emperor's army had been defeated in a cruel war and Italian troops had occupied all major centres. Immediately after the conquest of the capital Addis Ababa on 5 May 1936, Ethiopia was annexed to the Italian colonial empire. In the subsequent spatial reorganization of the *Africa Orientale Italiana* (AOI), it was merged with the Italian colonies of Eritrea and Italian Somaliland with six major regional divisions. Italian rule was, however, mostly confined to the urban centres.[2] Apart from an administration, which the historian Bahru Zewde described as 'top-heavy bureaucratic machinery', there was 'a mania for creating committees and commissions'.[3] The one that concerns us most in this chapter is the Sports Bureau for the Natives (*Yeager tewelajoch ts'ihfet bēt*), hereafter referred to as the Sports Bureau. Established in 1937, the Sports Bureau operated directly under the Directorate for Political Affairs (*Direzione Superiore Degli Affari Politici*). It was located near St. Paul's Hospital and in the neighbourhood of the newly built quarter

---

[1] Ethiopia joined the League of Nations on 28 September 1923. For motives and expectations concerning this international body, see Antoinette Iadarola, 'Ethiopia's Admission into the League of Nations: An Assessment of Motives', *The International Journal of African Historical Studies*, 8:4 (1975), 601–22. The original version of the speech was published as 'Firē kenafir ze k'edamawī Hayle Sillasē niguse negest ze Ītyop'ya' [Important words by His Majesty Haile Selassie King of Kings of Ethiopia] *Berhanena Selam* 1944 EC, 1951/52, pp. 119–35. An English translation of the text is available in *Selected Speeches of His Imperial Majesty Haile Selassie First 1918–1967* (Addis Ababa, 1967), pp. 304–16 and in Haile Selassie, Emperor of Ethiopia *My Life and Ethiopia's Progress, 1892–1937: The Autobiography of Emperor Haile Selassie I.*, Edward Ullendorff (trans. and annotated) (Oxford, 1976), pp. 298–312.
[2] Bahru Zewde, *A History of Modern Ethiopia, 1855–1991* (Oxford, 2001), p. 163; Paul B. Henze, *Layers of Time: A History of Ethiopia* (London, 2000), p. 223.
[3] Bahru, *History of Modern Ethiopia*, p. 162.

for the 'natives' (*Addīs yeager tewelajoch ketema*), today still called *Addīs Ketema*.[4]

Tamirat Gebremariam and Benoît Gaudin have already viewed the theme of sports in Ethiopia during the Fascist occupation from the vantage point of how the Sports Bureau for the Natives implemented its policy through competitions in the capital and the town of Harar.[5] This chapter instead analyses the role of sports as a Fascist propaganda tool by looking at their representation in Amharic newspapers as directed by the government of the Italian occupation. It argues in the first part that the regime applied this strategy because it worked so well in Italy to create consensus on the Fascist project. Looking at the Ethiopian case, the second part of the chapter introduces the Amharic media. By focusing on specific kinds of sports and venues, the chapter continues to explore the ways that sports news was used as a vehicle to reach consensus with the Italian 'civilizing' mission and the fit colonial subject in the context of the Fascist occupation.

Sports and 'New Man' Fantasies

Scholars of the Fascist period in Italy have convincingly described the use of sports as a political instrument for creating consensus on the Fascist ideas and practices that targeted Italy's physical and spiritual regeneration, as well as its subsequent militarization.[6] It is very likely that the conceptualization of a fit collective organism influenced policy and propaganda in the colonies, too. During the Fascist occupation of Ethiopia, some of the ideas around Italian regeneration met with a very specific context of an existing local attempt at modernization. As was demonstrated in the previous chapter, the Ethiopian drive to become modern included physical education and sports as a form of leisure. In order to understand this entanglement, it is worthwhile to have a closer look at developments in Fascist Italy.

There, a comprehensive sporting programme had begun in 1928. It included a reform of physical education in schools, the creation of sports academies, and the building of sports facilities such as play-

---

[4] 'New city for the natives'; 'New City': Sintayehu Tola, 'The History of St. George Sport Club' (Unpublished BA thesis, Addis Ababa University, 1986), p. 14.
[5] Tamirat Gebremariam and Benoît Gaudin, 'Sports and Physical Education in Ethiopia during the Italian Occupation, 1936–41', in Michael J. Gennaro and Saheed Aderinto (eds), *Sports in African History, Politics and Identity Formation* (New York, 2019), pp. 196–205.
[6] Sarah Morgan, 'Mussolini's Boys (and Girls): Gender and Sport in Fascist Italy', *History Australia*, 3:1 (2006), 04.1–04.12, https://doi.org/10.2104/ha060004 [accessed 15 September 2021].

grounds and stadiums. Former nationwide sporting bodies, such as the *Federazione delle Associazioni Sportive Cattoliche* (Catholic Sports Association), were disbanded or incorporated into the Fascist sports structures. Shortly before the rise of Fascism in Italy, the existing socialist forces split into those who labelled sports as a secondary issue or even a 'moral and spiritual danger for class solidarity'[7] and those who promoted it as a tool for class struggle. Thus, Fascism could fully exploit sports as a means to create a community and to secure power.[8] Its propaganda machine disseminated ideas about Italy as a modern organism and the *Italiano nuovo* (New Italian) as its ideal builder. The regime hoped that through the 'synthesis of virility, violence, combat and struggle … the *Italiano nuovo* would spiritually and physically regenerate the nation, thereby completing the "moral" unification'.[9] With racial ideologies gaining ground in the 1930s, sports was seen as a means of 'perfecting the race' and sports instructors as 'biological engineers and builders of the human machine'.[10]

There seems to be consensus in the literature that the *Italiano nuovo* was conceptualized as *homo sportivus*,[11] a perfectionist and, if necessary *Italiano duro*[12], citizen-soldier ready to fight to the death. As this chapter will demonstrate, the discourse about sports of the Italian Fascist regime directed at an Amharic-speaking audience in Ethiopia discussed physical fitness and competitive sports also as a means to achieve a higher level of civilization. In contrast to propaganda directed at Italian citizens, sports news in Amharic did not emphasize militaristic qualities but produced a moralistic discourse about sports and virtues. This discourse supported the general aim of the Fascist educational policy in Ethiopia, which regarded schools as 'a political instrument for the peaceful penetration and moral conquest of the native population'.[13] Since physical education was thought about in terms of military gymnastics and drill, it most probably linked up to existing ideas about physical education in the Italian colony of Eritrea in the

---

[7] Simon Martin, *Football and Fascism: The National Game under Mussolini* (Oxford, New York, 2004), p. 21.
[8] Ibid., pp. 22–3.
[9] Ibid., p. 28.
[10] Patrizia Dogliani, 'Sport and Fascism', *Journal of Modern Italian Studies*, 5:3 (2000), 327.
[11] Paul Dietschy, 'Sport, éducation physique et fascisme sous le regard de l'historien', *Revue d'histoire moderne et contemporaine*, 55:3 (2008), 73.
[12] Martin, *Football and Fascism*, p. 199.
[13] 'Le scuola e le istitutioni educative', *Gli Annali dell'Afica Italiana* III, 1 (1940), p. 690, cited in Richard Pankhurst, 'Education in Ethiopia during the Italian Fascist Occupation (1936–1941)', *The International Journal of African Historical Studies*, 5:3 (1972), 366.

1920s, which conceptualized sports as part of military training with the definite aim of transforming 'natives' into Italian 'future soldiers'.¹⁴

Given the fact that sports played such a decisive role in Fascist Italy, its growing prominence in her colonies and occupied territories is not very surprising, especially from the 1930s onwards. The little we know about physical education in colonial Eritrea, which had been colonized in 1897, points to the fact that, in the 'native' schools – the first opened in 1911 – sports meant military drill.¹⁵ Organized sports such as football, cycling,¹⁶ and boxing¹⁷ seem to have been practised well before the 1930s, but racial politics denied Eritreans club membership. In the mid-1930s, the first 'native' football and cycling clubs were founded in the major towns. Following the Fascist occupation of Ethiopia, successful Eritrean cyclists featured highly in the Ethiopian sports scene, and therefore also on the sports pages, probably serving as an example that Italian rule results in good athletes.

Sports News and the Emerging Fascist Press in Ethiopia

There is an increasing body of literature that describes how sports news became an integral part of the propaganda machine in Italy. Newspapers, cinemas, and, most importantly, radio played a decisive role in creating ideas about the 'New Italian'.¹⁸ The relevant literature shows how sports reporting, with its history going back well into the late nineteenth century, was not only completely reconfigured from the 1920s onwards. Rather, it displayed an increasingly racist character. We might expect a similar influence on the local sports news in Amharic. Despite the fact that the Italian Fascist regime saw Africans as an infe-

---

¹⁴ Tekeste Negash, *Italian Colonialism in Eritrea, 1882–1941: Policies, Praxis and Impact* (Stockholm, 1987), pp. 71, 72, 87.
¹⁵ Tekeste, *Italian Colonialism in Eritrea*, pp. 71, 72, 87. It would be interesting to know if the Swedish Mission School (run up to 1932) taught gymnastics as it did in Addis Ababa.
¹⁶ Fikreyesus Amahazion, 'Pedaling History: Eritrea's Teklehaimanot and Kudus in Tour de France', *TesfaNews*, 6 July 2015, www.tesfanews.net/eritrea-pedaling-history-at-tour-de-france [accessed 15 September 2021]; Yishak Yared, 'History of Football Sport in Eritrea at a Glance', www.shabait.com/about-eritrea/art-a-sport/2718-history-of-football-sport-in-eritrea-at-a-glance-part-i [accessed 15 September 2021].
¹⁷ Katrin Bromber, 'Improving Physical Self: Sport, Body Politics, and Ethiopian Modernity, ca. 1920–1974', *Northeast African Studies Journal*, 13:1 (2013), 71–99.
¹⁸ For this issue, see Eleonora Belloni, 'The Birth of the Sport Nation: Sports and Mass Media in Fascist Italy', *Aloma Revista de Psicologia, Ciències de l'Educació i de l'Esport*, 32:2 (2014), 53–61; Dogliani, 'Sport and Fascism'; Martin, *Football and Fascism*.

rior race, however, the press was not keen on voicing such statements explicitly in its sports sections. The editors rather turned this racial attitude into a language of normalizing the policy of racial segregation after the seizure of Ethiopia in 1935. Sports news in Amharic became a means 'to construct the myth (still in vogue today) of fascist colonialism as benign form of colonial rule [and] fascism as a positive colonial influence'.[19] Arguably, sports news served as a vehicle for reaching consensus on the Italian civilizing mission and the fit colonial subject in the context of Fascist occupation. The fact that the language used was Amharic and the style made efforts to exploit local modes of expression indicates that the target audience was a (new) colonial subject; partly educated and absolutely loyal to the Fascist regime.

By 1938, two Amharic newspapers published by the Italian Colonial Government provided extensive information about the latest sporting events in urban settings, especially Addis Ababa, and the diffusion of sports in the occupied territory. The weekly, at times bi-weekly, *YeK'ēsar Mengist Mel'iktenya* (The Messenger of Caesar's Government)[20], was launched on 13 March 1938 and sold at a price of 50 santeem. It mainly contained news on political developments in Italy, the colonies and, from 1940 onwards, the war. After one year of its existence, the editors hoped that the newspaper would soon pass its 'childhood', increase its readership, and become a member of the 'newspaper family'. The editorial emphasized the weekly's function

> to proclaim that the sick will recover, the prisoners will be released, the poor will become rich[21] ... and, by saying so, to [report] on the development of the country, the richness and health of the people, the cleanliness of the town, the straightening of roads, which was generously done by the Viceroy of Ethiopia for us so that Ethiopia could have a share in modern civilization.[22]

In the first year of its existence, sports news were confined to visuals only. In the second year, the number of pages increased from two to five and sports often occupied a whole page. With Italy's entry into the war

[19] Federico Caprotti, 'Visuality, Hybridity, and Colonialism: Imagining Ethiopia through Colonial Aviation, 1935–1940', *Annals of the Association of American Geographers*, 101:2 (2011), 387; for a substantial critique see Angelo Del Boca, *Italiani, brava gente? Un mito duro a morire* (Milan, 2005).
[20] 'Caesar' refers to the Roman Emperor (100–44 B.C.E.) and, thus, to the government of the Italian occupatio government and not to the Ethiopian emperor who bears the title Neguse Negest (King of Kings).
[21] Luke 4:18, 'The Spirit of the Lord is upon me, because he has anointed me to proclaim good news to the poor. He has sent me to proclaim liberty to the captives and recovering of sight to the blind, to set at liberty those who are oppressed' (English Standard Version).
[22] 'Huleṭenya amet' [The second year], *YeK'ēsar Mengist Mel'iktenya*, 3–9 megabīt 1931 [13–18 March 1939]. Neither newspaper used page numbers.

in 1940 and resources being scarce on all fronts, the number of pages decreased and, accordingly, the space for sports news. However, the topic never disappeared completely.

In May 1939, the administration launched a monthly magazine of seventy to eighty pages that they called *YeRoma Birhan* (The Light of Rome). Readers could purchase it in an ordinary copy for 5 Lira, or a high-gloss copy for 10 Lira. They could also opt for annual subscriptions. The magazine provided information in text and visuals about the Italian colonial possessions in the Horn of Africa. It focused on development through news on trade and religious matters, reported about official visits and reserved ten to fifteen pages for sports. In both newspapers, articles on sports were, with the exception of those by Abeba Abte and Taddesse Roba,[23] usually not signed by the author.

YeK'ēsar Mengist Mel'iktenya and *YeRoma Birhan* were published by the *Direzione Superiore Degli Affari Politici* of the *Governo Generale dell'Africa Orientale Italiana*. Dr. Umberto Franzina acted as *Direttore responsabile* of these publications. The linguistic mastery was, however, ensured by Afewerk' Gebre Īyesus, the famous writer of the first Amharic novel. His close affinity to the Italians made him a controversial historical figure. In 1938 he became the editor of *YeK'ēsar Mengist Mel'iktenya*, to which he regularly contributed 'propaganda articles scornful of both Ethiopia and the patriots' which gained him the title *Afe K'ēsar* (Mouthpiece of Caesar).[24] In February 1940, a ten-page article informed the readership about the production and distribution of both newspapers. According to the text, the whole process from writing and editing, typesetting and printing, binding and packaging was done in Addis Ababa. From there, an airplane transported the newspapers to post offices in other towns, where they reached their readers by land mail.[25] In Addis Ababa, distribution was via a network of neighbourhood headmen.[26] Except for a notice that the offset printing machine was able to produce 20,000 issues of *YeK'ēsar Mengist Mel'iktenya* within one hour, nothing

[23] Taddesse Roba, 'KeAddīs Abeba iske Holeta yetederegew yebīsīklēt ishk'ididim' [Cycling race from Addis Ababa to Holeta], *YeK'ēsar Mengist Mel'iktenya*, 13–19 mīyazya 1932 [21–27 April 1940]. Abeba Abte, 'Tillik' t'k'im yalew ch'ewata' [The great benefit of sports], *YeRoma Birhan*, 1:5, 22 t'ik'imt 1932 [28 October 1939].
[24] Bahru Zewde, *Pioneers of Change in Ethiopia: The Reformist Intellectuals of the Early Twentieth Century* (Oxford, 2002), p. 56; Yonas Adamassu, 'Afewerk' Gebre Īyesus', in Siegbert Uhlig (ed.), *Encyclopaedia Aethiopica*, 1 (Wiesbaden, 2003), p. 123.
[25] 'YeK'ēsar Mengist Mel'iktenya gazēt'ana YeRoma Birhan yetebalew bewer beweru yemīmet'aw indemin indemītatemu t'ik'īt masreja' [A short explanation about how the *YeK'ēsar Mengist Mel'iktenya* newspaper and the monthly called *YeRoma Birhan* are printed], *YeRoma Birhan*, 2:3 yekatīt 1932 [11 February 1940].
[26] *YeK'ēsar Mengist Mel'iktenya* 11–16 mīyazya1931 [23–29 April 1939].

is known about concrete circulation figures. The editors emphasized that they primarily used photographs sent by the readers, along with letters to the editor.

The articles on sports fall into three categories. The first group of texts focuses on the benefit of sports for building a civilized personality in terms of a loyal, responsible, colonial subject. A second category comprises reports on the establishment of sports structures and the spread of individual kinds of sports in the empire. The largest number of articles is concerned with extensive reporting on tournaments, including detailed descriptions of emerging star athletes. The newspapers' recurring references to Sunday as the day of sports, as 'rational leisure' for both athletes and spectators, hints at the readership editors had in mind. Arguably, the press targeted urban males who did manual or office work. The extremely low literacy rate amongst the urban population, and even more the extreme poverty, also made a wide reception of the Amharic press very unlikely. However, one can imagine that press circulated from one family to another and people were at least looking at the pictures. Therefore, analysing these newspapers primarily gives insight into Italian colonial imaginations about the importance of sports for their imperial project. Furthermore, taking up Charles Ambler's argument that sports news in African newspapers was an important source of entertainment, we can also assume that, during the Italian occupation, sports reporting, and especially visuals of cycling or football stars, provided a way to consume sports.[27]

Thus, acknowledging that sports news was designed along the lines of Fascist propaganda makes it possible to pose three bundles of questions that are instructive for this chapter: first, in how far did sports news legitimize the Italian Fascist occupation in terms of a civilizing project that targeted the mind through the body? What type of 'New Ethiopian' did they envisage? Second, which kinds of sports did the press project as suitable for Africans in general and Ethiopians in particular? How did sports news convey or attempt to create consensus between the Italian occupiers, the local nobility (including religious personalities), and the urban population? Who served which role? Third, what do these sports reports reveal about the spatial configuration of sports under the Fascist occupation? What was the role of sports-related propaganda in legitimizing racial and religious segregation? The following part discusses how the sports-related propaganda in Amharic brought ideas on sports as a physical activity and entertaining spectacle, and the potentially civilized, yet colonized *Etiope Nuovo*, home to its readership. Thus, it complements earlier

---

[27] Charles Ambler, 'Mass Media and Leisure in Africa', *The International Journal of African Historical Studies,* 35:1 (2002), 122.

works on the Italian Fascist understanding of its 'civilizing mission' and its implementation through the educational system in the colonized and occupied territories in Africa.[28]

Sports' Civilizing Mission

In October 1939, when *YeRoma Birhan* enthusiastically reported about the growing formation of organized sports structures in occupied Ethiopia, it defined the role of sports as 'the school of civilization'.[29] This explicit definition of sports as part of the civilizing process became a recurrent theme. Using the metaphor of the door-opener, the magazine emphasized that if

> sports means civilization in all civilized countries, a new good way of life in current time would be opened to the Ethiopian people. It strengthens the consciousness of the youth and prepares and enables them to receive new knowledge. Sports is a door-opener to wisdom and a main concern even in their dreams.[30]

Within this conceptual framework, sports was always more than a physical exercise and disciplining tool for the athletic youth and the spectators. Being presented as a way to 'progress for all', irrespective of their social background, it became a powerful mode of governance by involving large parts of the urban population. The press equated sports' importance with that of the 'vocational training Ethiopians received in Italy'.[31] In contrast to these vocational trainees, who also included young women,[32] exercising and consuming sports seems to have been reserved for the male populace only. Cultural constraints might have been the main reason that women (both Italian and Ethiopian) neither appeared as athletes in the press nor as spectators, but only in religious or family contexts. Obviously, the modern Italian athletic woman could not serve as a model for the colonial civilizing mission in Ethiopia.[33]

---

[28] For Ethiopia, especially see Paulos Milkias, 'Mussolini's Civilizing Mission, and Fascist Political Socialization in Occupied Ethiopia, 1936–41', in Siegbert Uhlig (ed.), *Proceedings of the 15th International Conference of Ethiopian Studies* (Wiesbaden, July 2006), pp. 328–36.
[29] 'Yesport dirijitina yehaymanot timhirt' [Sports organization and religious education], *YeRoma Birhan*, 1:5, 22 t'ik'imt 1932 [28 October 1939].
[30] 'Yeigir kʷas ch'ewata kampīyonato mejemer' [Start of the football championships], *YeRoma Birhan*, 2: 4, mīyazya 1932 [10 April 1940].
[31] 'Yesport dirijitina yehaymanot timhirt' [Sports organization and religious education], *YeRoma Birhan*, 1:5, 22 t'ik'imt 1932 [28 October 1939].
[32] 'Yefetil mekīna lememar wede It'alīya ager silehēdut yeĪtyopya sētoch' [On the trip of Ethiopian girls to learn the handling of spinning machines], *YeRoma Birhan*, 1:4, 17 meskerem 1932 [27 September 1939].
[33] Gigliola Gori, *Italian Fascism and the Female Body: Sport, Submissive Women*

Male Ethiopian youth being the target of the physical culture initiatives, the editors felt that they should especially address parents and relatives to include them in the Italian civilizing discourse. Parents were reported to have understood the benefit of sports for bodily and mental development and, thus, for a good life. Further elaborating on this issue, *YeRoma Birhan* argued that

> relatives of the youth, mothers and fathers are grateful to the government and are very happy that with the beginning of sports children have understood civilization. They can observe that [their children] have become obedient, love work, and respect those who are older, do not behave improperly on the street, and refrain from bad actions.[34]

Reporting on physical education and athletic competitions in the Wollo province, the magazine characterized organized sports as an antidote to laziness[35] and misdeeds. It serves, as the author continues, to educate young people to become responsible individuals who care for their families.[36] Apart from these benefits, another article in the same issue emphasizes that excellent physical and mental performance on the sports ground and at school will increase the honour and reputation of the athlete and his family. According to the editors 'it is his pride and prize if he reads his name in the newspaper and many people follow his story'.[37]

Apart from the virtues of a disciplined youth, ideas of the balanced subject (most forcefully propagated by the YMCA after the end of the occupation) became part of the civilizing physical culture discourse. In October 1939, the newly established Patriarch of Ethiopia Yohannis I[38] emphasized that the dissemination of sports competitions was in line with the Holy Scripture. Referring to Apostle Paul's reasoning about righteousness, self-control and finding the right path the Patriarch explained that in order 'to gain honour you have to follow the right path and be in competition to each other'. He emphasized that the benefit of the various competitions went well beyond the strengthening of the body. 'It is well known that when body and health are strong, soul and

---

and Strong Mothers (London, New York, 2004); Sarah Morgan, 'Mussolini's Boys (and Girls)'.
[34] 'Mīkenawenew dirijit' [Executive organization], *YeRoma Birhan*, 1:4, 17 meskerem 1932 [29 September 1939].
[35] Overcoming laziness – usually attributed to youth but not to 'the native' in general – by acquiring various kinds of knowledge is a recurrent topic in the press, which might in future deserve a more systematic study.
[36] 'BeDessē ketema yetederege sport' [Sports in Dessie town], *YeRoma Birhan*, 2:1, 20 tahsas 1932 [30 December 1939].
[37] 'Yesewinet maṭenkeriya ch'ewata' [Sports for strengthening the body], *YeRoma Birhan*, 2:1, 20 tahsas 1932 [30 December 1939].
[38] For biographical details see Stéphane Ancel, 'Yoḥannəs I', in *Encyclopaedia Aethiopica*, 5 (Wiesbaden, 2014), p. 80.

spirit are purified and in balance. Therefore, we help and fully support that the youth is strengthening their soul and bring their spirit into perfection'.[39] Since the youthful body enjoyed competition, it was a 'renewal of life'.[40] Opening a bicycle race in his honour, Yohannis I stressed that the embodied knowledge, gained through training and competition, was as important as religious and secular knowledge.[41] Having understood its potential, the Orthodox Church used the sports craze for religious purposes, too. It sent teachers to the places where the youth gathered for physical activities to give them religious instruction.[42]

As well as stressing the importance of physical exercise for a healthy body, the press provided explanations of exactly what happened to the human body if one did or did not do sports. These contributions focused on the problem of 'thick blood', which could not circulate appropriately through the body and eventually lead to cramped muscles and the inability to move.

> If you spend your day sitting your blood gets thick, and if your blood gets thick your nerves get knotted. After that you get tired and weak and finally this leads to illness. And if you are not doing anything, bad thoughts come into your brain. Sports, however, whether one is doing it or watching it, neither harms health nor life and keeps away bad thoughts from your brain. The one who loves sports is the one who lives in joy.[43]

YeK'ēsar Mengist Mel'iktenya further stressed that young athletes had to be prevented from smoking and drinking so that they would be able to combine strength and speed and eventually be 'real youth'.[44]

Turning to the spectators' side, articles on sports recurrently emphasized that the weekly competitions were an ideal site to 'see' civilization. Apart from rule-bound movement, ideas of useful leisure, clothing, and greeting were markers that went beyond athleticism proper. Reporting from the spectators' perspective about the great benefit of Sunday competitions, one author emphasized that the work-free Sunday was no

---

[39] 'Mel'ikit Yohannis hawarya' [Message of Patriarch Yohannes], *YeRoma Birhan,* 1:5, 22 t'ik'imt 1932 [28 October 1939].
[40] Ibid.
[41] 'Yet'ik'imt 8 k'en amus siletederegew yebīsīklēt ishk'ididim' [The bicycle race held on Thursday, 8 t'ik'imt], *YeRoma Birhan,* 1:5, 22 t'ik'imt 1932 [28 October 1939].
[42] 'Yesport dirijitina yehaymanot timhirt' [Sports organizations and religious education], *YeRoma Birhan,* 1:5, 22 t'ik'imt 1932 [28 October 1939].
[43] 'Yetenīs ch'ewata silemesfafat' [On the spread of tennis], *YeRoma Birhan,* 2:2, 3 yekatīt 1932 [11 February 1940].
[44] 'Yesport sira sile mesfafatinna yetemelkachochu bizat ilet ilet iyakele silemehēdu' [On the expansion of sports activities and the steady growth of athletes and spectators], *YeK'ēsar Mengist Mel'iktenya,* 1–8 senē 1932 [9–15 June 1940].

longer empty or lost time, but time for useful recreation. He continues that competitions had become a major topic to discuss with colleagues at work on Mondays. Finally, watching cycling races inspired him to learn how to ride a bicycle.[45]

The spread of sports, and especially sports competitions, also saw the spread of sports clothing and team uniforms (*meleya libs*). Various articles praised the Italian government for handing out shirts and trousers. Linking these to the issue of civilized behaviour, they emphasized that this also included keeping these clothes clean.[46] Perceived (mis)use prompted remarks such as a jersey not being

> everyday clothing and should be kept as a holy thing and handled with care. It is absolutely necessary that everything which is handed out by the government has to be handled with respect. One has to learn it by heart in order to always remember this care.[47]

Several articles directly linked the topic of the uniform or team jersey to that of 'civilized greeting' in competitive athletic contexts. Writing about the ceremonies for receiving trophies or prize money, the authors stressed that 'youth in a sports uniform conveyed [to the Italian governors] in a civilized manner the Roman salute [*besilt'anē akwahwan tet'egtew yeRoma selamta*]'.[48] The salute was but one reference to the Italian 'motherland'. According to Polson Newman, who visited Ethiopia during the Italian occupation, 'everywhere we went the natives stood up and almost all gave the Fascist salute'.[49] Arguably, greeting was a symbolic act that contributed to the functioning of sports as part of creating consensus on the colonial project. Uniforms did not only serve as symbols of loyalty or order: they also worked as symbols of prestige. Thus, the African officials of the Sports Bureau had a uniform with an 'orientalizing' headgear – the fez.[50]

The discourse that linked sports to civilization also included the establishment of organizational structures. At the top level, sports for the 'natives' was directly administered under the *Direzione Superiore Degli Affari Politici*. The Sports Bureau coordinated physical edu-

---

[45] Abeba Abte, 'Tillik' t'k'im yalew ch'ewata' [The great benefit of sports], *YeRoma Birhan*, 1:5, 22 t'ik'imt 1932 [28 October 1939].
[46] 'Mīkenawenew dirijit' [Executive organization], *YeRoma Birhan*, 1:4, 17 meskerem 1932 [29 September 1939].
[47] 'Yesewinet mat'enkeriya ch'ewata' [Sports for strengthening the body], *YeRoma Birhan*, 2:1, 20 tahsas 1932 [30 December 1939].
[48] 'Meskerem 20 k'en be Addis Abeba siletederegew liyu liyu ch'ewata' [On the various competitions held in Addis Ababa on 20 meskerem], *YeRoma Birhan*, 1:5, 22 t'ik'imt 1932 [28 October 1939].
[49] Cited in Pankhurst, 'Education in Ethiopia', 394.
[50] See visuals explicitly drawing the attention of the reader to the head gear in the subtitle in *YeRoma Birhan*, 2:4, 2 mīyazya 1932 [10 April 1940].

cation in schools and teams, which were sponsored by notables, as well as sports activities outside existing formal structures. *YeRoma Birhan* argued that the spread of competitive sports had made this formalization necessary. In this respect, it promoted Shoa province as a good example and 'an encouragement for the other provinces of the Empire'.[51] Apart from Addis Ababa, smaller towns with a strong Italian presence founded local sports organizations. In December 1939, for example, *YeRoma Birhan* reported on the town of Dessie.[52] Despite sports' recent introduction, spectators liked to admire the athletic youth in various competitions. Dessie's athletes were grouped into four divisions, the cycling teams forming the strongest. In order to organize the two-to-three hundred sportsmen into teams, the sports officials founded a competitor organization called *mereb* (net).[53] Only two months later, the magazine published the names of those sports enthusiasts who had 'founded an association in order to spread sports in their country to improve the training of their children so that they reach a higher level of civilization'.[54] As the quote indicates, the authors not only reported on the spread of sports as such, but linked the theme of higher levels of civilization to ideas of intensification of the training and perfection.

In order to provide readers with a sense of how to measure civilizational progress under the Italian occupation, *YeRoma Birhan* began to publish, although rather irregularly, statistics on registered athletes as well as the number of competitions and rewards. Thus, we can read that in 1939 Addis Ababa had one thousand registered athletes. In contrast, *YeK'ēsar Mengist Mel'iktenya* came up with the much more modest figure of 154 football players and seventy cyclists for the capital. Sports bureaus in the smaller towns of Fiche, Ankober, Debre Birhan, Woliso, and Indaba had all in all 3,000 athletes registered for competitions.[55] From October 1939 to February 1940, nearly 4,300 men participated in 49 bicycle races, 54 running competitions, 3 horse races, and 15 football matches, receiving 940 awards.[56] Furthermore, statistics and

---

[51] 'BeShewa ager sport silemesfafat' [On the spread of sports in Shoa], *YeRoma Birhan*, 1:5, 22 t'ik'imt 1932 [28 October 1939].
[52] Dessie lies 390 km north-east of Addis Ababa in the Wollo province and functioned as an important administrative centre under Italian occupation.
[53] 'BeDessē ketema yetederrege sport' [Sport in Dessie town], *YeRoma Birhan*, 2:1, 20 tahsas 1932 [30 December 1939].
[54] 'Yesport mahber' [The sports association], *YeRoma Birhan*, 2:2, 3 yekatīt 1932 [11 February 1940].
[55] 'Yesport dirijitina yehaymanot timhirt' [Sports organizations and religious education], *YeRoma Birhan*, 1:5, 22 t'ik'imt 1932 [28 October 1939].
[56] 'Barat wer wisṭ' yetederege yesport ch'ewata' [Sports competitions held within the last four months], *YeRoma Birhan*, 1:5, 22 t'ik'imt 1932 [28 October 1939]; 'Yesport sira sile mesfafatuna yetemelkachochu bizat ilet ilet iyakele

reports included exact figures regarding financial support of sports events. Interestingly, the newspapers classified sponsors into Muslim and Christian dignitaries, especially highlighting the role of the Muslim community. This was in accordance with general Italian politics towards Ethiopia, which attempted to exploit the fact that Haile Selassie promoted Christians over Muslims. When Alawiya El Morgana and the so-called sharifs from Asmara visited Addis Ababa in December 1939, the administration organized several sports competitions, including a high-class cycling race.

The same article stresses that the Muslim notables donated 27,000 Lira for 'strengthening the athletic youth and for spreading sports'.[57] However, they were not the only ones. Sponsorship was a general topic. The donation of more than 5,000 Lira by Christian and Muslim notables from Dessie was described not only as a good idea as such, but that 'it is desirable that this idea [extends] throughout the Empire for the spread of sports as a superior activity. Especially in Addis Ababa this should be a telling example'.[58] Interestingly, there is only one reported case of an Italian bicycle producer (Bianchi) sponsoring a trophy for the winner of a cycling race.[59] Instead, the discourse on the spread of competitive sports and the role of the local nobility as sponsors tapped into the existing trope of the benevolent notable. By doing so, the press depicted them as local (financial) drivers of progress and civilization.

However, if the general propaganda emphasized the positive role of sports and physical education for civilizing the colonized, which kinds of sports were useful for this mission? The sports news suggests that not all forms of physical activity met the editors' ideas of civilizational progress. While tennis was perceived as the 'food for the civilized people' and an 'honourable kind of sport' (*kibir yalew yetenīs ch'ewata*),[60] so-called traditional games were not considered suitable and, thus, rarely discussed at all. Even existing local styles of global competitive physical culture, such as wrestling or hockey, were rarely mentioned and if they were, editors were explicitly derogatory.

---

silemehēdu' [On the expansion of sports activities and the steady growth of the number of athletes and spectators], *YeK'ēsar Mengist Mel'iktenya,* 1–8 senē 1932 [9–15 June 1940].
[57] 'BeAddis Abeba yetederege sport' [Sports done in Addis Ababa], *YeRoma Birhan,* 2:1, 20 tahsas 1932 [30 December 1939].
[58] 'BeDessē yesport sira indīsfafa yetederege yegenzeb irdata' [Financial support for the spread of sports in Dessie], *YeRoma Birhan,* 2:1, 20 tahsas 1932 [30 December 1939].
[59] 'Des yemīyaseny shilimat' [A pleasing award], *YeRoma Birhan,* 1:5, 22 t'ik'imt 1932 [28 October 1939].
[60] 'Yetenīs ch'ewata silemesfafat' [On the spread of tennis], *YeRoma Birhan,* 2:2, 3 yekatīt 1932 [11 February 1940].

In earlier times, youth played *genna* [hockey] and adults did horse races during *Mesk'el* without rules and knowledge: in our country ... a game without rules does not give pleasure but is only shocking. And it is well known that if man only follows the character of his father then his knowledge will be limited forever.

We clearly know why Europeans are civilized. They have broken with the traditions of their forefathers. They do what they consider being right and do not let chances pass ... Among the civilized people, sports is a possibility to civilize man.[61]

Sports news in both *YeRoma Birhan* and *YeK'ēsar Mengist Mel'iktenya* exclusively reported about modern sports, or, in the case of horse races, versions with stricter rules. Similar to other contexts of colonial sports policy, the Italian administration promoted those sports that were already prominent in Italy itself, i.e. cycling, football, and to a certain extent, athletics. Thus, the next section will discuss how the press explained the value of these kinds of sports for inducing an imagined consensus amongst different parts of the urban local population and the Italian colonial administration.

Of Cycling Races, Football Matches, and Athletics

As Patrizia Dogliani convincingly demonstrated, the Fascist system tried to turn Italians into a nation of sportsmen, fans, and spectators. Arguably, the situation in urban centres of the occupied or colonized territories was not much different after 1938. By organizing regular sports events and reporting about them, the Italian administration attempted to offer sports as 'entertainment, an escape from the daily problems. ... Living through the exploits and victories of athletes ... was a way of forgetting anxieties over the future and daily hardship'.[62] While radio broadcasts (especially those of football matches) had raised sports enthusiasm in Italy since 1927, sports was consumed live in the African possessions.

Bicycle races and football matches became magnets for the male public. Thus, they featured prominently in the sports news. Interestingly, the Italian success in both football and cycling was never presented in the Amharic press. With the exception of two photographs showing Italian football players in Addis Ababa and Jimma,[63] both *YeRoma Birhan* and *YeK'ēsar Mengist Mel'iktenya* exclusively focused on local sporting talent.

[61] Ibid.
[62] Dogliani, 'Sport and Fascism', 333.
[63] 'Jīmma liyyu liyyu ch'ewata' [Jimma: various games], *YeK'ēsar Mengist Mel'iktenya*, 20 hidar 1931 [29 November 1938]; 'YeAddīs Abeba yekarabīnērī kifil futbol (igir kʷas) tech'awachoch' [Players of the Addis Ababa carabinieri football team], *YeK'ēsar Mengist Mel'iktenya*, 30 tahsas 1931 [8 January 1939].

Cycling and the Production of Heroes

Right from the beginning of sports reporting under the Italian occupation in 1938, admiration of cyclists' skill and speed filled the pages. 'They flew like the wind and very much impressed the spectators'.[64] They were able to handle skilfully the difficulties of a round course. Through knowledge, experience, and hard training the athletes melded with their bicycles to become an effective racing unit. Thousands of spectators lined the streets of Addis Ababa's newly built native quarter or filled the Jan Mēda racing grounds in order to admire and celebrate the new African heroes.

There seems to be agreement that cycling started in Ethiopia under the Italian occupation. Knowledge of the sport, its organizational structure as well as the appeal of races to the local population had already existed in colonial Eritrea. Apart from the Cycling Commission of Eritrea, which was founded in 1936 and dominated by Italians, Eritreans established their own cycling team in 1937.[65] Due to the Fascist segregationist policy, Eritrean athletes were barred from participating in the first cycling race in Asmara in 1937. It took them two more years to be allowed to race in local events against Italian athletes. When Gebremaryam Gebru won the first Eritrean Cycling Championships in 1939, it was not only proof of local athletic strength, but his victory also shattered the myth of Italian colonial and racial superiority.[66] Although it is difficult to establish exactly if and how Italian sports administrators had learned their lesson for occupied Ethiopia, there was not a single Italian cyclist reported to have participated in a local race. Instead, Eritreans mostly won the trophies and enjoyed a celebrity status. Despite the lack of an explicit document of proof, the idea is still appealing that Eritreans' cycling success created an argument for the colonial civilizing project, i.e. that Eritrea had already been colonized since the late nineteenth century and therefore Eritreans were more used to the sport than Ethiopians were.

Racing in and around Addis Ababa was grouped into straight and round courses. Straight-course races consisted of two parts. Depending on the existence of asphalt roads, athletes raced from Addis Ababa to Holeta (22 kilometres to the north-west), Addis Alem (56 kilometres to the west) or Sendafa, which is located 40 kilometres to the north-east

---

[64] 'Beturīzm bīsīklet yetederege ishk'ididim' [The race on Tourism bicycles], *YeRoma Birhan*, 1:5, 22 t'ik'imt 1932 [28 October 1939].

[65] Old Asmara Eritrea, 'History of Cycling Races in Eritrea', Facebook, 13 July 2015, www.facebook.com/OldEritreaAsmara/posts/1513403132253616 [accessed 15 September 2021].

[66] Fikreyesus Amahazion, 'Pedaling History: Eritrea's Teklehaimanot and Kudus in Tour de France', *TesfaNews*, 6 July 2015, www.tesfanews.net/eritrea-pedaling-history-at-tour-de-france [accessed 15 September 2021].

on the Addis Ababa–Asmara highway (today, the Adigrat highway). Notables accompanied them in their cars and handed over trophies to the winners of the first part of the race. After a thirty-minute break, they raced back to the capital, fighting for the overall victory in the tournament. Since Addis Ababa is surrounded by mountains, the athletes had to deal with uphill and downhill challenges, which gave the competitions an extra thrill. Circular track courses usually took place at the Jan Mēda racing grounds on a 3-kilometre circuit,[67] in the newly built native quarter near the market area on an 8-kilometre circuit,[68] or in Tekle Haymanot neighbourhood.[69] While the distance and the hilly terrain were the main challenges on the straight courses, the round courses were reportedly even more difficult since they 'demand[ed] great skill and knowledge to enter the bend or to turn the handlebar'.[70]

Furthermore, races were divided into the bicycle categories *kurs* and *turismo*. *Kurs* cycling competitions used racing bicycles (*yeshert' bīsīklēt*) or simply fast bikes (*fet'an bīsīklēt*), and were probably equipped and named after Tullio Campagnolo's recent invention, the *Corsa* gear changing system.[71] The reported racing dream, however, was the *abīyanko lenjono* (most probably a *Bianco Legnano*), a white racing bike produced by the Emilio Bozzi's legendary company.[72] Due to their experience, Eritrean cyclists dominated the *kurs* bike racing scene in Addis with champions such as Kassa Fidel, Kassaye Irisom, and Mulugeta Kassa giving top performances in every other event. Local athletes, often recognizable by their Oromo names, excelled more on *turismo* bikes. Races on these ordinary bicycles (*tera bīsīklēt*) were usually shorter in distance.

According to the sports news, races were held all year round, even during the long rainy season between June and September. The main reason was, of course, the much celebrated infrastructural improvement. Reporting on the Addis – Sendafa – Addis race of 14 August 1939, *YeRoma Birhan* explained that

---

[67] 'BeAddis Abeba yetederege liyu liyu ch'ewata' [Various games performed in Addis Ababa], *YeRoma Birhan*, 1:3, 6 nehasē 1931 [12 August 1939].
[68] 'Yebīsīklēt ch'ewata' [The bicycle competition], *YeRoma Birhan*, 1:4, 17 meskerem 1932 [29 September 1939].
[69] 'Yebīsīklēt ishk'ididim' [The bicycle race], *YeRoma Birhan*, 1:5, 22 t'ik'imt 1932 [28 October 1939].
[70] 'BeAddis Abeba yetederege liyyu liyyu ch'ewata' [Various games performed in Addis Ababa], *YeRoma Birhan*, 1:3, 6 nehasē 1931 [12 August 1939].
[71] Chris Boardman, *The Biography of the Modern Bike: The Ultimate History of Bike Design* (London, 2015), p. 51.
[72] In contrast, Legnano bicycles were branded by 1930s through their lizard green colour, not white (Breaking Away, 'The History of Legnano', 10 April 2013 https://condorino.com/2013/04/10/the-history-of-legnano [accessed 15 September 2021]).

people were afraid that because of the bad weather the competition would be cancelled ... One should not think that the shower of the night together with the rain of the previous week had turned the street into mud. It is made of asphalt and therefore a nice, perfect and well-arranged street.[73]

However, most of the races, especially those counting for the Shoa Championships (introduced in 1939) were held after September.[74] The press depicted the racing cyclists not only as well-trained and successful athletes, but as those who 'cherish the name of our country'.[75] The author does not indicate which country he meant, but his text shows very well that sporting success is never individual, but at the service of a greater entity. Together with acts of symbolism such as the Roman salute and/or greeting the Italian flag displayed at awards ceremonies, successful athletes became icons of Italy's successful civilizing mission. Furthermore, athletic success directly resulted in coaching obligations. The star of the scene, Kassa Fidel, was ordered to organize and train *sefer* teams (from various Quarters) of at least five cyclists and to train them for the Shoa Championships.[76]

The performance of cycling stars also served to address inappropriate behaviour. The otherwise celebrated Kassa Fidel,[77] for example, was repeatedly criticised whenever he did not race to expectations. Points of critique ranged from too much belief in his own final sprinting abilities, to going out with friends the night before a race. When he was absent from a competition without prior notice or permission, *YeRoma Birhan* commented that he 'violated the fixed and civilized rules for competitions and this has to be condemned. In sports it is absolutely necessary to keep discipline and order ... In any case, vanity and shyness are detrimental to sports'.[78] Again, others were criticised for not having

---

[73] 'Yebīsīklēt ishk'ididim keAddīs Abeba Sendafa derso milash' [Bicycle race in the Addis Ababa-Sendafa-circuit], *YeRoma Birhan*, 1:3, 12 nehasē 1931 [12 August 1939]. According to Seyoum Mulugeta, this highway was built by workers from Italy/Sicily who lived in Campo Alogo area in Addis Ababa.

[74] 'Yebīsīklēt ch'ewata' [The bicycle competition], *YeRoma Birhan*, 1:4, 17 meskerem 1932 [29 September 1939]: this informed the readership that in 'future, the winner of the race, if he has also won all the other competitions, will be awarded the title of the *kampiyoni*. In the Italian language, the *kampiyoni* is better than all the others and, therefore, named the *captain* of the competition'.

[75] 'YeShewa yesport ch'ewata mesfafat' [The spread of sports competitions in Shoa], *YeRoma Birhan*, 1:3, 6 nehasē 1931 [12 August 1939].

[76] 'Sport mesfafat' [The spread of sports], *YeK'ēsar Mengist Mel'iktenya*, 1–7 mīyazya 1932 [14–20 April 1940].

[77] The press usually portrayed Kassa Fidel, the winner of the first Shoa Championships in 1939, as a hard-working, modest, strong, skilful, and efficient cyclist. Editors left no doubt that he was the *wanna limadu*, the most experienced amongst the top-level athletes.

[78] 'Yebīsīklēt ishk'ididim keAddīs Abeba Sendafa derso milash' [Bicycle race

confidence in their own strength, wasting their energy on downhill pedalling or not keeping their bicycles in order.[79] By criticising successful athletes, the press reminded their audience that remaining at the top was a hard business of daily labour and self-discipline.

Out of this criticism, sports reporting developed into an advisory platform. Besides a very general emphasis on discipline, training, and confidence, editors also explained important practical issues. One of them was the question about when to start racing in major competitions. Under the rubric *Misgana* (Acknowledgement), the magazine thanked the fourteen-year-old Mulugeta Demse for abstaining from participation in major races and instead waiting for 'his' time to come. Editors praised him as 'an intelligent child who knows that cleverness is for short term and wisdom is for long term. Today he does cycling exercises and in future, when he has become stronger, he wants to compete on equal terms.[80]

The great success of the new sport in the occupied and colonized territories also attracted colonial administrators, local notables, and economically powerful personalities to use the sports scene for their own purposes. Arguably, for the Ethiopian nobility, including the clergy, sports competitions were an ideal opportunity to demonstrate their position within the colonial system and to link their personality to a modern or European idea of what it meant to be civilized. In contrast to Italy, where Mussolini himself was portrayed as the sportsman number one, notables used the well-established system of letting others sweat on their behalf. Intentionally or not, the start and finish of the races with straight courses, such as Addis Ababa – Holeta – Addis Ababa, was next to their houses, thus actively participating in the spatial configuration of sports in the city. During the Shoa Cycling Championships of 1939/40, the best local cyclists formed teams sponsored by and racing on behalf of notables such as *Ras* Seyoum Mengesha, *Ras* Kebede Guebret, and *Ras* Haylu Tekle Haymanot.[81]

Probably because of his economic potential, *Commendatore* Saleh Ahmed Kekiya also ranked amongst those notables often mentioned on the sports pages. Saleh was a wealthy merchant born in Hirghigo in 1904, at that time a village in the Northern Red Sea region of Eritrea. During the Italian colonial and Fascist period in the Horn of Africa, he was granted the honorific title *Commendatore* and with it the *Ordine*

Addis Abeba – Sendafa and back], *YeRoma Birhan*, 1:3, 6 nehasē 1931 [12 August 1939].
[79] 'Lesport tech'awachoch yemīt'ek'im mikir' [Useful advice the competitors in sports], *YeRoma Birhan*, 2:2, 3 yekatīt 1932 [11 February 1940].
[80] 'Misgana' [Acknowledgement], *YeRoma Birhan*, 2:4, 2 mīyazya 1932 [10 April 1940].
[81] 'Yetedenek'e sport' [An admired sport], *YeRoma Birhan*, 1:4, 17 meskerem 1932 [29 September 1939].

coloniale della Stella d'Italia (Colonial Order of the Star of Italy).[82] Saleh frequently conveyed trophies or financial gifts to winners. As the owner of a racing team that competed in various cycling championships in Shoa and Eritrea,[83] he contributed to the emerging process of professionalization in sports. Arguably, this athletic professionalism began during the Italian occupation with cycling, and was able to develop due to a suitable mixture of promoting cycling as a civilizing (Italian) sport and, perhaps, the local nobility's wish for recognition. Given the fact that Italians never regarded notables such as *Ras* Siyyum Mengesha as being fully trustworthy,[84] it is difficult to judge the part they really played in bringing about a consensus on the Fascist project in the Horn of Africa. On the propagandistic level, however, their public appearances with high-ranking figures of the Italian occupation forces such as General Guglielmo Ciro Nasi (especially during his time as Governor of Shoa, 1939–40) and their receiving of the Fascist Roman salute by the young athletes visibly contributed to using sports to create a political consensus.

Football's Moral Value

In contrast to cycling, football had already been established in Ethiopia by the first half of the twentieth century. The early 1930s saw the emergence of Ethiopian teams in the capital (and most probably in other Ethiopian towns) with the legendary St. George football club (also called Arada, after the neighbourhood), founded in 1935.[85] By the advent of the Italian occupation, there existed at least four teams named after their neigh-

---

[82] This order was given to personalities for their outstanding merits in the Italian colonies. The article, 'The praiseworthy help of Comendatore Saleh Ahmad Kekiya' [Komendatore Saleh Ahmad Kekiya yaderegut yemīyasmesegin irdata] in the Amharic weekly *YeK'ēsar Mengist Mel'iktenya* 30 hamlē–27 nehasē 1932 [6 August – 2 September 1940]), praised him for his donation of 150,000 Lira for the families of colonial soldiers who were wounded or killed during the operation against British Somaliland, and is accompanied by a photograph that shows Saleh Ahmed Kekiya with this order on his left chest. After the defeat of the Italians in East Africa, the British interned him as an alleged Italian spy, but soon released him and in 1944 conferred the title of *pasha* on him. Having returned from Addis Ababa to Eritrea in the late 1940s, he became prominent as vice-president of the Unionist Party and was elected as a representative of the Unionist Party for the Hirghigo and Zula districts to the Eritrean Assembly on 26 March 1952 (British Archives, 'Leading Personalities in Eritrea (1950)', 16 January 2003, www.ehrea.org/leaders.php [accessed 15 September 2021]).

[83] 'Yebīsīklēt ch'ewata' [The bicycle competition], *YeRoma Birhan*, 1:4. 17, meskerem 1932 [29 September 1939].

[84] Hanna Rubinkowska, 'Ras 'Siyyum Mengesha', Siegbert Uhlig (ed.), *Encyclopaedia Aethiopica*, 4 (Wiesbaden, 2010), p. 646.

[85] Solomon Addis Getahun, 'A History of Sport in Ethiopia', in Svein Ege, Harald Aspen, Birhanu Teferra, and Shiferaw Bekele (eds), *Proceedings of the 16th International Conference of Ethiopian Studies* (Trondheim, 2009), p. 411.

bourhoods: Arada, Gulele, K'ebana, Intot't'o, and Sidist Kilo. According to the sports news these five teams dominated Addis Ababa's football scene during the Italian occupation. They had adult teams, youth teams, and junior teams. With the exception of the rainy season, when playing fields turned into marshes, spectators and players enjoyed matches in the capital on Sundays on the premises of the Jan Mēda racing grounds and, from April 1940 onwards, also on the newly built sports ground in the 'native' quarter.[86] Special occasions such as the Shoa Championships (1940) added matches on Thursdays.

The re-organization of football under the Sports Bureau also generated attempts to imprint the Italian presence by renaming the existing teams in Addis Ababa and Asmara. In the capital, St. George/Arada became Littorio Wube Squadra, Gulele was changed into Consolata, K'ebana was renamed Villa Italia, and Sidist Kilo became Piazza Roma. The Asmara-based Hamassēn team was baptised Arita and K'ey Bahir became Savoia.[87] However, following the sports news on football in both *YeRoma Birhan* and *YeK'ēsar Mengist Mel'iktenya*, the naming practice was not effective at all. Thus, editors resorted to the established neighbourhood names of the teams, at least for Addis Ababa.[88] Furthermore, with the introduction of team uniforms, shirt colours or patterns served as synonyms to connect local sports reporting to a globalized style.

Instead of insisting on the new names for established teams, the Sports Bureau concentrated on the 'right' labels for the new junior teams [*tek'olk'oloch sk'wadrawoch*]. Fully in accordance with the pedagogical line of the civilizing project, the junior teams were named after favourable character traits: *mefak'ir* (love), *ti'igist* (patience), *tigat* (diligence), *met'en* (modesty, balance), *imnet* (faith, confidence), and *tihtina* (modesty, civility, politeness). In an extensive article, *YeK'ēsar Mengist Mel'iktenya* explained how these categories were to be understood. It stressed that, by internalizing these traits, children were regarded as superior to all other wealth.[89] Talking about the same issue, *YeRoma Birhan* argued that '[o]n the way to the next step to civilization, the juniors will be on the forefront and their team names shine in their consciousness like a spiritual light'.[90] Making a connection to local naming practices, it emphasized that when

---

[86] 'Baddīsu yehager tewelajoch ketema yeteseraw yeigir kwas mech'awecha bota temerek'e' [Inauguration of the playing field in the new native quarter], *YeRoma Birhan*, 2:4, 2 mīyazya 1932 [10 April 1940].
[87] Sintayehu, 'The History of St. George Sport Club', pp. 14–15.
[88] 'Yeigir kʷas ch'ewata kampiyonato mejemir' [Start of the football championships], *YeRoma Birhan*, 2:4, 2 mīyazya 1932 [10 April 1940].
[89] 'Liyu liyu yehone yesewinet maṭenkarīya ch'ewata' [Various games to strengthen the body], *YeK'ēsar Mengist Mel'iktenya*, 14–20 megabīt 1932 [24–30 March 1940].
[90] 'Yeigir kʷas ch'ewata' [Football], *YeRoma Birhan*, 2:4, 2 mīyazya 1932 [10

> a mother gives a name to her child, e.g. *Ashennafī* [winner] and *Belayneh* [you above others], she does not know if in real life he becomes a victor or stands above all the others. However, she supposes that wishing is finding ... Since the Sports Bureau is like a mother for the junior players, it gave them [these] names so that they put them into action.[91]

Such explanations do not simply reveal ideas about how moral and physical reforms go hand in hand. They also demonstrate the appropriation of a familiar practice as a discursive hook, putting the aim of colonizing the minds and bodies of the occupied peoples into practice. As an administrative arm of the Fascist administration, the Sports Bureau (not the parents) should monitor the moral and physical transformation of the most malleable generation. Consequently, the idea that young people are on the frontline of progress, and need careful, age-specific preparation, points to a differentiated understanding of youth, according to its degree of malleability. Using the metaphor of the tree, *YeK'ēsar Mengist Mel'iktenya* argued that 'if a tree has grown wayward, it will be difficult to straighten it. It either breaks or remains bent. It is impossible to correct somebody or give him advice, if he was not corrected during childhood and bad character traits were eradicated'.[92] The project itself, however, most probably failed due to the severe shortage of coaches for an increasing number of junior teams.[93]

Whereas news about the junior teams focused on the moralizing aspects or on organizational matters, extensive reports on the adult matches represented early attempts to convey the excitement of the game. This excitement was augmented by featuring one particular player: Yidnek'achew Tesemma (1921–87), the legendary father of Ethiopian football. Born in Jimma, he attended the Tafari Mekonnen School in Addis Ababa, which was well known for its sports programme before the occupation. The school had its own football team and Yidnek'achew excelled there.[94] Later, he became a founding member and the star of St. George football club. Alongside an excellent goalkeeper, whom the press compared to a hawk, and the other teammates, Yidnek'achew led the scene during the occupation period. The Amharic newspapers admired him for his skill in keeping the ball close to his foot while quickly passing by the defenders of the opposing team. The spectators

---

April 1940].
[91] Ibid.
[92] 'Liyu liyu yehone yesewinet mat'enkarīya ch'ewata' [Various games to strengthen the body], *YeK'ēsar Mengist Mel'iktenya*, 14–20 megabīt 1932 [24–30 March 1940].
[93] 'YeShewa yesport ch'ewata mesfafat' [The spread of sports competitions in Shoa], *YeRoma Birhan*, 1:3, 6 nehasē 1931 [12 August 1939].
[94] Solomon, 'A History of Sport in Ethiopia', 11.

were reported as cheering 'he keeps the ball; he does not let it go!'[95] In his short history of athletics in Ethiopia from 1985, Yidnek'achew also explained about his participation as an amateur athlete during the Fascist occupation for financial reasons. There, he excelled in pool vaulting, high jump, as well as 100-metre races.[96]

Yidnek'achew's prominence and excellence, but also his education and linguistic abilities (including Italian), made him attractive to the Sports Bureau.[97] There, he translated the football rules into Amharic.[98] Most probably, his translations correspond with the contributions on this issue in the press.[99] Yidnek'achew continued his athletic and administrative career after the end of the Italian occupation. In fact, he became the most influential figure in Ethiopian sports and one of the most prominent sports leaders on the African continent. His professional development through very different historical periods (Fascist occupation, Haile Selassie period, socialism), arguably free of any ruptures, demonstrates very well a more general observation that, in the Ethiopian sports system, continuities were much stronger than ruptures.

Working Out the Nobility: Mass Gymnastics and Athletics in Physical Education

Whereas competition, with its inherent binary system of victory and defeat, focused on success, mass gymnastics, and especially its display, conveyed a projection of the 'New Ethiopian' as part of an organic whole. Gymnastic shows by school children (boys and girls) on special occasions, such as the visit of the Swedish Crown Prince Gustav Adolf to Ethiopia in 1935, had already served the purpose of demonstrating the Ethiopian empire's physical fitness along the lines of an accepted 'Western' form. The Italian sports officials were able to tap into this visual experience and shape it according to their needs. Again, schools provided the ideal site to train and publicly display gymnastics. Arguably, gymnastics was the site to instil an allegedly higher ethical concept in a selected group of malleable youth of noble descent and, thus, ennoble physical fitness as such. News about physical education also referred to the spectators standing beside the field. In the city of Gondar, for example, on

---

[95] 'Mejemerīya silatederegew yeigir kʷas ch'ewata' [First (report) on the football match which took place], *YeRoma Birhan*, 1:5, 22 t'ik'imt 1932 [28 October 1939].

[96] Yidnek'achew Tesemma, *YeĪtyop'ya atletīks tarīkina wit'ēt* [History and results of Ethiopian athletics], in YeĪtyop'ya 'atletiks federēshin (eds), *Arengwadēw gorf* [The green torrent], 5 t'ir 1977 [13 January 1985], p. 27.

[97] Sintayehu, 'The History of St. George Sport Club', p. 15.

[98] Paul Rambali, *Barefoot Runner* (London, 2008), p. 44.

[99] 'Yeigir kʷas ch'ewata denb' [Rules of the football game], *YeRoma Birhan*, 1:5, 22 t'ik'imt 1932 [28 October 1939]; 'Yeigir kʷas ch'ewata' [Football match], *YeRoma Birhan*, 2:4, 2 mīyazya 1932 [10 April 1940].

Thursday and Sunday morning, youth gather on the field next to the market below the Fasīledes Palace in order to learn warm-up exercises. The children of the notables and the children of the poor are diligent in learning to warm up. On school days, these youngsters come first to the sports ground and dwell there in brotherhood and love, laughing, playing, and kidding with each other. Once the teacher comes, they stand still, orderly, and straight like civilized people and give their teacher the Roman salute. Relatives and friends, who accompany the children, stand beside the field and watch with joy how their children skilfully work during the lesson. It is well known that sport fills the spirit of the youngsters with positive thoughts and adds skilfulness to their bodies. Thus, it is a true symbol of civilization.[100]

Mass gymnastics, the training held in schools, became a site for showing hierarchically enforced physical perfection, i.e. 'the gymnastic learning youth [lining] up [with] their Italian teachers and Ethiopian sergeants [giving] them orders and people from the streets [watching] with joy the quickly performed drill'.[101] Regular advertisements in the weekly *YeK'ēsar Mengist Mel'iktenya* gave the time – almost always stated in European instead of the East African time measurement[102] – and place of compulsory gymnastic exercises for school children in Addis Ababa. These reveal that physical education was mostly reserved for the offspring of the nobility (*lemekwanintina leshumamint lijoch*). These advertisements were able to directly address them since their parents were the target audience and readers of the newspaper.

Athletic competitions also featured in the press, although not filling the sports pages to the same extent as cycling and football. They included running, high jump, and long jump. As we know from Yidnek'achew Tesemma's historical sketch on athletics in Ethiopia, other technically more complicated disciplines, such as pole vaulting, were part of competitions, but they never featured in the news.[103] Instead, running enjoyed great popularity, especially amongst children, and received good media coverage. Children ran distances according to age categories, with 80 metres for the younger and 150 metres for the elder ones. There was no mention of any middle or long-distance running, neither as part of school competitions nor as any such event for adults. The

---

[100] 'BeGonder sport silemīmarut hits'anatoch' [About physical education for children in Gondar], *YeRoma Birhan*, 1: 4, 17 meskerem 1932 [29 September 1939].
[101] 'BeDessē ketema yetederrege sport' [Sports in Dessie town], *YeRoma Birhan*, 2:1, 20 tahsas 1932 [30 December 1939].
[102] As in other African languages, Amharic has the six-hour difference in expressing the time compared to European time measurement. Calculating time starts at sunrise with two twelve-hour periods.
[103] Yidnek'achew Tesemma, 'YeĪtyop'ya atletīks tarīkina wit'ēt' [History and results of Ethiopian athletics], in YeĪtyop'ya atletīks federēshin (eds), *Arengwadēw gorf* [The green torrent], 5 t'ir 1977 [13 January 1985], 27.

running fever in the capital resulted in enormous turn-outs. According to *YeRoma Birhan*, when 600 children participated in the New Year's competition at Jan Mēda (11 September 1938), referees had difficulties identifying the winner of the race.[104] Reports intermittently stressed that running was not just running, but that athletes had to know how to run a competition, and that they received the necessary support from their physical education instructors.

Besides fun and fame, running competitions on public holidays also became attractive due to the meal provided after the run or even the money that young athletes received from one of the organizers (usually a notable). Thus, on the occasion of *Buhē*, a non-religious feast that foregrounds children,[105] a huge running competition took place in the Tekle Haymanot neighbourhood on Sunday, the 14 nehasē 1932 (20 August 1939). When afterwards, the *Mikittil T'ek'lay Shum* (Deputy Mayor) Birhane Mark'os, who was the patron of the competition, gave some money to the children, they

> divided the money and shouted: 'Cinema! Cinema!' And since the cinema was nearby, they ran together to the cinema. It is very pleasant to see that the children went to the cinema together after they had received the money. Why? If a cycling race called sports or any other activity is useful for strength and health, and if one watches films from which one gains learning and knowledge, then the benefit gained from both [sports and cinema] is inseparable.[106]

Without going into the details of Ethiopia's cinematographic history, this piece of information first of all shows that sports was linked to another form of modern entertainment. It further demonstrates that, quite similar to physical exercise, cinema was conceptualized as a knowledge provider. The film advertisements in *YeK'ēsar Mengist Mel'iktenya* reveal that the open-air screenings especially, which took place twice a week (Tuesdays and Saturdays) in the market area, were propaganda films, often celebrating the effectiveness of airborne battles.[107] Since the competition was on a Sunday, the children were most prob-

---

[104] '"Besra" ina "Bīza" letebalut lekristīyanina leislam kifil lesport tech'ewachoch lijoch yetederegelachew gibzha' [Reception for the athletes of Christian and Muslim teams called 'Besra' and 'Biza' teams], *YeRoma Birhan*, 1:4, 17 meskerem 1932 [29 September 1939].
[105] Akalou Wolde-Michael, 'Buhe', in *Ethnological Society Bulletin*, 7 (2011), pp. 57–63; Alula Pankhurst, 'Buhe: An Ethiopian Children's Festival', *Selamta: The Inflight Magazine of Ethiopian Airlines*, 28:3 (2011), 18–20.
[106] 'Yeigir iruch'a ishk'ididim' [Running competition], *YeRoma Birhan*, 1:3, 6 nehasē 1931 [12 August 1939].
[107] 'Silesīnīma t'k'iit masreja' [On the spread of the taste of cinema], *YeK'ēsar Mengist Mel'iktenya*, 20–27 mīyazya 1932 [29 March–5 April 1940]. Other contributions in this newspaper elaborated on the difference between film and photography, its benefit as useful recreation, and the role of the actor/actress.

ably referring to the cinema owned and run by the businessman *Ras Haylu Tekle Haymanot*, hereditary ruler of Gojjam and supporter of the Italian project of civilized fitness.[108]

Running defined by distances according to age categories indicates the further 'sportization'[109] of athletics during the Italian occupation. With regard to cycling and the establishment of sponsored racing teams, we might even speak of emergent professionalization. These processes included the introduction or intensification of sports-related temporal-spatial regimes. The next section of this chapter will discuss how the press presented these regimes to its readership. I further argue that the newspapers legitimized religious and racial segregation through sports during that period.

Standardization and the Production of Segregated Sportscapes

Attempts to turn modern sports into a tool to enforce a specific version of the civilized-cum-colonized personality in occupied territories went hand in hand with processes of sportization, i.e. regulating games through rules and standards set and supervised by legitimizing and regulating institutions. An organizational structure with the Sports Bureau at the top was established to legitimize and guarantee adherence to the strict spatial and temporal regimes that characterize modern competitive sports. Fully acknowledging that this process had begun well before the Italian occupation, there are very clear indications that rule-bound behaviour as well as 'the fierce temporal-spatial disciplines of measurement and record-breaking'[110] were intensified during this period and supported by sports reporting in the newspapers. With the attempt to develop sports in Shoa into a good example for the other provinces, hope was articulated that 'in future each of the exercises to strengthen the body will be standardized for the whole province'.[111] This became all the more necessary with the introduction of football and cycling championships at the provincial level in 1940.

---

[108] Chrystal L. Johnson, 'Reshaping Urban Environments in Ethiopia: Exploring Life through the Use of Space in Four Addis Ababa Kebele' (Unpublished Ph.D. dissertation, University of Wisconsin-Milwaukee, 2008), p. 126.
[109] 'Sportization', a term coined by Norbert Elias, refers to the transformation of folk games into modern sport by codifying rules, writing them down, and strictly enforcing them in an effective manner.
[110] John Bale and Chris Philo, 'Introduction: Henning Eichberg, Space, Identity and Body Culture' in John Bale and Chris Philo (eds), *Body Cultures: Essays on Sport, Space and Identity by Henning Eichberg* (London, New York, 2002), p. 12.
[111] 'BeShewa ager sport silemesfafat' [On the spread of sports in Shoa], *YeRoma Birhan*, 1: 5, 22 t'ik'imt 1932 [28 October 1939].

As early as October 1939, *YeRoma Birhan* felt the need to publish the basics of football.

> In the following, we explain to our readers how the game of football functions. 22 youngsters are grouped into two teams of 11 each. After that a construction which resembles a door is put up at either end of a field which is conveniently large. A 'door keeper' called *portiere* prevents the ball from going into the door. In front of him stand the back, who are called *terzini [sic]*. And in front of them there are three youngsters in the middle: one right, one left, one centre ... The game starts when the referee signals with his whistle 'Start!' and the teams line up. The team which scores several times is the winner.[112]

The magazine continued to elaborate on specific issues in reports on matches. In one case, the corner kick rule was explained by referring to the *gebbere* rule in the local game of *gebeta*.[113] In April 1940, *YeRoma Birhan* explained that the championships were organized according to the rules and regulations of the Italian Football Federation. These clarified issues such as age groups (children, youth, and adults), the respective duration of games, clothing requirements, and registration procedures. Furthermore, the article explicitly thematised civilized behaviour including punctuality and not starting any quarrels with fans or spectators, which could result in severe punishment.[114]

Sportization also meant the introduction of strict registration procedures and deadlines for competitions. The second Shoa Championships scheduled for 1940–41 might serve as an example. Through advertisements in *YeK'ēsar Mengist Mel'iktenya*, the Sports Bureau informed readers that no registration was possible after the deadline (20 July 1940) and that participants should come and register well before the deadline. Furthermore, the list of players with which a football team was registered could not be changed after the fact.[115] Spectators and fans were recurrently provided information about the colours and patterns of the team jerseys in detailed descriptions and, from 1940 onwards, through photographs, which were produced as a souvenir for each team that had registered for the match.

Apart from football, cycling became highly regulated with the advent of the Shoa Championships, with an elaborate system of points published in the press.[116] Horse races, in and outside the capital, were also

---

[112] 'Yeigir kʷas ch'ewata denb' [Rules of the football game], *YeRoma Birhan*, 1:5, 22 t'ik'imt 1932 [28 October 1939].

[113] 'Yeigir kʷas ch'ewata' [The football game], *YeRoma Birhan*, 2:1, 20 tahsas 1932 [30 December 1939].

[114] See rule (h) in 'Yeigir kʷas ch'ewata' [Football game], *YeRoma Birhan*, 2:4, 2 mīyazya 1932 [10 April 1940].

[115] 'Yesport ts'ihfet bēt mastawek'īya' [Announcement of the Sports Bureau], *YeK'ēsar Mengist Mel'iktenya*, 23 senē 1932 [30 June 1940].

[116] 'Yebīsīklēt kampyonato 3nya git'mīya program' [Programme of the third

reported to follow strict rules. In preparation for the races in Wollo and Yeju in February 1940, for example, *YeRoma Birhan* reminded its readership that jockeys 'must turn up personally two days before the race in their respective administration buildings, and have their name, their weight, the weight of their horses registered'.[117] The regularity of reporting on horse races and its exact organization might also derive from the fact that horse races were very important for Ethiopian nobles before the Italian occupation.[118] As already remarked upon in the section on athletics, rules for running competitions related age to distance.

Apart from the disciplining effect inherent in the sportization process, the attempts to transmit them via the Amharic-language, Italian-run periodicals offer insight into where exactly the formalized places for sports were located. Some of the bicycle races started in front of police station A 10 in the native quarter, or opposite the Printing House and the Propaganda Bureau. The equipment (bikes, shirts, shoes, caps) was collected in the courtyard of the *Residente*'s house.[119] Others used the houses of notables such as *Commendatore* Saleh Ahmed Kekiya and *Ras* Haylu Tekle Haymanot as start and finish lines.[120]

Tamirat and Gaudin even commented that, insofar as 'sport and physical education are concerned, the Italian occupation cannot be precisely labelled a colonizing process, since it did not provoke any deep societal or cultural changes in the occupied country'.[121] They obviously overlooked the spatial-temporal regimes in competitive sports, as such, coupled with spatial-temporal regimes enforced through a policy of racial and religious segregation. Plans for urban development produced by Italian architectural bureaus for various Ethiopian towns during the Italian occupation indicate that sports infrastructure was part of colonial town planning. As will be further elaborated in Chapter 5, *Sports' Material Infrastructure and the Production of Space*, these plans included a stadium or at least a *zona sportivo*. As racial segregation was increasingly enforced, separate venues emerged, where the 'native' population could compete and consume sports. Jan Mēda, the former imperial racing grounds, extend-

---

race of the cycling championships], *YeK'ēsar Mengist Mel'iktenya*, 12–19 mīyazya 1932 [21–27 April 1940].

[117] 'BeWollonna beYeju silemĭdderegew yehager tewelajoch yeferes shert' program' [Programme of the native horse races in Wollo and Yeju], *YeRoma Birhan*, 2:2, 3 yekatīt 1932 [11 February 1940].

[118] For a history of equestrian sports in Ethiopia see Ethiopian Equestrian Association, *Ethiopian Riders and their Horses* (Addis Ababa, 2005), pp. 82–109.

[119] 'Yesport ts'ihfet bēt mastawek'īya' [Announcement of the Sports Bureau], *YeK'ēsar Mengist Meliktenya*, 10 t'ik'imt 1932 [20 October 1940].

[120] 'Kaddīs Abeba iske Holeta yetederegew yebīsīklēt ishk'ididim' [The bicycle race from Addis Ababa to Holeta], *YeK'ēsar Mengist Meliktenya*, 12–19 mīyazya 1932 [21–27 April 1940].

[121] Tamirat and Gaudin, 'Sports and Physical Education', p. 203.

ed its original function by adding facilities for football, round course cycling, and athletics. Its size allowed huge crowds of spectators to watch the events. However, the rising number of young athletes, and especially the introduction of the Shoa Football Championships in 1940, required additional sports facilities. As early as December 1939, *YeRoma Birhan* emphasized the necessity of having more sports fields for both athletes and spectators and that, therefore, the government had planned a sports field in the new 'native' quarter.[122] Two months later, it informed the reader that the work had started and would be complete before the kick-off. The place itself was advertised as a convenient and centralized leisure space: 'This place is built according to a good plan, because it is surrounded by a beautiful, strong wall; because beautiful trees are planted and because it is situated in the centre of the quarter. Thus, it is convenient in all respects for spectators and athletes'.[123]

On Sunday, 30 April 1940, the new playing field was inaugurated in the presence of high-ranking personalities: the *Residente* of Addis Ababa, Dottore Baschieri, the Deputy Mayor, *Dejazmach* Yohannis Jotu, and a Muslim Qadi. According to the press, the place was decorated with flags, and masses of people watched the inauguration ceremony and the matches of the six teams. The article stressed the amazement of the spectators about the comfort of the place, with its trees making it possible to consume sports even during the hot hours of the day.[124]

Building the sports ground in the centre of the new native quarter further strengthened a sports policy based on racial and increasingly religious segregation. Young athletes were grouped by faith into sections called *Bīza* (for Muslims) and *Besra* (for Christians). Although it is not clear how effective this separation was, *YeRoma Birhan* reported that, by September 1939, nearly two thousand sportsmen were competing in the *Besra* section in Shoa.[125] Allegedly conveying a sense of true sportsmanship, even under conditions of segregation, the magazine argued that

> sports competition is a medium to love and like each other. For the one who is observing them, it is a great joy to see that young people of different religious and ethnic backgrounds feel a brotherly bond and care during the cycling race. The best youngsters from [the provinces

[122] 'Yesewinet mat'enkerya ch'ewata' [Sports for strengthening the body], *YeRoma Birhan*, 2:1, 20 tahsas 1932 [30 December 1939].
[123] 'Yesport ch'ewata makenawonya bota badīsu yeager tewelaj sefer silemederajitu' [On the preparation of the sports field in the new quarter for the natives], *YeRoma Birhan*, 2:2, 3 yekatīt 1932 [11 February 1940].
[124] 'Badīsu yehager tewalajoch ketema yeteseraw yeigir kʷas mech'awecha bota temerek'e' [Inauguration of the playing field in the new quarter for the natives], *YeRoma Birhan*, 2:4, mīyazya 1932 [10 April 1940].
[125] 'BeShewa yesport ch'ewata silemesfafatu' [On the spread of sports competitions in Shoa], *YeRoma Birhan*, 1:4, 17 meskerem 1932 [29 September 1939].

of] Shoa, Amhara, Eritrea, and of Muslim background will be grouped into four teams.[126]

On the occasion of the Ethiopian New Year (11 September 1939), the Bureau of the Directorate for Political Affairs staged its segregationist sports policy at Jan Mēda by giving a reception for the young athletes of the *Besra* and *Bīza* teams. Coming from all parts of the empire, they appeared in their uniforms and 'carrying their symbols'.[127] News reports not only legitimized religious segregation amongst the athletes, but extended this discursive strategy to the local sponsors as well. Both *YeRoma Birhan* and *YeK'ēsar Mengist Mel'iktenya* published separate lists of Muslim and Christian notables with the exact amounts of money they had contributed. Furthermore, whenever a major sports event featured in the news, articles grouped the attending notables into Christian and Muslim. Whether effective or not, the newspaper legitimized a policy of segregation in sports by attaching a kind of normality to it.

Contrary to the 'New Italian' in terms of militaristic qualities and racial perfectionism, the Amharic press constructed *Etiope Nuovo* along the lines of a civilizing project. Within this frame, it conceptualized sports as door-opener and knowledge associated with (Western) civilization. Through sports news, the editors made unmistakably clear that it was the still malleable male youth who would, through (self-)discipline and guidance, advance in this direction. Since guiding competence lay with the Fascist government, parents and relatives could only support, but never guide. To civilize meant to break with traditions and to transform with outside help, i.e. colonialism. Arguing in favour of naming junior football teams after favourable character traits such as love, patience or diligence, presented the Sports Bureau (representing the government) as the (caring) mother. This argumentative strategy of 'care' was also underpinned by the topic of clothing; i.e. providing sportswear. As the sports news made clear, 'care' was not provided at random, but relied on a functioning and rapidly expanding bureaucratic structure. Naming practices and explanations about clothes were part of a discourse that conceptualized the 'New Ethiopian' as a balanced subject in terms of good health, a strong body, and purified soul. The moralistic and quasi-religious language not only emphasized the sacredness of the human body, but also the role of competition as the 'renewal of life' for both athletes and spectators. In this respect, the newspapers

---

[126] 'Yetedenek'e sport' [An admired sport], *YeRoma Birhan*, 1:4, 17 meskerem 1932 [29 September 1939].
[127] '"Besra" ina "Bīza" letebalut lekristiyaninna le'islam kifil lesport tech'awachoch lijoch yetederegalachew gibzha [Reception for the athletes of Christian and Muslim teams called 'Besra' and 'Bīza' teams], *YeRoma Birhan*, 1:4, 17 meskerem 1932 [29 September 1939].

argued that civilization could be 'seen'. Even through the consumption of sports, ordinary leisure turned into useful recreation. Every Sunday gave a chance to belong to those who were already marching on the path to civilization.

The sports news published in *YeRoma Birhan* and *YeK'ēsar Mengist Mel'iktenya* reveals that only specific sports were considered suitable to civilize through active participation or consumption. On the spectrum between tennis, which was described as the most civilized of all sports, and *genna,* which served as an example for the uselessness of local sports practices, cycling, football, and athletics dominated the media scene. Their popularity in Italy and the resulting vast media coverage provided the editors of the Amharic press with valuable knowledge about the propagandistic value of sports. It goes without saying that the unifying, militaristic, and increasingly racialized discourse of Italian sports reporting would have had contrary effects undermining the production of loyal colonial subjects through sports. Even the construction of sporting heroes such as cyclists had to be carefully monitored.

Whereas football served the civilizing project as a magnet for young adults and children, gymnastics was the site for instilling an allegedly higher ethical concept to a selected group of malleable youth of noble descent and, thus, ennobling physical fitness as such. Apart from the introduction of cycling and further promotion of football, the Italian Fascist occupation intensified the existing process of sportization with its strict spatial-temporal regimes and gratification systems. The Sports Bureau enhanced and supervised the institutionalization of sports by organizing a growing system of provincial and local associations regulated according to the rules valid for Italian sports federations. In the eyes of propaganda, this development opened additional possibilities for recognition by the Fascist government in Rome; obviousely the ultimate indicator that Ethiopia was now on the right path. *YeRoma Birhan* stressed that

> the good reputation of these sporting activities [including local financing through donations] which strengthen the body have already reached Rome, which is a good sign ... By understanding activities that strengthen the body as a serious matter and by internalizing style and method, the children of our country will be healthy people who respect the law and ideally cherish the name of our ruler as well as the government in Rome.[128]

Being more specific, *YeK'ēsar Mengist Mel'iktenya* informed its readers that the Italian newspaper *Le Colonie* had written about the positive development of sports in Ethiopia, especially football and cycling. It argued that

---

[128] 'Sport yegenzeb irdata leset't'u sewoch yetenegere yemisgana k'al' [Acknowledgement to persons who gave financial support to sports], *YeRoma Birhan,* 1:3, 6 nehasē 1931 [12 August 1939].

this had been achieved through administrative effort, athletic diligence, and an increasing consensus about the benefits of sports.[129]

Sportization's temporal and spatial regimes also effected the implementation of a previously unknown extent of segregation along racial and religious lines. Sports reporting legitimized and actively supported this policy by normalizing it through two argumentative tropes: the civilizing value of the new facilities in the segregated neighbourhoods, and the importance of sportsmanship between the segregated groups. It falls into the realm of speculation to judge the extent to which the Italian Fascist sports policy had lasting effects in terms of racial segregation, or if it deepened existing splits amongst Ethiopians. Its legacy, and here I agree with Tamirat Gebremariam and Benoît Gaudin, lies more in the structural improvements to a competitive system and the further promotion of physical education and modern sports as markers for the modern subject. Such a statement, however, overlooks the fact that this subject was conceptualized within a colonial framework. Thus, I assume that the sporting 'New Ethiopian' for the post-liberation context was different. Looking at physical education and the re-organization of the Boy Scout movement, the next chapter discusses the ways in which the Ethiopian government attempted to create the 'New Man' for the 'New Era'.

---

[129] 'Beītyop'ya yesport mesfafat beT'alian ager gazēt'och lay yits'afal' [Also Italian newspapers write about the dissemination of sports in Ethiopia], *YeK'ēsar Mengist Mel'iktenya,* 27 mīyaza–2 ginbot 1932 [5–11 May 1940].

3
Muscular Reconstruction: Urban Leisure, Institutionalized Physical Education, and the Re-establishment of Boy Scouting (1940s–1960s)

The socio-political context in post-liberation Ethiopia was marked by a multitude of agendas and possibilities. On the national level, Haile Selassie tried to reduce the power of the occupying British military administration – after the final defeat of the Italian troops in 1941 – and checkmate any attempt by local notables to threaten his authority and legitimacy. Within this difficult situation, life continued for adults, youth, and children in the empire. Drawing on a wide range of examples, this chapter analyses the role of sports in educational and leisure contexts.

The existing literature on modern sports in post-liberation Ethiopia reduces athletic activities primarily to football.[1] Without any doubt, the game was very popular amongst the local male population as well as amongst the members of the British Military Mission (BMME), which remained in the empire until 1951. Thus, it is no wonder that football became one of the main drivers behind re-organizing sports in absence of an authority, such as the Sports Bureau for the Natives, which had coordinated athletic activities during the Fascist occupation. Matches were being played as early as 1942, and the Ethiopian Football Federation was founded in 1943 – a year before the establishment of the Ethiopian Sports Confederation.[2]

---

[1] Solomon Addis Getahun, 'A History of Sport in Ethiopia', in Svein Ege, Harald Aspen, Birhanu Teferra, and Shiferaw Bekele (eds), *Proceedings of the 16th International Conference of Ethiopian Studies,* vol. 2 (Trondheim, 2009), pp. 409–18; Bezabih Wolde and Benoît Gaudin, 'The Institutional Organization of Ethiopian Athletics', *Annales d'Éthiopie,* 23 (2007–2008), 479; Richard Pankhurst, 'Sports', in Siegbert Uhlig (ed.), *Encyclopaedia Aethiopica,* 4 (Wiesbaden, 2010), p. 729; Tamirat Gebremariam and Benoît Gaudin, 'Sports and Physical Education in Ethiopia during the Italian Occupation, 1936–41', in Michael J. Gennaro and Saheed Aderinto (eds), *Sports in African History, Politics and Identity Formation* (New York, 2019), p. 203; Paulos Milkias, *Ethiopia, Africa in Focus* (Santa Barbara, Denver, Oxford, 2011), p. 376.
[2] Ethiopian Football Federation, *Football in Ethiopia* (Addis Ababa, 1968), pp. 19–22.

Reports in Ethiopian newspapers such as the *Ethiopian Herald* and *Addīs Zemen*, as well as photographs located in the Institute of Ethiopian Studies, suggest that modern sports proliferated mostly in the armed forces via the influence of foreign military advisors. The army established its athletic club in 1945. In 1948, the Imperial Body Guard and Police Force followed suit. During the 1950s, the Air Force founded its sports club and opened its training camp at Debre Zeit air base for athletes 'deprived of any facilities and installations'.[3] Furthermore, armed forces personnel promoted sports in the educational system. First, by teaching 'drill' as a form of sports in schools; retired army officers were involved in physical education until its systematic introduction by a governing institution in the late 1940s. Second, the re-established Boy Scout Association formed a strong link between army and educational system, which became most apparent in the form of the Department of Physical Education and Boy Scouting within the Ministry of Education and Fine Arts (MoE), established in 1950.

Looking at sports through structures and institutions only, however, does not do justice to the multiple engagements of Ethiopians and members of the foreign communities with modern sports as (urban) leisure. The 'New Ethiopian' of the post-liberation period was by no means only the educated, disciplined, and physically fit subject, but also a personality that belonged to an emerging 'leisure class'. Thus, this chapter starts with a section on modern sports as urban leisure. Although it draws heavily on memoirs by male writers, they do offer more than football narratives. These memoirs also provide an idea about both spatial-temporal and material conditions for sports as leisure.

The chapter continues with a section on articulations and implementations of politics that influenced modern physical culture after the expulsion of the Italian occupation forces. It argues for the application of a wide lens to discover the multiple ways of shaping youth as loyal citizens and 'torchbearers of progress'. Since modern education viewed schools as ideal places to instil necessary character traits, the section deals with the establishment and work of the Department of Physical Education and Boy Scouting. The development of physical education as an integral part of the curriculum at all levels demanded qualified physical education teachers. Their training and acceptance was by no means easy, as the chapter will show. They joined forces and built a sports-related network – the Ethiopian Inter-School Athletic Association (EISAA). Through a refined system of competitions from the provincial to the national level, the Association served as the most powerful instrument for promoting modern sports in most parts of the empire. In the final section, the chapter deals with the re-established Boy Scouts as part of the Ethiopian educational system. Arguably,

---

[3] Bezabih and Gaudin, 'The Institutional Organization', 478.

the Ethiopian movement shifted away from its emphasis on national defence to a broader, demilitarized form of civic engagement and fitness through adventure.

Reconfiguring Urban Sportscapes

Of Open Fields and Swimming Pools

Grasping the everyday lives of people of different social strata is difficult, but to some degree traceable through written memoirs, interviews, newspaper reports, and images. Apart from press information, these sources often lack exact figures. However, they offer a personal view of the past that often surprises the reader. Michel Lentakis's *Ethiopia: A View from Within* opens such a window beginning with the immediate post-liberation period.

Being a good player and enthusiastic football fan, his memoirs are full of football stories. He describes the growing football craze amongst the urban male population and the unboundedly aggressive behaviour triggered by the sport. Thus, he not only mentions the usual play between the children of the Greek families who resided near the railway station and Ethiopian boys outside the compound, but also the violence involved.

> Football was also a game that we adored and almost every afternoon we would play football games in the wide plains [beyond *Casa Populare*, marking the Southern boundary of Addis Ababa well up to the 1950s] for hours, without a referee or real goal posts, always full of arguments and often ending in fist-fights or stone throwing gang wars.[4]

Whereas he speaks of wide, open fields for enjoying the game, other sources suggest the absence of playing grounds. Prevented from using existing ones, such as those in Jan Mēda, Medfenya Gibī, Filwoha, or school compounds in Addis Ababa, Ethiopian football enthusiasts asked the owners of appropriate fields for access. 'In some areas where good playing fields exist, the owners of the land did not permit them to play in it. Whenever the players were found playing in such fields, they were whipped and sometimes imprisoned by Arada Zebenya (city police)'.[5]

However, football was not the only sports-related form of leisure in town. For those who could afford it, the bicycle became both a means of transport to school as well as a tool for sporting leisure activities.

> Outside the railway compound there was an Ethiopian who rented out old bicycles by the hour. We had all become experts with bicycles, performed acrobatics, jumping on and off like the Cossacks do while

---

[4] Michel B. Lentakis, *Ethiopia: A View from Within* (London, 2005), p. 109.
[5] Sintayehu Tola, 'The History of St. George Sport Club' (Unpublished BA thesis, Addis Ababa University, 1986), p. 11.

riding, standing with one foot on the bicycle seat and one foot in the air, and other tricks.[6]

As shown in the previous chapter, bicycle races had gained enormous popularity in and around the capital. Although races stopped after the dismantling of the Sports Bureau, which was the main driver organizing races during the Fascist occupation, the love of cycling continued. Besides the associations for football, boxing, and athletics, the Ethiopian Cycling Federation is one of the oldest in the country. In the 1950s, races were already taking place in Addis Ababa and Asmara[7] as well as in smaller towns such as Dire Dawa or Mek'ele. In 1956, when Ethiopia sent its first Olympic team to Melbourne, it included four cyclists.[8]

The 1950s also saw the development of leisure facilities that allowed for water sports. Whereas children went to Mekanissa or the two rivers within Addis to have their first swimming experience, the 1955 Master Plan for Addis Ababa documented and projected a quite lively water sports scene. Apart from military and school facilities, people could use swimming pools in hotels such as the Ghion. There, the warm Olympic-sized swimming pool and the 'apparatus for diving from varied heights' had become a real attraction.[9] The facility is reported to have served about 300 people per day. Another swimming facility was offered by the Hilton Hotel, which was smaller in size. Both invited guests to swimming lessons and offered the necessary equipment for rent.[10]

Furthermore, the planners proposed developing natural facilities in satellite towns. Debre Zeit, until 1955 and since the 1990s known under its Oromo name Bishoftu, is one of the prominent examples. The town lies approximately fifty kilometres south-east of Addis Ababa and was well connected to the capital by an asphalt road. Since 'the Lake and Hotel at Bishoftu are part of the Open Space System of Addis Ababa in that many travel there for rest and recreation' the planners argued, 'Addis Ababa would, therefore, benefit from the development of Bishoftu Lake as a Lido'.[11] The plan was put into practice and, later, Ras Hotel was constructed on the banks of Lake Hora at Debre Zeit, adjacent to the emperor's Fairfield Palace. It offered facilities for many rich residents of Addis Ababa who spent their weekends sailing or using the very few motorboats 'which only the very rich could afford'.[12] In 1956,

[6] Lentakis, *Ethiopia*, p. 105.
[7] In 1950, Eritrea was federated with Ethiopia.
[8] 'Ethiopia at the 1956 Summer Olympics' https://en.linkfang.org/wiki/Ethiopia_at_the_1956_Summer_Olympics [accessed 15 September 2021].
[9] Sylvia Pankhurst, 'The Changing Face of Addis Ababa', *Ethiopia Observer*, 4:5 (1960), 164.
[10] Tadesse Negash, 'Swimming Pools in Addis Ababa', no date, IES 839e.
[11] Getachew Mahiteme Selassie, The Master Plan for Addis Ababa, 1956, IES 711.4 GET, p. 62.
[12] Lentakis, *Ethiopia*, p. 152.

a West German documentary on Ethiopia highlighted the 'highest sailing club in the world' and featured the 'first swimming school' in Ethiopia, located there.¹³ The comment, however, that swimming was largely alien to Ethiopia, ignores existing swimming practices of lake and river communities, both as a survival technique as well as pastime. Arguably, a documentary that aimed at displaying a modern empire, sports, and pastimes had to also be modern, i.e. organized and allegedly 'Western' in style. In 1964, swimming had become such a marker for useful recreation that the *Ethiopia Observer* advertised swimming facilities in and around Addis Ababa as an important element of tourism promotion in the country. In addition to Bishoftu/Debre Zeit, it highlighted Hagere Hiwot (Ambo), approximately 125 kilometres west of Addis Ababa, as a 'hot spot' of water sports.¹⁴ The place had developed into a 'spa' and gained fame for its healthy climate and mineral water resources. An Olympic-sized swimming pool of warm water offered ideal circumstances for the sport. Furthermore, Lake Langano provided facilities for water-skiing,¹⁵ and the hot springs at Wollisso (114 kilometres south-west of Addis Ababa) offered water sports and recreation to those who could afford it.

However, there was also critique about recreation at the swimming pool. Casting an analytic eye on the leisure routines of the urban population who frequented the Sodere resort,¹⁶ the *Addis Reporter* commented that there is 'nothing exciting in spending the whole afternoon in or around a crowded swimming pool with all kinds of people staring at you and with all kinds of senseless sounds bugging your ears'.¹⁷ Whereas swimming in hotel pools and sailing in modern boats were reserved for a rich 'leisure class', clubs of the so-called foreign communities reached out to many people in those communities and beyond. Despite its importance for the sporting scene, this section leaves out the Ethio-British Army Club. It belongs to the broad field of sports in the Ethiopian armed forces, which deserves a comprehensive study and a publication of its own.

---

¹³ *Äthiopien: Kaiserreich zwischen Gestern und Morgen*, film, directed by Dej. Makonnen Deste. Bayrischer Rundfunk, Deutschland, at 51:02:00, 54:55:00, www.filmothek.bundesarchiv.de/video/593861?q=Kaiser+Haile&xm=AND&xf%5B0%5D=_fulltext&xo%5B0%5D= CONTAINS&xv%5B0%5D= [accessed 15 September 2021].
¹⁴ 'Ethiopia. A Tourist Paradise', *Ethiopia Observer*, 8:3 (1964), 194–208, 202.
¹⁵ Lentakis, *Ethiopia*, p. 327.
¹⁶ Sodere is located 127 kilometres south-east of Addis Ababa. The swimming pool has been fully operational since 1963, https://web.archive.org/web/20110528232845/http://130.238.24.99/library/resources/dossiers/local_history_of_ethiopia/s/ORTSOB.pdf [accessed 15 September 2021].
¹⁷ Tereffe Asrat, 'The Excitement Game of Leisure', *Addis Reporter*, 21 April 1969, 17.

Clubbing and Sporting

Members of the so-called foreign communities (many of them actually had Ethiopian citizenship) used the sports facilities at their clubs. These included ball-game fields, swimming pools, tennis courts, and more. Greek graduates of the Comboni College – a British boarding school for boys in Khartoum that had won fame through sporting success – started holding basketball tournaments on the premises of the old Greek club opposite the Ras Desta hospital.[18] Apart from the Young Men's Christian Association (YMCA), which later hosted the Ethiopian Basketball Federation and trained the national team, the Greek club promoted the game exactly at the time when it came to Ethiopia. Before the construction of the sports facilities within the (new) Greek Club building near Bole Road, they rented a hall near Omedla Clinic for practising basketball, as well as billiards, table tennis, chess, and other board games.[19]

The Armenian community also put up a strong basketball team, which trained at the Armenian club. In 1945, members of the Ararat football team had raised the money to buy the estate and, thus, facilitated the establishment of the club. In contrast to the Greeks, who dominated the Ethiopian national scene after having recruited players from Greece, the Armenian team included Ethiopians and, at a later stage, American Peace Corps members. In order to have the proper facilities, members and sports enthusiasts enlarged the existing tennis court at the Armenian club and transformed it into a basketball court. This shift seems to have not raised problems since courts existed on the compounds of wealthy Armenian families for private matches on Saturdays. As early as 1947, the club hosted basketball and volleyball matches against the teams of the Imperial Body Guard and Olympiacos SC. They entertained the sporting community such that 'the event ended with the serving of refreshments and dancing'.[20]

Apart from football, basketball, and lawn tennis, the Armenian club offered and excelled in judo during the late 1950s and early 1960s. Armen Mardikian, who had received his black belt from Japan, became the president of the judo club in 1957/58. The first training location was in Arada, where the United Printers is today.[21] Later, it moved into the Armenian club. What was arguably the first judo club in Ethiopia occupied the part of the building, which currently houses the restaurant. When Armen Mardikian left Ethiopia, Gino Pecol (Italian,

---

[18] Lentakis, *Ethiopia*, p. 150.
[19] Ibid., p. 273.
[20] 'Sports', *Ethiopian Herald*, 24 February 1947, 3.
[21] Arada Sub-city Kebele 02 House 476/77 Dej. Jote Street, https://web.archive.org/web/20110528232845/http://130.238.24.99/library/resources/dossiers/local_history_of_ethiopia/s/ORTSOB.pdf [accessed 15 September 2021].

and one of Armen's pupils) took over and moved the judo school to the Italian club Juventus.[22]

In the mid-1950s, the Italian community created its club, Juventus, which included a *circolo sportivo* with tennis and basketball courts and football fields, just near the *Campo Alogio* – a football field specifically created for the Italian workers during the Fascist occupation (see Chapter 5, *Sports' Material Infrastructure and the Production of Space*). Later, the Italian community built and managed the *Rece* – a recreation centre near the Italian Club. It became very popular for its go-cart and bowling facilities.[23] Apart from these locations, members of the Italian community also met informally at *La Gare* to practice wrestling.[24]

An institutionalized British cultural presence in Ethiopia in the form of the British Council began in 1934. With the growing number of British citizens in the Ethiopian capital, who had come within the framework of the BMME or as experts, the community established an Anglo-Ethiopian Club. It was located on the premises of the British Institute and inaugurated by the emperor himself on 23 January 1943. In 1945, branches opened in Dessie, Harar, and Jimma. The monthly programme included a variety of sports and mind games. Bridge and other card games were as popular as chess evenings, darts, or Miss E. Sandford's regular organized dancing lessons. The club also held table tennis and lawn tennis tournaments, which turned out to be 'the least successful section'.[25] From 1943, the Red Cross organized a gymkhana on the paddock of the British Legation. According to the 1944 programme, it combined sports and spectacle by offering riding competitions such as 'pole bending' and an 'Addis vale hunt spectacle'.[26]

The picture of sports as recreation in associational contexts would be incomplete without mentioning the Indian community. The Indian Association, established in 1937, held its sports tournaments at the Indian Association School in Addis Ababa, which commenced work in 1947. The community also had its own football team, which, however, did not feature prominently.[27] Arguably, the Association became even stronger with the influx of numerous Indian teachers, many of them specializing in physical education, in the 1950s.

Probably, all foreign legations practised or promoted sports in one way or another. However, they did not feature much in the Ethiopian sports scene. Even though the Soviet Cultural Centre and, later,

[22] Interview with Vartkes Nalbandian, Addis Ababa, 27 February 2014.
[23] Interview with Paulos N. Donikian, 5 March 2014.
[24] I am grateful to Giuliano Cicoria for drawing my attention to this fact.
[25] Anglo-Ethiopian Club, British Institute and Anglo-Ethiopian Club, Report 1 January – 31 December 1945, ENA 1.2.18.13, p. 17.
[26] Second Annual Red Cross Gymkhana 1944, ENA 1.2.18.13, p. 57.
[27] Indian Community Sports Tournaments: Prize Distribution, 1959, Indian Community A.A., ENA 1.2.43.09.

the Yugoslav Club also had sports sections, they never appeared in sports news.[28]

A discussion of sports as leisure or 'useful recreation' that separates the foreign communities from one another and, most importantly, from the Ethiopians, is to present an incomplete if not wrong picture however. It ignores the diverse engagements and cooperation amongst these communities with people who could not rely on strong associational structures and, most importantly, with Ethiopians. However, the clubs' popularity had its flipside. In 1946, for example, the Anglo-Ethiopian Club faced such a wave of membership applications that the organizing committee discussed who should count as 'Anglo' or 'Ethiopian'.[29] Overall, the clubs were open to others, and often mixed teams secured sporting success.

Sports produced spaces of productive encounters. Bowling might serve as an example. Without giving any specific date, Michel B. Lentakis remembers the existence of three bowling centres

> one in the Ghenet Hotel, another next to the Ethiopia Hotel [most probably the one in the basement of Ambassador Theatre[30]], and the third and biggest with ten lanes – on the road to the industrial area, the 'rece'. All these to start with catered to the American advisers and their families, who numbered to almost 2,000. Soon, the Italians, Greeks and Ethiopians formed their own teams and joined the party. An international bowling league was formed and a strong annual competition started, involving all three bowling centres.[31]

Whereas bowling facilities became places of encounter, motor rallies demanded the joining of forces. Apart from car races, which had been organized since the 1950s, it was the Ethiopian Highland Rally (first held in 1965), which gained fame beyond the empire. Paulos N. Donikian, a motor race enthusiast himself, remembered that besides the many sponsors the rally 'was organised by the Italian Juventus Club'.[32] The approximately 3,000-kilometre long circuit included large parts of both the empire and Eritrea, which Ethiopia annexed in 1961. Thus, the Ethiopian Highland Rally provides an excellent example of how a sport produced imperial space. Chapter 5, *Sports' Material Infrastructure and the Production of Space*, gives a more detailed picture of the event.

Although the history of (successful) sports teams in Ethiopia is mostly associated with those of the foreign communities, army sports

---

[28] The Yugoslav Club in Addis Ababa, ENA 1.2.67.05.
[29] E. F. Collier, 1 June 1946, 109, ENA 1.2.18.13.
[30] In an interview (5 March 2014) Paulos N. Donikian mentioned a bowling facility in the basement of the Ambassador Theatre, which caught fire and was destroyed.
[31] Lentakis, *Ethiopia*, p. 338.
[32] Interview with Paulos N. Donikian, 5 March 2014.

clubs, or the YMCA (which is the topic of the next chapter) systematic training and competition within a nation-wide structure mushroomed primarily through the educational system. The next section looks at the structural development of physical education.

Anchoring Athletics in Education

The Department of Physical Education and Boy Scouting

The importance of systematic physical education at all educational levels translated into the National Physical Education Programme in the mid-1940s. For its implementation, the MoE[33] employed the Egyptian Copt Michel Wassef, who had already served as a physical training instructor at the Tafari Makonnen School. As a graduate of the Higher Institute of Physical Education in Cairo and active member of the Egyptian Boy Scout movement, the superintendent was more than an expert on the promotion of sports in schools.[34] As part of a network of sports officials, Michel Wassef became one of the nodal points of a system that actively promoted physical fitness and useful recreation amongst Ethiopian youth. His work included active engagement in the re-establishment of the Ethiopian Boy Scout movement as well as his assignment as the first secretary of the Young Men's Christian Association (YMCA) in Ethiopia (1947–51).

In the late 1940s, an institution replaced the National Physical Education Programme: The Department of Physical Education and Boy Scouting within the MoE. The legendary Onni Niskanen, who later gained fame as coach of the marathon champion Abebe Bikila, became its first director in 1950. Niskanen, who was Finnish by birth, had come to Ethiopia as part of the Swedish military mission in 1946. He worked as a sports officer at the Cadet Training School of the Imperial Body Guard and at the Air Force base in Debre Zeit. Two years later, he was assigned to the post of physical education teacher at the Haile Selassie I Secondary School in Kotebe.

During this teaching engagement, Niskanen was already assigned to create a Department of Physical Education and Boy Scouting. He served as its director from 1950 to 1954 and from 1956 to 1959.[35] His former

---

[33] The Ministry of Education and Fine Arts had been established in 1930.
[34] Memorandum about the Extension Project into Ethiopia, N. Kelada, February 1947, KFYA, Y.USA.9-2-37, YMCA International Work in Ethiopia Box 1, correspondence 1946–1947–1948.
[35] Tek'ewame Wolde Ts'adik', *Yesewinet magolmesha timhirt beītyop'ya. T'inatawī ts'ihuf* [Physical Education in Ethiopia: A Scientific Approach] (Addis Ababa, 1978 EC, 1986), p. 24; Viveca Halldin Norberg, *Swedes in Haile Selassie's Ethiopia, 1924–1952* (Uppsala, 1977), p. 214.

school service, his active engagement in developing sports as a subject (including the training of Ethiopian PE teachers), as well as his capacity as Acting Commissioner of the Ethiopian Boy Scouts (1948–54) and Member of the National Council of the Boy Scout Association of Ethiopia (1948–61) had made him an ideal candidate for the position.

Onni Niskanen contributed considerably in developing the PE curriculum for Ethiopian schools. The first PE curriculum was elaborated for grades one to six in 1947 and officially enacted a year later. Following European and US curricula, it suggested a gradual development from 'free movement' and plays with or without music for a general strengthening of the body to gymnastics, athletics, and ball games.[36] However, problems arose not only because the instruction guides and books were in English, but also and mainly because they had nothing to do with the realities in Ethiopia, especially with regard to the 'cultural' perception of sports.[37] This was also true for the PE curriculum for secondary education, which the ministry developed in the 1950s. Later, the curriculum more or less copied the template for US secondary PE education and largely neglected the organization and facilities of Ethiopian secondary schools.

Whereas most of the PE teachers in the 1940s and early 1950s came from abroad, the situation had changed in the late 1950s. At that time, Ethiopia already had well-educated Ethiopian PE teachers and PE courses even at the university level. However, these Ethiopian practitioners were largely excluded from curriculum development.[38] Furthermore, the curriculum did not assign specific time slots for PE, which were necessary to systematically develop the proposed physical skills in athletics, ball games, swimming, camping, and hunting. Thus, PE teachers were forced to improvise rather than systematically teach their subject. Tek'ewame Wolde Ts'adik' explains this gap between the curriculum and the realities on the ground by emphasizing that the curriculum was designed to match international standards in order to apply for development aid from international organizations such as UNESCO and UNICEF.[39] In a very creative way, instructors at the University College, headmasters, and teachers developed lesson plans in order to facilitate physical education at their respective schools. They had to work against a rather negative perception of sports as a punishment for pupils who had misbehaved. Physical education teachers and other responsible persons had to grapple with diverse difficulties in explaining to their students the important

---

[36] Tek'ewame, *Yesewinet magolmesha timhirt*, p. 25.
[37] Ibid., p. 26.
[38] Ibid., p. 27.
[39] Ibid., p. 28.

ideas around sports and the positive effects of physical education for health and a holistic development.[40]

However, those responsible for implementing PE policies not only faced difficulties transmitting positive ideas about sports and a systematic approach to physical education: the Department of Physical Education and Boy Scouting also grappled with financial constraints. It had to operate with a decent budget of 25,650 Birr per annum between 1948 and the early 1960s – with a minimal increase when schools began multiplying rapidly in the 1960s.[41] Thus, schools faced chronic shortages of teaching aids in general as well as for sports, which remained a field broadly neglected until the mid-1970s, particularly because it heavily relied on material imported from abroad.

The Training of PE Teachers

In order to re-establish a modern education system after the Italian occupation, the government hired headmasters (especially for junior secondary schools) and teachers (including physical education) from abroad. Interestingly, PE teachers often came from the country of origin of the respective headmaster and, with them, the diverse approaches to what sports at school means. Thus, the Haile Selassie I Secondary School in Kotebe followed the Swedish model, sports instruction at Tafari Makonnen School was dominated by Canadian ideas, and at General Wingate Secondary School a British sports instructor taught according to the British system. The Empress Menen School for Girls added physical education to its curriculum as early as 1946, which seems to have been taught by a Swedish teacher as an additional assignment. In 1949, the school appointed a Mrs. Ferno as a full-time PE and sports teacher. In an official history of the school, which was prepared on the occasion of its Silver Jubilee in 1956, this step was portrayed as 'an outward sign of a long-held belief that girls should receive mental and social training in their school career'.[42] Very conveniently, the home-making classes made the sports clothes and other equipment for the gymnastic performances. Arguably, sporting life at schools was not only limited to physical activity as such. It was much more complex and exceeded athletics, gymnastics, or ballgames. As shown in Illustration 1, Haile Selassie I Secondary School even had a swimming pool.

---

[40] Ibid.
[41] Ibid., p. 38. In the 1960s, 1 Eth$ / Birr equalled US$ 0.40. At that time, a sub-professional civil servant received a monthly salary between 75 and 525 Eth$.
[42] The History of the Empress Menen School, 1931–1956 in Commemoration of the Silver Jubilee (Addis Ababa, 1956), p. 56.

1. Swimming pool at Haile Selassie I Secondary School, today Kotebe College of Teacher Education, probably early 1960s (courtesy of Institute of Ethiopian Studies).

Reidar Dittman, who taught music there in the late 1940s, commented that the Ethiopian boys are 'interested in all sorts of sports, and particularly in soccer-playing and swimming. They have a great liking for all kinds of games; few places I have seen so many good ping-pong players! And when we introduced chess, we really made a hit with them'.[43] This perception very much resonates with the situation at other places such as the YMCA – which is extensively dealt with in the next chapter – where sports included board games, especially chess.

In addition to developing the first PE curriculum and taking responsibility for creating the necessary administrative structures, the MoE began training local PE teachers. As early as 1950, the MoE stressed that there exists in 'every school a qualified physical training instructor' supervised in larger schools by foreign PE teachers.[44] The training of PE teachers had commenced in summer 1948.[45] At this point, the his-

---

[43] Dittmann to Barnett, 24 March 1950, KFYA, Y.USA.9-2-37, YMCA International Work in Ethiopia Box 1, correspondence 1950/51.
[44] David Abner Talbot (ed.), *Imperial Ministry of Education Year Book* (Addis Ababa, 1950), p. 56.
[45] Tek'ewame Wolde Ts'adik', 'YeĪtop'ya akal maselt'enyana sport tarīk' [The History of the Physical Education Teachers Education], in: Mekonnen Amdie/

toriography offers more than one narrative. The first one explains that the cinema hall 'Ejersa Goro', which was located on the present science campus of Addis Ababa University (Arat Kilo), was the venue where Shiferaw Agonafir, Kifle Belay, and Mulugeta Wolde Giorgis (later also joined by Lakew Yigletu and Yidnek'achew Tesemma) gave training to approximately one hundred soldiers.[46] These soldiers became the first Ethiopian PE teachers and their teaching is appropriately remembered as 'drill' (*meserserīya*). Later, most of their Ethiopian instructors went to Sweden to receive training at the Royal Gymnastics Central Institute, returning to Addis with a diploma as 'Gymnastic Director'.[47]

A second narrative says that Onni Niskanen organized a two-month course for forty teachers from twenty-two schools in Addis Ababa in 1948, and for fifty-four teachers from schools from different parts of the empire in 1949. They received training in various kinds of sports. From the mid-1950s, the course took place at the sports facilities located on the premises of the Haile Selassie University College – today the Science Faculty.[48] A third narrative suggests that the *Kiremt* (summer) course, which started in 1949, was composed of volunteers and selected personnel from the army, the Imperial Body Guard, and the police forces. Their successful participation opened the possibility for employment as a PE teacher after their discharge from the armed forces. Except for the volunteers and the armed forces personnel, the costs for the *Kiremt* course were covered by the MoE.[49] Lakew Yigletu, who had gained experience as a teacher in Harar, was promoted to headmaster of the Menelik II School. Arguably, he became the main driver behind the *Kiremt* courses in Addis Ababa, which in the late 1950s still targeted teachers with a minimum knowledge of physical education and at least two years of teaching experience. They were trained on the premises of the Menelik II School. Successful participation resulted in a salary increase of 50 Ethiopian Birr.[50] Despite the financial incentives, this specific project petered out after three years. However, the *Kiremt* course as such seems to have continued until 1974 with a short break between 1965 and 1968.

Tilahun Gebrekristos (eds) Collection of research papers presented on different conferences organized by Ethiopian Physical Education and Sport Professionals' Association in 1993 & 1994 (Unpublished MS. 1995), p. 24.

[46] Apart from Yidnek'achew Tesemma, they went to Sweden and, in the case of Shiferaw Agonafir, to Israel for higher education in the field of sports.

[47] Interview with Shiferaw Agonafir, 8 June 2011.

[48] Tek'ewame, *Yesewinet magolmesha timhirt*, p. 29.

[49] Lakew Yigletu, cited in Tek'ewame, *Yesewinet magolmesha timhirt*, p. 32.

[50] 'Yeand amet yejīmnastīk memhiran kors' [One-year physical education course], Tenth Annual Track & Field Meet 1958–59, 17. IES 796 ADD ETH. All issues of the journal are catalogued under the same reference number. On the comparative value of the salary increase, see fn. 41.

Given the scarcity of time, subjects such as anatomy, physiology, or psychology could not be taught.[51]

Despite the urgent need for sports teachers, especially after the publication of the PE curriculum for grades one to six, the newly founded Teacher Training College, which was located on the premises of the Police College on Gefersa Road, did not include PE as a subject. Thus, schools in the Ethiopian capital relied on foreign teaching personnel, such as Onni Niskanen at the Haile Selassie I Secondary School or Mrs. Ferno at the Empress Menen School.[52] Summer courses continued in Addis Ababa and Harar, which primarily included experienced and newly trained teachers as well as instructors of the Imperial Body Guard. In 1952, the most successful participants, with selected graduates of the secondary schools, went to Sweden to receive higher training in physical education.[53]

In 1955, Onni Niskanen left Ethiopia and returned to Sweden. L.D. Casbon, who taught PE at Sandford School in Addis Ababa,[54] replaced him as head of the Department of Physical Education and Boy Scouting. During his time in office, the *Kiremt* course for experienced teachers and novices shifted to Harar.[55] With the establishment of the Haile Selassie I Military Academy in Harar (1957–77), one of the most modern of its kind on the continent, the city became an important centre of physical training, too. It is, however, not clear if PE students could use the modern training facilities. *Blood and Steel*, the academy's yearly publication, reveals nothing in this respect. During Casbon's time in office, a group of students was sent to Great Britain in 1957, where they received further PE training.[56]

After the successful completion of his study in Sweden, Lakew Yigletu began working in the MoE and was appointed director of the Department of Physical Education and Boy Scouting in 1957. In 1959, Shiferaw Agonafir, who was at that time already a PE instructor at Haile Selassie I University, Addis Ababa (HSIU), launched a one-year university course with foreign teaching personnel.[57] During the first year, twenty-seven teachers and one Air Force cadet (who had a clear leaning towards gymnastics) were admitted. In the second year, the composition of the course changed slightly. Of the forty-three participants, three were women and two were pupils who had already passed

---

[51] Lakew Yigletu, cited in Tek'ewame, *Yesewinet magolmesha timhirt*, p. 33.
[52] Ibid., p. 24.
[53] Ibid., p. 30. Amongst them Gorfu Gebre Medhin, Kifle Belay, Mulugeta Wolde Geurgis, Lakew Yigletu, Shiferew Agonifir, and Melash Yetayew.
[54] I am grateful to Peter Garretson for drawing my attention to this fact.
[55] Tek'ewame, *Yesewinet magolmesha timhirt*, p. 30.
[56] Tek'ewame mentions Belay Amikael, Berhan Dereso, Tek'wame Wolde Ts'adik', and later Neguse Seyfu Wolde Yohannis and Imru Hailu.
[57] Tek'ewame, *Yesewinet magolmesha timhirt*, p. 31.

the tenth grade and showed a liking for and ability to teach physical education and sports. Recruitment of female teachers and pupils also continued during the third year.[58]

Despite the successful graduation of 119 PE teachers, it became obvious that the course had to be administered, and therefore recognized, as college-level education. Therefore, a two-year course in physical education (major) and health (minor) was established within the Faculty of Education at HSIU in 1965. One of the drivers behind this project was an American with the name Bozma.[59] During a short research stay (financed by the Fulbright Program) at the Faculty of Education (HSIU), he realized there was a lack of PE teacher training. In addition to working out a PE teacher course plan, he also prepared an application to the Fulbright Program – the international educational exchange programme sponsored by the US government. After securing the financing for a course director, i.e. Bozma himself, and a decent three-year budget for implementing the course, the MoE opened the two-year course at the Faculty of Education (HSIU).[60] With the tremendous assistance and help of the university sports director, Shiferaw Agonafir, the course lasted over three years before it was stopped due to budget problems or, in fact, lack of interest from both officials and students.

With the expansion of the secondary school system, however, the need for Physical Education teachers became a severe problem, which forced the MoE to resume the two-year diploma course. The Addis Ababa College of Teacher Education (established in 1959 as part of Haile Selassie I University College), started PE courses again in 1969. The college was located on the premises of the Technical School (Tegbare Ed School)[61] around Mexico Square. Sisay Zeleke became the first department head. After having successfully passed the entrance exam, students could take a so-called 'composite major' in health and physical education, Ethiopian language (most probably Amharic or Ge'ez), and English. In 1971, after the second curriculum reform, physical education was grouped with mathematics, and home economics within the Division of Sciences.[62] When attendance remained low and the number of graduates could not come near to meeting the demands of the secondary schools, the Education Planning Task Force suggested offering 'music, physical education, arts and crafts, and home economics ... to in-service teachers in the Advanced Elementary Program

---

[58] Ibid., p. 34.
[59] Ibid. Unfortunately, no further information on this person could be found.
[60] Ibid., p. 36. Shiferaw Agonafir remarked that the PE course was established with the help of the Americans (Interview with Shiferaw Agonafir, 8 June 2011).
[61] A vocational school around Mexico Square, founded in 1943.
[62] Public Relations Office Addis Ababa: General Information on KCTE'S Twenty-Six Years of Training Experience (1969–1996); MoE, KCTE'S 1174, p. 1.

as selective possibilities'.[63] This plan was scheduled for implementation in summer 1973.[64]

All these planning and implementation processes took place in parallel with an education sector review conducted by the MoE with the World Bank, the International Bank for Reconstruction and Development, and the International Development Association in 1971. Its task was to evaluate the results of the 'Ten-Year Plan for the Controlled Expansion of Ethiopian Education' drawn up in the mid-1950s. It would go far beyond the limits of this book to make any elaborate statement on this very critical and detailed report published in 1972 (the revised version appeared in 1973). The following comments are limited to the few mentions of physical education or sports as recreation.

In the (revised) 1973 report, the section on the political aims of education highlighted sports as an activity 'which can be used to cultivate tolerance, team spirit, cooperation and fair play'.[65] Thus, sports went into the Guidelines on Curriculum Content of the Minimum Formation Education as a tool to increase physical coordination, thereby 'producing' healthy individuals and citizens who are fair and cooperative. Overall, the report gave little attention to physical education. Its call for a basic change towards an 'Ethiopianization' of the content of education, including the promotion of Amharic as the medium of instruction at all levels, did not include physical culture. This stands in contrast to earlier mentions of the inclusion of 'native' games such as *gittya, genna,* and *meket* in physical education practice at schools.[66] Systematic instruction on how to teach 'low-organized sports', as it is currently called, at faculties of education or teacher training colleges was not considered at all, neither in the report nor elsewhere, and an explicit re-evaluation of local sports practices had to wait until the late 1970s.[67]

---

[63] Education Planning Task Force Report. HSIU, 15 May 1973, MoE, 371.207 MIN861.
[64] Ibid., p. 51.
[65] Ministry of Education and Fine Arts, Report of the Education Sector Review. Education – Challenge to the Nation, Draft Revised Edition (Part C) (Technical Papers: Extracts from Task Force Reports and other Documentation), November 1973, p. 128, MoE, 378 Ac.1525 SH-32, 349, 354, 357.
[66] Talbot, *Imperial Ministry of Education*, p. 59.
[67] Following a proclamation in 1975 to establish sports competitions with a view to promoting and coordinating traditional sports in Ethiopia, as well as to scientifically and systematically register and study traditional sports, significant work was undertaken through the involvement of Tefere Mekonnen (then the Sport Commission's staff in charge). Until 1978 a group of sports experts studied the existing provinces and registered 293 traditional sports. The results were published in Tefere Mekonnen, *Nebbar sport*, [Traditional sports], Library of the Ethiopian Sports Commission (Addis Ababa, 1973 EC, 1980/81).

Ambitious Plans Meet Local Realities

Arguably, the main reason for the lack of interest in the subject was its low recognition. There seems to have been a generally negative attitude towards sports teachers, especially in their work places. As Girma Cheru (who later gained fame as the father of bodybuilding in Ethiopia) remembered, '[a] sports teacher had the reputation of someone with no qualification. Since he only spends his time with children, he needs neither promotion nor additional courses ... In practice, pressure was put on him'.[68] Former PE teachers and sports officials explained that if other classes were cancelled, the physical education teacher had to include the affected pupils in their classes. Thus, courses were overcrowded and the training of technical disciplines nearly impossible.[69]

Apart from overcrowded classes, there was the problem of insufficient teaching aids. Not only books, but also all kinds of equipment for teaching and practising modern sports had to be imported (although tax-free) from abroad. Whereas the annual budget of 25,650 Eth. Birr[70] might have been a good start in the late 1940s, it was definitely insufficient in the 1960s, when the number of schools had tremendously increased without an equivalent budgetary amendment. In this respect, Lulusegged Alemayyehu (headmaster of Medhane Alem School until 1967) commented that, in the school year 1965–66, 'Medhane Alem School had only 1,000 Eth$ to spend for physical education, hand-craft education, and gardening for 2,500 students ... These financial limitations put great stress upon a director who is concerned about the efficient operation of his school'.[71] Furthermore, there were scarce proper outdoor and indoor sports facilities in urban areas due to rocketing land-prices. A regulation that demanded every school construction plan to include proper sports facilities did not exist. In order to ease the situation, headmasters ordered pupils to level suitable parts of the school compound (if available) for doing sports. In 1952, the Amha Desta School in Addis Ababa even organized a ground-levelling competition between the classes.[72]

Despite the difficulties, modern sports found its way into schools throughout the country, but not always in the same way. Depending on the facilities and the engagement of individuals, it could take the

[68] Wendimu Negash Desta, 'Girma Cheru – gʷolmasaw sportenya II' [Girma Cheru – a fully accomplished athlete], *Yekatīt*, tahsas, 1974 [December 1981], 36.
[69] Interview with Shiferaw Agonafir, Alemu Miteku (former head of the Ethiopian Boy Scout Association), Zora Yarsu (athletics coach, former member of the Ethiopian Olympic Committee), Telahun Woldehana (sports teacher) in Addis Ababa, 18 June 2011.
[70] Tek'ewame, *Yesewinet magolmesha timhirt*, p. 38.
[71] Lulusegged Alemayyehu, 'A Descriptive Analysis of the Administration of Education in Transition in Ethiopia' (Unpublished Ph.D. dissertation, University of Southern California, August 1969), p. 190.
[72] Third Annual Track & Field Meet 1952, 19.

form of physical education, club activities,⁷³ or community oriented events.⁷⁴ Pupils of the Atse Gelawdeos Comprehensive School in Nazareth seem to have adored their PE teachers in the early 1970s for providing instruction in a great variety of sports ranging from basketball and table tennis to acrobatics.⁷⁵ Prince Makonnen Haile Selassie Comprehensive Secondary School in Dire Dawa boasted of extracurricular activities such as the 'Swimming Club' being amongst its pupils' favourite pastimes.⁷⁶ Enthusiasm and personal investment were the foundation for the establishment of a system of school competitions that gradually spread and connected the empire through sports.

The Ethiopian Inter-School Athletic Association

The history of athletics in Ethiopia would be incomplete without giving the Ethiopian Inter-School Athletic Association (EISAA) its due place. The idea of interschool competitions and its implementation through systematic planning began in 1948.⁷⁷ Sports teachers and administrators from home and abroad had realized that, although physical education was a compulsory subject, the implementation of the curriculum was unsatisfactory. Founded in 1949, the EISAA served to do more than organize athletic competitions between schools, however. The Association 'grew from the desire of all directors and sports masters in Ethiopian Schools to see the development of sports properly guided and not allowed to take the haphazard course it had been taking since 1933 EC [1940/41]'.⁷⁸

Apart from the severe shortage of physical education teachers and sports grounds in urban areas as described in the previous section, the 'haphazard course' was the result of a chronic lack of equipment. In order to get a better picture of the situation, the Association launched a study on the development of sports equipment most suitable for the local (Ethiopian) environment in 1950. Turning a problem into an opportunity, the EISAA restricted the supply of footballs, basketballs, softballs, and volleyballs to educational institutions participating in the Annual Track & Field Meet.

---

73 Several school yearbooks located at the IES present sports club activities in text and visuals.
74 Ministry of Education, Education – Challenge to the Nation, p. 422.
75 *Year Books of the Atse Gelawdeos Comprehensive School*, Nazareth, IES 371.805 NAZ ATS, 1970–72.
76 *School Bulletin*, Prince Mekonnen Haile Selassie Comprehensive Secondary School, Dire Dawa, May 1971, IES 371.805 DIR PRI, 2.
77 Tek'ewame, *Yesewinet magolmesha timhirt*, p. 39.
78 Second Annual Track & Field Meet 1951, 3, IES 796 ADD ETH. All issues of the journal are catalogued under the same reference number.

In his capacity as director of the Department of Physical Education and Boy Scouting, Onni Niskanen became the main driver behind the establishment of EISAA.[79] He paved the way for the 'pioneers' of physical education in Ethiopia, both Ethiopian and foreign, to become active EISAA members. Onni met with all sports teachers and headmasters of participating schools at the Annual General Assembly to decide on the Association's policy. Apart from government schools, mission schools and schools of the so-called foreign communities were also eligible for EISAA membership. The executive committee consisted of six members with a chairperson directly nominated by the Minister of Education.[80]

The Association conducted competitions at all levels according to the rules and regulations of the International Amateur Athletics Federation (IAAF)[81] of 1953, including some minor adjustments 'to meet the local conditions'.[82] Classification of athletes into 'senior', 'intermediate', 'junior', and 'invitation' is but one example. Whereas 'senior' and 'invitation' athletes comprised pupils of a higher age, 'junior' and 'intermediate' applied a mathematical guideline multiplying height (in cm) by weight (in kg).[83] Such adjustments accommodated the fact that exact ages were usually not known and that children entered school at very different times in their lives, not necessarily at a specific age.

In the broader picture, the EISAA pushed for the introduction of competitions in athletics and ball games according to (adapted) international standards through the education system. It also served to enforce ideas of fair play and good sportsmanship. Playing by rules was intended to change the partly negative association of sports such as football and boxing with criminal behaviour. The Association's journal reported that Asfa Wossen School (Addis Ababa) disciplined their volleyball players through weekly matches with staff members. Continuing, it noted that, since 1953, the inter-school competition had separately assessed and rewarded 'play according to rules'.[84] Slogans such as 'Have a calm spirit if you win and a smiling face if you lose' – a rough translation of the English slogan 'Be modest in victory; be cheerful in defeat' – joined visuals in the journal.[85]

In the early years, only Addis Ababa schools participated in EISAA competitions. In 1951, thirty-two educational institutions were already sending teams to compete in athletic disciplines (short-distance and relay races, high jump and long jump, shot put, and javelin) and in football. In the school year 1953–54, Harar province followed

[79] Tek'ewame, *Yesewinet magolmesha timhirt*, p. 40.
[80] Second Annual Track & Field Meet 1951, 3.
[81] Renamed International Association of Athletics Federations in 2001.
[82] Seventh Annual Track & Field Meet 1955–56, 12.
[83] Sixth Annual Track & Field Meet 1954–55, 14–16.
[84] Third Annual Track & Field Meet 1952, 19.
[85] Second Annual Track & Field Meet 1951, 3.

in the same way and, one year later, football matches were organized amongst schools from various provinces.[86] An analysis of the EISAA journal suggests that school sports competitions took place in all provinces from 1962 onwards. Apart from publishing the results of the final competition in Addis Ababa, the EISAA journal also provided information in texts and visuals about the sports meets at the provincial level. The government supported the EISAA with up to 90,000 Ethiopian Birr per year for co-financing the participation of athletic youths from the provinces.[87] This meant, in practice, that mostly rich provinces such as Sidama, Kaffa, Harar, and Wollega, as well as Eritrea, could send their athletes to the finals in Addis Ababa.[88]

Furthermore, sponsors such as the private sporting outfitters Tewfic Sports House, House of Sports, and Samuel Beheshelian and Sons donated money or gifts in kind. In turn, they had the opportunity to place advertisements in the annual EISAA journal.[89] However, they were not the only ones. Advertisements ranged from Volkswagen to the Assco Shoe Factory, with companies often using the language or symbols of sports to advertise their products. In 1957, for example, Ethiopian Airlines addressed the readership with the slogan – 'Always pick a winner'.[90]

The increasing enrolment of girls, especially at government schools, facilitated their participation in and visibility on the athletic scene. Empress Menen School in Addis Ababa became especially active in the field of sports. Female athletes participated in gymnastic performances on several occasions, including non-competitive events,[91] and became very successful in the EISAA finals. From the 1950s onwards, progress and gender equality were sometimes symbolized in newspapers and books by female athletes in short sporting attire. Girls participated in mixed gymnastic performances during the annual EISAA finals in Haile Selassie I Stadium. As to whether they always had the consent of their families, that is a matter of debate. As elsewhere, the ideal woman in Ethiopia was associated with reserved behaviour. In contrast, informal conversations with women who went to school during the 1960s revealed that short sportswear and mixed performances were no problem at all.

---

[86] Seventh Annual Track & Field Meet 1955–56, 23.
[87] Tek'ewame, *Yesewinet magolmesha timhirt*, p. 41.
[88] Comment by Seyoum Mulugeta, 21 March 2018.
[89] Mentioned in Lentakis, *Ethiopia*, p. 275.
[90] Eighth Annual Track & Field Meet 1956–57.
[91] In 1955, more than 250 older girls participated in the gymnastic display during the Silver Jubilee Anniversary of Haile Selassie's Coronation: The history of the Empress Menen School, 1931–1956 in commemoration of the Silver Jubilee' (Addis Ababa, 1956), p. 77.

Physical education in Ethiopia and elsewhere always served the gradual, but massive inculcation of ideas about the modern physically fit citizen. The EISAA finals became a space for identifying athletic talent for top-level competitions on the world scene. From 1956, Ethiopia participated in the Olympic Games and literally 'raced' to fame in Rome four years later. Thus, in 1960 the EISAA General Assembly decided to intensify the training and to organize a competition with the best athletes from the Army Sport Clubs, the police, and the university colleges. The assembly further discussed the future of successful athletes after they completed school. Since not all sporting talents might choose a career in the armed forces, vocational training centres or colleges, the EISAA put the foundation of a civil sports club on the agenda.[92]

Finally, and importantly, the EISAA finals served as a display of political power through the involvement of politicians in sports. They took place in presence of the emperor and high-ranking officials in the Haile Selassie I Stadium in Addis Ababa. Winning teams and individuals received their trophies and plates from his hands. Haile Selassie's role in competitive sporting events remained an important aspect of performing a visibly modern and enlightened monarch, showing interest and guiding the youth. The programme included gymnastic shows as well as the performance of extraordinary athletic disciplines such as pole vaulting. Arguably, mass gymnastics served as a physical expression of identifying with and being part of a youthful, strong, healthy, and disciplined Ethiopian nation. The presence of heroic groups such as Korean War veterans dressed in their uniforms as guests of honour during the closing celebrations of the Third Annual Track & Field Meet in 1952 may have also served to demonstrate Ethiopia's military potential.[93] However, as Chapter 1 argued, the Boy Scout Association of Ethiopia provided the space where physical fitness and pre-military training found their strongest expression.

The Boy Scout Association of Ethiopia

Re-establishment within an International Framework

During the Italian occupation, Boy Scout activities had come to a standstill in Ethiopia. The experience of the Fascist youth movement Wolves of Ethiopia, which trained and paraded on and off school grounds, had

---

[92] Tenth Annual Track & Field Meet 1958–59, 20.
[93] Third Annual Track & Field Meet 1952, 8. Between 1951 and 1953, 6,037 Ethiopian soldiers and officers fought as part of the UN forces in Korea and formed the so-called Kagnew Battalion. Kagnew/*K'anyew* was the name of *Ras* Makonnen's warhorse. *Ras* Makonnen – Haile Selassie's father – fought as a general under *Ats'ē* Menelik II.

produced a lasting negative attitude amongst Ethiopians towards any paramilitary activity at schools. In 1957, the emperor still saw a need to emphasize in public that the Ethiopian scouts had actively resisted the Italian occupation.[94]

Discussing the militarism in Baden-Powell's movement, Michael Rosenthal argues that the training of 'serviceable citizens ... to follow orders in war time' does not automatically turn them into 'war Scout[s]'. Instead, scouting produces a role model of 'absolute loyalty, an unbudgeable devotion to duty, and the readiness to fight, and if necessary, to die for one's country'.[95] These virtues made the movement adaptable to both war and peace time contexts.

As early as 1942, the Greek community in Addis Ababa continued their active pre-occupation engagement by forming patrols at the new community school in the Eriba Kentu area.[96] Michel B. Lentakis remembers that

> some Greeks who had come from Egypt persuaded our schoolteachers to allow boys to become Scouts; we joined the movement with all our heart, and about 120 boys formed the first Scout troop in Ethiopia. We were both happy and proud to wear our Scout uniforms and learned everything about being a Scout and the movement's principles, and we paraded on Sundays, going to church on foot singing Scout songs in a martial way.[97]

Other schools in the capital and, probably in other Ethiopian towns such as Dire Dawa, commenced scouting activities through private initiative, too. Mignon Innes Ford, headmistress of Princess Zenebe Work School, formed girl patrols.[98] Although girls were at the forefront of re-establishing scouting in Ethiopia, plans for a Girl Scout/Guide Association of Ethiopia did not emerge prior to the 1950s. Thus, existing girl guides participated in the activities of the Boy Scouts. In Eritrea, scouts were active in the government schools in Asmara and Massawa by the

---

94 Haile Selassie I, 'Address to the Boy Scout Movement 6 June 1959', in The Imperial Ethiopian Ministry of Information (ed.), *Selected Speeches of His Imperial Majesty Haile Selassie First, 1918 to 1967* (Addis Ababa, 1967), p. 648.
95 Michael Rosenthal, *The Character Factory: Baden-Powell and the Origins of the Boy Scout Movement* (London, 1986), p. 162.
96 Lentakis, *Ethiopia*, p. 99; during the *Derg* (socialist military rule 1974–91), the building became the central statistics office.
97 Ibid., p. 101. Boy Scouting had already begun in 1919 and gained momentum in the early1930s. See Chapter 1, *The Emergence of Ethiopia's Modern Sports Scene (1900–1935)*.
98 Mignon Innes Ford had come to Ethiopia in the 1930s as part of the Pan-African movement: Giulia Bonacci, 'Back to Ethiopia: African-American and West-Indian Returnees in Ethiopia (1896–2010)', in Kwesi Kwaa Prah (ed.), *Back to Africa, 2. The Ideology and Practice of the African Returnee Phenomenon from the Caribbean and North America to Africa* (Cape Town 2012), pp. 360–61.

late 1940s. In 1948, non-government schools such as *Kidist Mariam* (Orthodox), *Agazian* (private), or *Kidane Mehret* (Catholic) asked the Scouts Bureau in Asmara for help to establish their own patrols. Scoutmasters propagated the movement in Mendefera, Keren, Dekemhare, and Hirghigo (near Massawa). The Eritrean movement cooperated with the US military base Kagnew Station and saw further connection to the Ethiopian Association.[99]

In 1948, work on re-establishing the Boy Scout Association began. This meant that all the necessary structures and committees, such as a national council and an executive board, had to be built, a charter drafted, and scoutmaster courses started. Haile Selassie, who considered scouting to be militarized youth training, had personally requested its re-establishment and provided the necessary funds to get the process under way.[100] The implementation of the project demanded people who had a career within the armed forces, its sports sector, and the Ethiopian school system. They had to have enough experience as scouts and, if they were expatriates or members of the foreign communities, good contacts to their home associations.

Within the MoE, the Canadian Dr. Robert N. Thompson was identified as the ideal person to facilitate the re-establishment process. Having served as an instructor in the Commonwealth Air Training Plan during the Second World War, Thompson and his family were relocated to Ethiopia through the offices of the Sudan Interior Mission in 1943. He worked in the Ethiopian Air Force and later became a secondary school teacher and headmaster of Haile Selassie I Secondary School.[101] In 1948, Thompson was seconded to the MoE, where he acted as Director of Provincial Schools until 1952. His personal connections to the armed forces as well as to various decision makers and potential allies within the Ethiopian educational system were as important for the job as his experience as a scout. Thus, Haile Selassie's favourite son, Prince Makonnen, Chief Scout and Patron of the movement in Ethiopia, assigned Thompson to act as commissioner in the absence of a national council. He gave the Canadian free rein in choosing the right personnel to re-establish the Ethiopian scout movement.[102]

Thompson primarily based his choice on the candidates' previous experience as scouts and on their political influence. Thus, the first

---

[99] 'Tarīk mimisrat ts'ehyane funot āb ērtra' [The history of the foundation of the Scouts Zehyawiane Funot in Eritrea], *Awet. Sportawī mets'hēt* [Success. Sport Magazine], 6 (1968), 18-19, IES, 796 AWA PER. I am grateful to Lula Mebrahtu und Tekle Mebrahtu for translating the article from Tigrinya into German.
[100] *Addīs Zemen,* 13 tik'imt 1941 [23 October 1948].
[101] Robert N. Thompson, 'Down a Memory Lane from Ethiopia', in *World Scouting,* 4 (1965), 1, 10.
[102] Crown Prince to R.N. Thompson, 10 January 1948, RNT TWU.

boards and committees consisted of Ethiopians (mostly high-ranking individuals from diverse ministries as well as the armed forces), members of the so-called foreign communities (mostly Indian and Greek), and expatriates from Sweden, North America, Egypt, France, Britain, and Sudan who served in various capacities in the educational sector.[103] Most of them were also active in other capacities. Onni Niskanen, Aberra Jembere, and Michel Wassef, who belonged to the group of very active board members, had functions within the Red Cross Society and the YMCA of Ethiopia and, thus, facilitated cooperation between these organizations. In 1949, Aberra Jembere[104] was appointed as general secretary, Akalework Haptewold (Vice-Minister of Education) acted as chairman and Thompson became deputy commissioner.[105] In late 1950, a national council, consisting nearly entirely of high-ranking Ethiopian officials, and an executive council, with a multinational membership, commenced work. In the same year, the charter and the constitution were drafted, approved and published. The Ethiopian government officially recognized the Boy Scout Association in 1950.[106] After a delay of almost twenty years, Ethiopia finally became a member of the World Organization of the Scout Movement in 1969.

'Be Prepared!' Through Physical Fitness

With its emphasis on physical fitness, it seemed more than logical to combine scouting with physical education and to establish a Department of Physical Education and Boy Scouting within the MoE. Haile Selassie later commented on this step that even

> in the future, the development of the physical and spiritual strength of Our nation is dependent on her youth obtaining Scout and military training along with their academic studies, thus combining in themselves the heroism and spirit of determination of their fathers with military training and modern scientific knowledge; and it is for this reason

---

[103] R.N. Thompson to Col. J.S. Wilson (Director, Boy Scouts International Bureau, London) 5 December 1949, RNT TWU.

[104] According to Jon Abbink, Aberra Jembere had studied law and public administration at HSIU. Later, he worked in administration, administrator, as a lawyer, and teacher. 'Until 1974 he held various positions and public functions in Ethiopia, among them Secretary General (Vice Minister) of the Ethiopian Council of Ministers, Head of Legal and Parliamentary Affairs in the Prime Minister's office with the rank of Minister of State (until 1974), administrator of the Haile Selassie I Foundation, Secretary General of the Ethiopian Orthodox Church head office, and Director of the Ethiopian Red Cross Society.'(Jon Abbink, 'In memoriam Aberra Jembere (1928–2004)', *Aethiopica*, 7 (2004), 190. I am grateful to Norris Lineweaver for drawing my attention to this source).

[105] R.N. Thompson to Aberra Jembere, 27 July 1949, RNT TWU.

[106] R.N. Thompson to H. Pratten, New York, 22 November 1950, RNT TWU.

that We have commanded Our Vice-Minister of Education to establish facilities for military training in all Our educational institutions.[107]

The implementation of this dream required, first of all, qualified scoutmasters. In July 1949, a six-week scoutmaster's training course was held on the premises of Tafari Makonnen School. It provided elementary scoutmasters' training combined with physical training that continued on a regular basis.[108] The *Yearbook of the Ministry of Education* of 1950 reveals not only an 'expanding zeal for Scouting' at schools, but that the physical education instructors supervised 'field trips and tracking' as 'open air pastimes'.[109] Later, the physical education teacher training at HSIU included scoutmaster courses.[110]

If Boy Scouting was associated primarily with physical fitness, we might ask which disciplines it promoted through its activities. Apart from endurance and physical strength, the focus lay on survival techniques such as swimming. Swimming was part of the scout training and had to be completed with a test. Boy Scouts who were organized in educational institutions in Addis Ababa, for example, went to camps at Lake Langano, in Debre Zeit, and Ambo, i.e. places with good swimming facilities.[111] Despite its emphasis on swimming, the Boy Scout Association of Ethiopia never actively promoted swimming as an organized sport. This was mainly done in military institutions. According to documents from the Ethiopian Swimming Federation (established in 1971 EC, 1978), formal competitions began in 1951 EC (1958) in different military camps.[112] Some of the secondary schools that had swimming facilities on their compounds, access to hotel pools, or to the facilities of a company such as the cement factory in Dire Dawa, also organized competitions. In contrast to competitions operating according to win–lose binaries, swimming in the Boy Scout Association meant survival, not sport.

Apart from drilling, marching, and other exercises as part of public spectacles such as the global military practice of the Guard of Honour, scouting focused on mental and physical fitness for survival. *Scouting for Boys*, the 'bible' of the movement, contains a whole chapter on 'Practices for Developing Strength' which is a combination of gymnastics and yoga.[113] More than anything else, scouting was hiking, camping, mountaineering, trekking, i.e. practices with the potential for adventure.

[107] Haile Selassie I, 'Address to the Boy Scout Movement', 649.
[108] Minutes Meeting of Executive Board, 28 July 1949, RNT TWU.
[109] Talbot, *Imperial Ministry of Education*, p. 59.
[110] Department of Health and Physical Education, Haile Selassie I University Catalogue, May 1965, IES 378.006 GEN, 196.
[111] Fik'ru Kīdane, *YePīyassa lij* [Child from Piazza] (Addis Ababa, 2009), p. 45.
[112] Mentioned in Mekonnen Sintayehu, 'Swimming in Ethiopia' (Unpublished BE thesis Kotebe College of Teachers Education, 1995), p. 27.
[113] Robert Baden-Powell, *Scouting for Boys: A Handbook for Instruction in Good Citizenship*, 7th edn (London, 2013), pp. 184–91.

Walking the Nation

Hiking and camping became part and sometimes even the epitome of the 'scouting way of life'. They offered the possibility to test theoretical and practical knowledge such as orienteering, and building necessary items out of what could be found in nature. Hiking firmly tied the human body to the soil in general, and to the national soil in particular. Although we can assume that most hikes explored the immediate surroundings, there were also documented round trips covering large parts of the Empire. Whereas the former served to integrate the city and the rural hinterland, trips around the country worked to instil nationalism – a function that scouting fulfilled in diverse political contexts in Africa, the Middle East, and elsewhere. As Jakob Krais argues for Algeria and the Middle East, it brought about specific masculinities that combined (anti-colonial) nationalism with physical fitness and religion, i.e. Muscular Islam or Muscular Christianity.[114]

From *Scouting for Boys* onwards, scouting literature gives hiking a prominent place and associates it with adventure and fitness. In 1955, the Department of Physical Education and Boy Scouting published the first booklet in Amharic on scouting in Ethiopia.[115] It advertised the movement to a wider Amharic-speaking audience by adapting the ideal scout to the Ethiopian context and its emphasis on obedience to any superior. The book further explains the requirements for achieving a specific rank. The second scout rank explicitly demanded participation in at least three hiking and camping events. Requirements for the first rank specified that applicants needed to be physically capable of completing a hike of at least 25 kilometres and accurately rendering the route as a hand-drawn map. Scouts from Addis Ababa, who attended the first training camp in Dire Dawa (1949), had to pass a 35 kilometres distance from Alemaya to Dire Dawa, which Onni Niskanen later declared an 'elite hike'.[116] Apart from technical training, endurance seems to have been an essential part of most of the exercises. Hikes could last several days. General Wingate School, for example, organized a 'one hundred kilometres march' from Ambo to Addis Ababa.[117] These marches always included exercises in first aid, camping, signalling, and extra portions of sports.

---

[114] Jakob Krais, 'Muscular Muslims: Scouting in Late Colonial Algeria between Nationalism and Religion', *International Journal of Middle East Studies*, 51:4 (2019), 567–85.
[115] Befek'ade Sillasē Fantaye, *Sile boy iskawt agelgilot ach'ir meglech'a* [On the Boy Scout service: A short explanation] (Addis Ababa, 1947 EC, 1954/55), p. 11.
[116] Onni Niskanen, The Boy Scout Camp in Dire*Dawa [sic] and Harar during August 1949, 15 September 1949, RNT TWU.
[117] I am grateful for this information to Seyoum Mulugeta, who attended the school during the early 1960s.

Good relations with army or police contingents in the area often helped with transport of equipment. Due to its excellent contacts with the BMME, for example, the Greek school received the necessary equipment such as tents, canvas, ropes, and poles to learn camping. The British military provided transport to camps at Mekanissa, Holeta, and Debre Zeit, where Greek scouts learned 'discipline and all the lessons that Scouts learn from booklets'.[118] Later, the Ethiopian armed forces gave support. The elementary school in Negele (Sidamo), for example, was provided transport by the Territorial Army's Fourth Brigade and scouts from the Secondary School in Yirgalem were accompanied by police sergeants.[119]

The additional military training within the Association would make Boy Scouts ideal candidates for a career in the armed forces. Early cooperation with the Imperial Ethiopian Air Force is a case in point. Sports events where the Boy Scouts specifically competed against cadets from the Air Force Training School in Debre Zeit took place during the first training camp in Dire Dawa (1949). As an award, eight members of the winning team – which happened to be the Boy Scouts – got a half-hour pleasure flight in one of the training aircraft of the cadet school.[120] Despite the sustained strong connection to the armed forces, the army and police had their own channels of recruitment.[121] The yearbooks of several educational institutions, which are located at the IES library, even suggest a demilitarizing tendency. Scouting could be found amongst other club activities, such as debating, volleyball or drama. By the 1960s, it had developed from pre-military training to a pastime that advertised outdoor activities and was active in social welfare. As the *Yearbook of the Haile Mariam Mamo Secondary School* emphasized, although 'this association is not able to help others with money, it is always assisting the community through labour and morale'.[122] The description of leisure activities at the Technical School in Addis Ababa highlighted 'hiking, helping people, [and] group work' as major scouting activities.[123] Haile Selassie I University promoted scouting activities as useful recreation for both, male and female students. However, asked about female membership in the Rovers' Club, Chairman Tesfaye Teferi 'doubted their physical strength to participate in the walks, that are arranged every two

---

[118] Lentakis, *Ethiopia*, p. 150.
[119] I am grateful for this information to Seyoum Mulugeta.
[120] 'BeDireDawa yeiskawtoch yeigir k^{w}as ch'ewat'a' [The football match of the scouts in Dire Dawa], in *Addīs Zemen*, 13 tik'imt 1941, 4 [23 October 1948].
[121] I am grateful to Bahru Zewde for drawing my attention to this fact.
[122] *Yearbook of the Haile Mariam Mamo Secondary School* (1958 EC, 1964), 11 IES 371.805 DAB HAI.
[123] Student Publications Technical School Addis Ababa, 1964–65, 70.

weeks right after supper. He proudly remarked that the stretch they [the boys] cover in one walk may be more than 10 km'.[124]

In some cases, hiking provided an ideal opportunity to display politics. In May 1953, for example, *Addīs Zemen* reported extensively on the emperor receiving thirty-five Boy Scouts from Ras Abate School in Kembata (in southern Ethiopia) in the MoE. Haile Selassie not only asked about the development of the school, but also expressed his expectations regarding the scouts' unconditional loyalty in accordance with the Scouting Oath, and ordered a pair of shoes for each of them as an imperial gift. He also allowed himself to be photographed with the boys, portraying himself as the 'emperor of the youth' as he stood amongst them, quite within their reach. Such media coverage was an attempt to convey the image of the emperor as the 'New Man' at the top – approachable to those youth who promised to become the vanguard in modernizing and strengthening the Ethiopian nation.[125]

For his personal engagement in supporting the Boy Scout Association of Ethiopia, the World Boy Scout Committee made Haile Selassie Honorary Patron of the World Boy Scout Movement on 30 May 1971.[126] With the downfall of the empire, the Ethiopian Boy Scout Association was again dissolved in 1974. Obviously, a movement that was loyal to God and emperor had no place in a socialist future.

The education of PE teachers reveals more continuity. The diploma course begun at the Technical School in 1972, continued until 1985 and awarded degrees to 344 male and 18 female students.[127] Following the transfer of the college to Kotebe in 1976 it was renamed the *Kotebe College of Teacher Education*; at that point, the MoE not only decided to include students from different regions per quota, but also shifted the balance between theory (40 per cent) and practice (60 per cent).[128] School competitions continued during the socialist period and a three-year *Spartakiade* system began in 1979, including all children between eleven and eighteen years of age. The aim was both to promote sports for

---

[124] Students Travel, Work, Sunbathe during Break, *The University Reporter*, 1:2 (1967), 3, IES 378 HSU PER.
[125] Yeras Abate timhirt bēt boy iskawtoch keKembata wede Addīs Abeba [Boy Scouts of Ras Abate school from Kembata to Addis Ababa], *Addīs Zemen*, 28 mīyazya 1945, 2 [6 May 1953].
[126] The certificate is located in the Ethiopian National Archive; Honorary Membership H.S.I, ENA 1.2.52.03.
[127] Tek'ewame, *Yesewinet magolmesha*, p. 36.
[128] Sisay Zeleke, *Yebalemuyawoch silt'ena beītiop'ya yeītyop'ya yesewinet magolmesha timhirtina yesport balemuyawoch mahber* [PE teacher training in Ethiopia, physical education classes, and the Sports Teachers Association], 1985 EC, 1992/3 and 1986 EC, 1993/4 (Addis Ababa 1987 EC, 1994/5), pp. 58–9.

proper development and to systematically search for sporting talent.[129] The organizational expertise came from socialist countries, primarily from the German Democratic Republic, which offered training courses to athletes, coaches, and sports foreign officials at the Deutsche Hochschule für Sport und Körperkultur (German University for Sports and Physical Culture, DHfK) in Leipzig, German Democratic Republic.[130]

This chapter began with sports as leisure or useful recreation in urban contexts. This narrative remains incomplete without considering the YMCA, which became active in Ethiopia in the mid-1940s. Reports on education mention the Association under the rubric 'informal' or 'non-formal' education, or 'uncoordinated programs'.[131] Its Future Citizen Schools made thousands of children literate. The Operation Better Boys became the first street worker programme in Africa.[132] Today, Ethiopians associate the history of this volunteer organization primarily with sports. Its former headquarters in *Arat Kilo* still serves as a meeting point for retired sports officials, physical education experts, and sports enthusiasts. The next chapter discusses the role of the YMCA in promoting sports beyond notions of Muscular Christianity.

---

[129] 'Ethiopia', *Olympic Review*, 233 (1987), 138.
[130] For a comprehensive description, see Lothar Kalb, *Sendboten Olympias: Die Geschichte des Ausländerstudiums an der DHFK Leipzig* (Leipzig, 2008).
[131] Ministry of Education and Fine Arts, Report of the Education Sector Review. Education – Challenge to the Nation, Addis Ababa, August 1972, HSIU, Five Year Plan 1967–1971 EC, genbot 1966 [May 1974], MoE, 378 Ac.1525 SH-32, pp. 349, 354, 357.
[132] Katrin Bromber, 'Make Them Better Citizens: YMCA Training in Late Imperial Ethiopia (1950s–1970s)', *Annales d'Ethiopie*, 32 (2018/19), 35–9.

4
Training Leaders and Athletes: The Ethiopian YMCA (1940s–1970s)

The long history of Young Men's Christian Association (YMCA) activities in Africa is heavily under-researched. Systematic studies only exist for South Africa. There, a YMCA branch in Cape Town, which was exclusively restricted to white members, opened in 1865. With the growing influence of the North American YMCA on a global level, Afro-American secretaries also started to work in Africa, including South Africa. So it was that, after the First World War, the enthusiastic Afro-American secretary Max Yergan successfully started to reach out to young non-white South Africans.[1] Prior to his South African work, the North American YMCA had dispatched him and two other Afro-American YMCA secretaries to Kenya, where they worked with African members of the Carrier Corps during the First World War.[2] In Nairobi, Theodore Roosevelt had already founded the first YMCA branch of the Kenya colony in 1910.[3] The French Alliance started YMCA activities in colonies such as Madagascar or Cameroon as early as 1924.[4] As I will argue in the first part of this chapter, the establishment of the movement in Ethiopia in the late 1940s was not primarily the result of an increased interest by the movement in Africa. In contrast, its initial organization as a sub-branch of the Egyptian YMCA is yet another example of how Ethiopia was conceived of as belonging to North Africa or the Middle East. Arguably, the growing presence of the movement, and most prominently its North American model, in African (post-)colonial states from the 1950s onwards, as well as the increased political interest of the United States in Africa, resulted in the relocation of the Ethiopian YMCA within the East African context.

[1] David Henry Anthony III, 'Unwritten History: African Work in the YMCA of South Africa', *History in Africa: A Journal of Method,* 32 (2005), 435–44.
[2] Jim C. Harper, *Western-Educated Elites in Kenya, 1900–1963: The African American Factor* (New York, 2006), p. 63.
[3] 'Brief YMCA History', www.ymca.int/member/ymca-in-africa/ymca-kenya [accessed 15 September 2021].
[4] Cameroon and Madagascar became members of the YMCA World Alliance in 1951 and 1968 respectively. 'History of Cameroon – YMCA', http://ymca-cameroon.org/who-we-are/our-history [accessed 15 September 2021]; 'Brief YMCA History'.

Facing socio-economic hardships in post-liberation Ethiopia, children and youth tried to carve out new possibilities. Many of them had lost their parents and family members. They often searched for chances in urban areas, and Addis Ababa became their prime destination. In order to survive, some youth operated in gangs. In the late 1940s, the Egyptian YMCA representative Naguib Kelada commented that one of the 'recognized curses there [in Addis Ababa] is the habit of drinking' and 'a great deal of laxity in sexual morality' due to 'the utter absence of any provision for the proper use of leisure time of youth'.[5] In contrast to ideas about youth as 'torchbearers of progress', as partly portrayed in the previous chapters, these young people were perceived as a problem.

Apart from other counter-measures, such as the Training School and Remand Home for Boys,[6] volunteer organizations were supposed to help change the situation. The already described Boy Scouts, as well as the Ethiopian Red Cross, targeted privileged youth as members through an educational system that was out of reach for most children. With its specific outlook on underprivileged male youth of all social strata and religious backgrounds, the YMCA provided spaces for what was perceived as proper use of leisure. On the educational front, the Association opened possibilities for thousands of children through its literacy programmes. Furthermore, the training of future leaders in Ethiopia and, especially, the United States helped to compensate for the immense loss of existing leadership during the Fascist occupation.[7] However, today most Ethiopians I have talked with no longer remember the 'Y' for informal education or leadership training, but as a hot spot for sports. This perception resonates with the general argument that sports and physical education were the 'Y's biggest international selling point'.[8]

---

[5] Naguib Kelada, 'The Ethiopian Project: The Field, Its Opportunities, Handicaps and Immediate Needs', Mainau, 4 July 1949, KFYA, Y.USA. 9-2-37, YMCA International Work in Ethiopia Box 1, correspondence 1946–49.

[6] This institution was established in 1958 and molded along the ideas of the correction homes in Britain. Located in the former Italian horse stables in the Lideta area of Addis Ababa, it was an attempt not only to separate juvenile delinquents from adult prisoners, but also to produce 'well adjusted, satisfied, contributing and responsible citizen[s]': Zenebu Kefelew, 'The Role of the Training School & Remand Home in Correcting Juvenile Delinquents in Ethiopia' (Unpublished senior paper, School of Social Work, Haile Selassie I University, 1973), p. 20.

[7] Katrin Bromber, '"Make Them Better Citizens": YMCA Training in Late Imperial Ethiopia (1950s–1970s)', *Annales d'Ethiopie,* 32 (2018/19), 19–40; Katrin Bromber, 'Education for Leadership: The YMCA in Late Imperial Ethiopia (1940s–1970s)' in Harald Fischer-Tiné, Stefan Huebner, and Ian Tyrrell (eds), *Mediating Modernity: Global Perspectives on the 'Secular' Work of the YMCA and YWCA (c. 1870–1970)* (Honolulu, 2020), pp. 237–58.

[8] Harald Fischer-Tiné, Stefan Huebner, Ian Tyrrell, 'The Rise and Growth of a Global "Moral Empire": The YMCA and YWCA during the Late Nineteenth and

This chapter specifically looks into the multiple functions of sports at the Ethiopian YMCA. It argues that activities, which ranged from sports as useful recreation for everybody to the creation of successful national athletes and teams, served to transform problematic youth into healthy, loyal citizens, successful athletes, and potential leaders. Following a brief description of the establishment of the YMCA in Ethiopia, the first section outlines the position of sports in the development of the organization in Ethiopia. It interrogates the drivers of the promotion of programmes and the influence of the North American secretaries from the United States and Canada, Ethiopian secretaries trained in the US, World Service workers, and Peace Corps volunteers. The second part of the chapter zooms in on actual sports practices and places; i.e. what kinds of sports were done and where? The final part discusses how the 'Y' became a site for forming new masculinities through bodybuilding as well as a training ground for alternative styles of wrestling.

The 'Y' Comes to Ethiopia

At the personal request of Haile Selassie, Ethiopia approached the World Alliance of YMCAs in 1946 to assess the feasibility of establishing a YMCA in the country. Its North American members perceived the organization's World Alliance as being too occupied with post-war reconstruction in Europe.[9] Thus, the International Committee of the Young Men's Christian Associations of the United States and Canada (hereafter referred to as the International Committee) stepped in.

The main idea was to establish the Ethiopian YMCA as an Egyptian sub-branch. Having received the green light from the World Alliance in Geneva, James K. Quay, the representative of the International Committee and the Senior American Secretary in Egypt, and Naguib Kelada,[10] Senior Secretary of the Egyptian National Council of the YMCAs of Egypt, arrived in Addis Ababa in early February 1947. They met with Haile Selassie and top-ranking Ethiopian government officials to discuss questions of local leadership. Explaining that the national YMCAs would ultimately have to rely on their own local personnel, the representatives emphasized that, in case of a positive reply to an invitation from the emperor, the World Committee 'would send one or more experienced secretaries to inaugurate the work and train

---

Early Twentieth Centuries', in Harald Fischer-Tiné, Stefan Huebner, and Ian Tyrrell (eds), *Spreading Protestant Modernity: Global Perspectives on the Social Work of the YMCA and YWCA, 1889–1970* (Honolulu, 2020), p. 7.

[9] James K. Quay to Dalton F. McClelland, 6 May 1946, KFYA, Y.USA.9-2-37, YMCA International Work in Ethiopia Box 1, correspondence 1946–49.

[10] Edward Said described him as 'a genial Copt' in his book *Out of Place: A Memoir* (London, 2000), p. 16.

Ethiopian young men to take over the responsibility as secretaries in Ethiopia'.[11] Quay and Kelada also indicated the possibility of using the YMCA Secretarial Training School in Egypt for this purpose. The Egyptian YMCA was supportive in networking and providing leadership training for the first general secretary of the Ethiopian YMCA, who was Egyptian.

However, the project failed, for various reasons, to provide the necessary material support for Ethiopia, especially for building the proper facilities.[12] Due to financial and manpower shortages in Egypt itself, the Ethiopian project was at the point of collapsing. Thus, Egypt approached the World Committee to assign the task of helping develop the work to a secretary from North America.[13] By directly asking the International Committee for support, Egypt could eventually step back as an active party without losing face. In February 1951, a North American secretary commenced his work in Addis Ababa. This shift strengthened the growing cooperation between Ethiopia and the United States (less Canada). It added social work and leadership training to other fields of soft power, such as higher education, in which the United States had been gaining ground during the Cold War. It found its most forceful expression in two general secretaries from the United States as well as in training programmes for local secretaries within and outside Ethiopia along the lines of the those of the International Committee. Even after the appointment of an Ethiopian general secretary in 1967, the influence of the United States remained very strong, and continued even after the downfall of the emperor in 1974.

(Pro)motors of YMCA Sports

The promotion of sports at the Ethiopian YMCA depended to a large extent on its secretaries, their enthusiasm, their training, and the networks they could build inside and outside the country. They often served in various positions and committees at the same time, and facilitated the establishment of the Ethiopian YMCA as a sports hub.

---

[11] Minutes of the First Meeting to Plan the Establishment of a YMCA, Addis Ababa, 8 February 1947, KFYA, Y.USA.9-2-37, YMCA International Work in Ethiopia Box 1, correspondence 1946–49.
[12] The financial issue was intermittently discussed between Addis and Cairo as well as with the World Alliance and the International Committee.
[13] Tracy Strong, World Alliance, to Dalton F. McClelland, 9 August 1949, KFYA, Y.USA.9-2-37, YMCA International Work in Ethiopia Box 1, correspondence 1946–49.

Michel Wassef and the Egyptian Knowledge Transfer

Michel Wassef, the first general secretary, was an Egyptian expatriate in his late twenties and well prepared to promote sports at the 'Y'. From 1942–47, Michel worked as Superintendent of the National Physical Education Programme for the Ethiopian Ministry of Education. He was a graduate of the Higher Institute of Physical Education in Egypt and active in the Egyptian Boy Scout movement. Naguib Kelada described him as a 'normal Coptic youth – more conventional than dynamic; but he has idealism and is strikingly unselfish and serviceable in his attitude',[14] while James K. Quay reported that Michel Wassef was an 'A1 man'.[15]

When his term of service with the Ethiopian government ended, Michel Wassef found himself in a position to join the YMCA staff.[16] He received intensive training at the YMCA in Cairo in early 1948. However, coming back to Addis Ababa to start a YMCA, he was fully aware that this would be a difficult task. 'From the very start he felt at a loss as to whom he could turn to for intelligent co-operation in this creative job, with no budget, no building, and no facilities to help demonstrate its aims and objectives'.[17] However, Michel Wassef managed to raise interest amongst high-ranking Ethiopians, members of the so-called foreign communities, as well as expatriates. Apart from his work as the first YMCA secretary in Ethiopia (1948–51), which he did under the direction of an Ethiopian YMCA board of managers, he also became a member of its physical committee. With Nerses Knadjan, Telahun Zerihun, and K.V. Krishnan, Michel Wassef began to organize sports in a slightly systematic way. By 1950, the Ethiopian YMCA already had volleyball, basketball, and table tennis teams, which later developed into one of the best in the country. The enthusiasm of the table tennis player is clearly visible in Illustration 2. During the early years of its existence, the YMCA also laid the ground work for the institution's fame in chess, organizing 576 tournaments in football, basketball, and table tennis and holding sixteen chess competitions.[18]

When it became clear that the Egyptian YMCA had neither the means nor the capacity to handle the Ethiopian YMCA as a sub-branch, the International Committee increased its engagement. In November 1949, the very energetic and supportive Ethiopian YMCA president, Lieutenant Colonel Tamrat Yegezu, had sent an official request to New

---

[14] Memorandum about the Extension Project into Ethiopia, Naguib Kelada, February 1947, KFYA, Y.USA.9-2-37, YMCA International Work in Ethiopia Box 1, correspondence 1946–49.
[15] James K. Quay to Eugene Barnett, 1 January 1947, p. 2, KFYA, Y.USA.9-2-37, YMCA International Work in Ethiopia Box 1, correspondence 1946–49.
[16] Memorandum About the Extension Project into Ethiopia, N. Kelada, February 1947, KFYA, Y.USA.9-2-37, YMCA International Work in Ethiopia Box 1, correspondence 1946–1949.
[17] Naguib Kelada, 'The Ethiopian Project'.
[18] First Annual Report & Statement of Accounts, 1950.

2. Table tennis at YMCA in the building of the Patriot Association, probably early 1950s, (Kautz Family YMCA Archives, University of Minnesota Libraries, Minneapolis, USA).

York for a North American secretary with experience in boys' work and programme development.[19] The plan was to replace Michel Wassef as general secretary, give him further training in the US, and keep him on as the physical education programme secretary.

Sports Development under a Non-Athletic Fraternal Secretary

The choice fell on Merlin Bishop, who took up his position as general secretary of the Ethiopian YMCA in February 1951. Bishop had gained international experience during his service abroad as a missionary of the Methodist Church in China, where he also became a staff member of the YMCA International Committee in 1945. Holding an MA degree in vocational education from Columbia University, Bishop worked

---

[19] Tamrat Yegezu to Dalton McLealand [sic], 7 November 1949, KFYA, Y.USA.9-2-37, YMCA International Work in Ethiopia Box 1, correspondence 1946–49.

as the principal of an industrial school in China and, later, became a faculty member of the Fukien Christian University. The International Committee recommended him for the post in Ethiopia because he was experienced in administration, group work, and the development of a programme for vocational and industrial training.[20] In August 1951, he arrived in Addis Ababa with his wife and daughter.

Merlin Bishop was never enthusiastic about Michel Wassef's work at the 'Y'. Although acknowledging his achievement in 'introducing the YMCA in Addis', Bishop complained about 'his lack of training and basic understanding of the philosophy, structure and purpose of the YMCA'.[21] Thus, Merlin Bishop seems to have been relieved about Michel Wassef's departure to the US for further training in 1952.[22] There is no indication that he ever returned to Ethiopia.

Sports and physical education did not count amongst the urgent matters that the new general secretary tackled up-front. His own way of life was rather unhealthy; a visitor suggested that 'somebody ought to get Bishop to stop doing so much smoking'.[23] Instead of sports, at the top of his agenda were the new YMCA building, the establishment of vocational training, adult education, and literacy programmes. Most importantly, however, was the development of local leadership. Merlin Bishop trained local secretaries nearly on a daily basis to instil 'team spirit' and an 'understanding of the history, structure of the YMCA and the technique of working with young people'.[24] The first group consisted of men in their twenties with an elite or at least educated family background. Aleme Selassie W. Emanuel, who had commenced work at the Ethiopian YMCA under Michel Wassef, received on-the-job training for the position of programme director.[25] Ewmetu Belay (20 years old),

---

[20] Dalton McClelland to Tamrat Yegezu and Michel Wassef, 21 March 1951, KFYA, Y.USA.9-2-37, YMCA International Work in Ethiopia Box 1, correspondence 1950/51.

[21] Merlin Bishop to Dalton McClelland, 7 October 1951, KFYA, Y.USA.9-2-37, YMCA International Work in Ethiopia Box 1, correspondence 1950/51.

[22] Telegram from Dalton McClelland to Naguib Kelada, 21 December 1951, KFYA, Y.USA.9-2-37, YMCA International Work in Ethiopia Box 1, correspondence 1950/51.

[23] Excerpt from a Memorandum, Emery M. Nelson to Paul B. Anderson, 17 January 1958, KFYA, Y.USA.9-2-37, YMCA International Work in Ethiopia Box 6, correspondence 1958.

[24] Merlin A. Bishop to Eugene Barnett, 22 January 1952, KFYA, Y.USA.9-2-37, YMCA International Work in Ethiopia Box 1, correspondence 1952.

[25] Aleme Selassie W. Emanuel's father, a former government official, had been killed during the Italian occupation. Before he joined the YMCA, Aleme had worked in the Government Office of Press and Information and had been active in raising funds for the Red Cross. Ewmetu Belay's father and two brothers had been killed during the Fascist occupation. He was the only staff member who had a secondary school education, and he was well-versed in Amharic, Arabic,

who had joined the YMCA in 1949, was made responsible for the boys' work, including the Junior Hi-Y, and other boys' groups in schools and on the streets. He also worked as a librarian. Girma Belew (23 years old) became a secretary of religious work and programme development. Ato Selassie (20 years old), who had joined the YMCA in 1950, took responsibility for the athletics programme.[26] In January 1954, the 23-year-old Ato Tenna began to lead the 'Y's' physical activities. He had joined the YMCA four years earlier, and was in his first secondary school year. Apart from directing volleyball on a daily basis, football on Fridays, and softball twice a week, he was also responsible for indoor games such as chess, draughts, and table tennis.[27] In 1954, when 'athletics' (as physical education and sports were called in the reporting language) took the lead in terms of events as well as attendees, systematic organization and development became a priority.

Marvin J. Ludwig and the Hey-Days of YMCA Sports

In order to ease the staffing situation, particularly with regard to athletics, Col. Tamrat Yegezu, the Ethiopian YMCA's president, sent an official request to the National Council of North American YMCAs, asking for an additional man from the US with 'certain skills, such as athletics and boys work training'.[28] In March 1954, the National Council presented seven candidates and singled out Marvin J. Ludwig as 'brilliant and with a background in physical education, but doing Boy's Work'.[29] He had graduated from Ohio Wesleyan University with a BA in physical education and graduate studies in sociology and group work.[30] Ludwig's background in physical educational, his experience as youth director of the YMCA in Marion, Ohio from 1949 to 1954, and the impression that he 'is little bothered by "personal difficulties"',[31] must have recommended him for the post, which he took up in October

---

French, and English. Girma Belew's father was a retired judge killed during the Fascist occupation. Ato Selassie's father worked as treasurer in the Ministry of Finance of Shoa Province. Report Dalton McClelland to Herbert P. Lansdale about his visit to Ethiopia, 13 November 1952, KFYA, Y.USA.9-2-37, YMCA International Work in Ethiopia Box 1, correspondence 1952.

[26] Report Dalton McClelland to Herbert P. Lansdale about his visit to Ethiopia, 13 November 1952.

[27] Dalton McClelland to Herbert P. Lansdale, 18 January 1955, KFYA, Y.USA.9-2-37, YMCA International Work in Ethiopia Box 1, correspondence 1955.

[28] Tamrat Yegezu to Lennig Sweet, 14 February 1955, KFYA, Y.USA.9-2-37, YMCA International Work in Ethiopia Box 1, correspondence 1955.

[29] Lennig Sweet to Merlin Bishop, 7 March 1955, KFYA, Y.USA.9-2-37, YMCA International Work in Ethiopia Box 1, correspondence 1955.

[30] 'YMCA Arat Kilo', Y Blog, www.ymca.8m.net [accessed 15 September 2021].

[31] Lennig Sweet to Merlin Bishop, 27 May 1955, KFYA, Y.USA.9-2-37, YMCA International Work in Ethiopia Box 1, correspondence 1955.

1955. However, running gym classes was not what Marvin Ludwig had come for. 'I want to work with a broad program of leadership training, including gym classes but much, much more. It is to leadership training that I shall give everything I have to give'.[32] In 1956, nineteen young men received special courses in physical education leadership.[33]

Nine months later, Ludwig assumed full responsibility from Merlin Bishop, who went on furlough. At this time, the Ethiopian YMCA had seven full-time secretaries who received daily training in matters such as finance, planning, community organization, and YMCA philosophy. Over 400 volunteer leaders attended courses in practical psychology and community organization as well as 'practical courses in physical education for coaches and leaders'.[34] Marvin Ludwig's physical education and boys' work flourished at the Addis Ababa YMCA. Furthermore, he successfully extended leadership training to the field of sports. In the late 1950s, the YMCA always offered leadership training in physical education with the lowest budget compared to training in programme secretarial issues, boys' work, and rural development. Nevertheless, Ludwig considered the physical education programme to be 'one of the finest, well-rounded programs in any YMCA' precisely because it consisted of 'leadership training courses in health, recreation, physical education and first aid as well as leadership techniques in methods of leadership and courses in officiating'.[35]

Merlin Bishop returned to Ethiopia in 1958 and resumed work in an increasingly difficult political-cum-Cold War environment. The Soviet Union, Yugoslavia, and Czechoslovakia had become very influential amongst the Ethiopian people – especially its youth. In comparison, the Point Four Programs in education, agriculture, and water resource management as well as the activities of the United States Information Service (USIS) were done on a 'modest scale as compared with the Communist countries'.[36]

---

[32] Quoted in Report by Kenneth I. Brown, Executive Director, The Danforth Foundation, 2, KFYA, Y.USA.9-2-37, YMCA International Work in Ethiopia Box 6, correspondence 1961.
[33] Merlin Bishop, Summary Review of Local Situation Section IV, 11, KFYA Y.USA.9-2-37, YMCA International Work in Ethiopia Box 5, correspondence 1958.
[34] The 1958 Participation Report, KFYA, Y.USA.9-2-37, YMCA International Work in Ethiopia Box 5, correspondence 1958.
[35] Marvin Ludwig, End of Term Report, May 1959 through July 1962, KFYA, Y.USA.9-2-37, YMCA International Work in Ethiopia Box 6, correspondence 1962–63.
[36] Merlin Bishop to Emmett Gissenaas (Executive Secretary YMCA, St. Louis), 16 March 1959, KFYA, Y.USA.9-2-37, YMCA International Work in Ethiopia Box 1, correspondence 1959.

In spring 1959, Merlin Bishop was worn out and worried. Although the Ethiopian YMCA was the fastest growing YMCA in the world, its financial situation was desperate to the point of not being able to pay salaries. Whereas YMCA president Col. Tamrat Yegezu had supported fund raising within and outside Ethiopia, a new president, *Balambaras* Mahteme Selassie Wolde Meskel (Minister of Finance), was not really interested in the organization. Bishop was suspicious about intrigues against himself. He no longer received private invitations or audiences with Haile Selassie and his officials, and also feared censorship.[37]

After Bishop resigned in late 1959, Marvin Ludwig became acting YMCA general secretary on 1 January 1960. Attempts to make Aleme Selasse W. Emanuel the first Ethiopian general secretary of the movement failed because he resumed work as general secretary of the Chamber of Commerce.[38] Later in 1960, and amidst the turmoil created by the attempted coup d'état in December of that year,[39] Alan McCann and his wife Grace from Sudbury (Ontario, Canada) arrived in Addis Ababa to commence work as youth secretary. They were apparently not able to establish themselves within the Ethiopian context and were replaced by John 'Jake' Smythe and his wife Betty in 1963.[40] Smythe had graduated with a degree in physical education from Sir George Williams College (Montreal, Canada), worked as the physical director at the Windsor YMCA (Ontario), and was counted amongst the three best physical directors in Canada.[41] Support from the top management of the organization increased again in 1961, when Col. Tamrat Yegezu resumed his earlier position as president of the Ethiopian YMCA.[42]

---

[37] Hugo Cedergreen to Joel Nystrom, 23 April 1959, KFYA, Y.USA.9-2-37, YMCA International Work in Ethiopia Box 1, correspondence 1959.

[38] Marvin Ludwig, End of Term Report, May 1959 through July 1962 KFYA, Y.USA.9-2-37, YMCA International Work in Ethiopia Box 6, correspondence 1962–63.

[39] During the abortive coup d'état on 13 December 1960, the YMCA was slightly damaged, although there is no indication that it was an explicit target. Marvin Ludwig to Joel Nystrom, 22 December 1960, KFYA, Y.USA.9-2-37, YMCA International Work in Ethiopia Box 1, correspondence 1960.

[40] Later, Marvin Ludwig recalled that moving the McCann's from Ethiopia was 'a very tense experience' and 'a trying period for the total YMCA'. End of Term Report, Marvin Ludwig to Joel Nystrom, 15 November 1965, 4, KFYA, Y.USA.9-2-37, YMCA International Work in Ethiopia Box 1, correspondence 1965.

[41] Cody S. Moffat to Marvin Ludwig, 5 June 1963, KFYA, Y.USA.9-2-37, YMCA International Work in Ethiopia Box 6, correspondence 1962–63. Before his deployment to Ethiopia, John Smythe had been president of the Physical Directors Society of Canada and secretary of the Physical Directors Society of North America. In his 1964 Report, Marvin Ludwig wrote very enthusiastically about Smythe's abilities. Marvin Ludwig to Joel Nystrom, 24 March 1964, KFYA, Y.USA.9-2-37, YMCA International Work in Ethiopia Box 1, correspondence 1964.

[42] Marvin Ludwig to Joel Nystrom, 5 June 1961, KFYA, Y.USA.9-2-37, YMCA

In contrast to Merlin Bishop, whose leadership gives the impression of a caring father figure, Marvin Ludwig applied 'persuasively aggressive leadership'.[43] This also included expanding the geographical scope of the movement. While Bishop concentrated on laying sound foundations in the capital, Ludwig conceptualized YMCA work on much broader lines, both within and beyond the empire. His term of office was marked by the spread of the Association into other parts of Ethiopia and Eritrea, where the Asmara YMCA officially opened on 19 November 1960. Fully aware of the Muslim context in which the 'Y' had to operate, Ludwig explicitly asked for the approval of local religious leaders. Due to the lack of facilities, sports did not play the same role as in other branches. The situation changed for the better when the Asmara YMCA opened its own new building in February 1968, which included a tennis court, a volleyball court, and a badminton court. Between 1967 and 1969, the number of sports meets increased from 57 to 125 and attendance rose from 1,785 to 11,810.[44] Such an increase was primarily the result of the enthusiastic work of local staff members and volunteers. When Owen R. Manchester, who had joined the Asmara YMCA in 1968, frankly admitted that he was the weakest in developing physical education leaders because he did not have the personnel skills to do so, the programme committee used their contacts to recruit PE teachers and other volunteers. Thus, the employment of a full-time physical director was high on their agenda.[45]

Similar to operating the YMCA in Muslim majority contexts by including relevant decision makers, Marvin Ludwig also tackled the influence of socialist countries head on. When the Soviet Union built a polytechnical institute with a capacity for 1,500 students in Bahir Dar, Ludwig explicitly declared the city and the local YMCA a 'challenging opportunity for the YMCA'.[46] With the permission of the Ministry of Education (MoE), the YMCA operated clubs at the institute, used classrooms for its activities, and had its office in one of the institute buildings before

---

International Work in Ethiopia Box 6, correspondence 1961. Thus, Ludwig was very disappointed when Smythe did not return from his home leave in 1967 to continue work as fraternal secretary in Asmara, but instead took up an executive position in the Central Branch Toronto. Marvin Ludwig to Joel Nystrom, 5 September 1967, KFYA, Y.USA.9-2-37, YMCA International Work in Ethiopia Box 2, correspondence 1967.
43 Report by Kenneth I. Brown, Executive Director, The Danforth Foundation (retired), 30 August 1961, KFYA, Y.USA.9-2-37, YMCA International Work in Ethiopia Box 6, correspondence 1961.
44 Eleventh Asmara YMCA Annual Report, 1968–69.
45 Owen R. Manchester to Millard Collins, 6 June 1968, KFYA, Y.USA.9-2-37, YMCA International Work in Ethiopia Box 2, correspondence 1968.
46 Marvin Ludwig, End of Term Report, May 1959 through July 1962, KFYA, Y.USA.9-2-37, YMCA International Work in Ethiopia Box 6, correspondence 1962–63.

it opened its own facilities on the shores of Lake Tana in 1965.[47] It is, thus, no wonder that Million Belete, director of the institute, advised its first graduates (1967) to spend their leisure time wisely, for example by 'helping in organisations like the YMCA'.[48] Furthermore, the Bahir Dar YMCA provided staff who were to run the recreation centre of the textile mill, which was managed by Yugoslav expatriates. In anticipation of Bahir Dar's importance in Cold War competition, Marvin Ludwig saw that this is 'the time and it [Bahir Dar] is a strategic location to prove our ability to do the job and do it well. Therefore, we are in the process of recruiting the best men we can find to fill this post'.[49]

With the establishment of three additional YMCA branches in Addis Ababa, fifteen branches in other Ethiopian towns, and one branch in Asmara throughout the 1960s, activities in the field of leadership and physical education diversified and centralized at the same time.[50] On the one hand, they were dictated by the needs and facilities of the respective locality. On the other, YMCA official guidelines still had to be followed. Vacation leadership courses, which were free to all YMCA members, seem to have been very much in demand. The Physical Education Committee, which included well-known sports personalities such as Lakew Yegeletu, Shiferaw Agonifer, and Onni Niskanen, ensured excellent work.[51] Abebe Bikila, the Olympic marathon champion, also worked for the committee and gave instruction to boys as to how they might better develop their physical prowess and to help to see other opportunities in recreation and sports.[52]

---

[47] Marvin Ludwig, Report about Last Four Months, 21 May 1964, KFYA, Y.USA.9-2-37, YMCA International Work in Ethiopia Box 1, correspondence 1964.
[48] 'Word before You Go', *Year Book Polytechnical Institute in Bahr Dar*, 1966–67, 6, IES 373 BAH POL.
[49] Marvin Ludwig to Joel Nystrom, 11 April 1962, KFYA, Y.USA.9-2-37, YMCA International Work in Ethiopia Box 6, correspondence 1962–62.
[50] YMCA branches existed in Addis Ababa (Central with two branches, New Market, Foundation, University), Adigrat, Asmara, Ambo (Student branch), Awassa, Bahir Dar, Debre Birhan, Dire Dawa, Gondar, Harar, Jimma, Wollamo Sodo, Mek'ele, Nekemte, Massawa, Adwa, Jijiga. In 1968, Marvin Ludwig commented that there were more requests for establishing new branches than personnel and financial capacities could meet. Marvin Ludwig to Millard Collins, 6 August 1968, KFYA, Y.USA.9-2-37, YMCA International Work in Ethiopia Box 2, correspondence 1968.
[51] According to the 1961 Annual YMCA Report, the Physical Education Committee consisted of Ato Taye Abate (Physical Education Secretary), Col. Mebratu Fesseha, Yidnek'achew Tesemma, Maj. Admassu Habte Mariam, Capt. Gebeyehu Dubbie, Lakew Yegeletu, Shiferaw Agonafir, Onni Niskanen, J. Velissariou, Megu Malkassian and Mr. Dabbous.
[52] Marvin Ludwig to Erika Stephan, SIGNAL-Verlag Baden-Baden, no date 1962, KFYA, Y.USA.35, Marvin Ludwig papers, Box 4.

In summer 1961, 189 pupils attended ten different courses in physical education, group work, and group dynamics. Short-term evening courses equipped young men who had started to establish Y clubs in rural areas with 'leadership knowledge' in psychology and group dynamics.[53] Participation was certified and celebrated in a 'Leadership Training Award Night'.[54] With regard to physical education, these celebrations included the winners of the intramural sports programme and a sportsmanship award. No doubt, this broad kind of training went far beyond the YMCA staff and member youths to include community leaders and assisted 'in the training of teachers to teach'.[55] In contrast to the organization's successful spread in the empire, Marvin Ludwig's ideas for developing the Addis Ababa YMCA into a broader African or at least East African leadership-training centre were not successful. Counterparts in the International Committee argued that Ethiopia was not African enough.[56]

During the second half of the 1960s, an increasing number of volunteers from the United States and Canada arrived at the Ethiopian YMCAs. They came as World Service workers, as Peace Corps volunteers[57] or, through exchange programmes with North American YMCAs, e.g. the Duncan YMCA. Most of them assisted in the physical education part of leadership courses. In 1967, for example, twelve Peace Corps volunteers worked at several YMCAs in the empire.[58] Since the YMCA provided lodging and meals for the World Service workers, officials in Addis Ababa preferred volunteers from the American Peace Corps, which provided these for their people. In 1973, Fraternal Secretary Lee Houser commented that these men 'cost the Ethiopian Association absolutely nothing', were 'all placed in provincial YMCAs' and

[53] Report by Kenneth I. Brown, Executive Director, The Danforth Foundation, KFYA, Y.USA.9-2-37, YMCA International Work in Ethiopia Box 6, correspondence 1961.
[54] Leadership Training Course, September 1963, KFYA, Y.USA.9-2-37, YMCA International Work in Ethiopia Box 6, correspondence 1963.
[55] Report about the last four months, Marvin Ludwig to Millard Collins, 21 May 1964, p. 4, KFYA, Y.USA.9-2-37, YMCA International Work in Ethiopia Box 1, correspondence 1964 (Janury–June).
[56] I discuss this issue more broadly in Bromber, 'Education for Leadership', pp. 246–47.
[57] The first American Peace Corps volunteers arrived in Ethiopia in 1962. In 1968, four hundred volunteers served in various locations, including the Haile Selassie I University, teacher training colleges, in agricultural and urban development, and as technical or legal assistants in government ministries. The Ethiopian programme was the largest in Africa and one of the largest in the world. Information for the new staff from US, KFYA, Y.USA.9-2-37, YMCA International Work in Ethiopia Box 2, correspondence 1968.
[58] Marvin Ludwig to Millard Collins, 7 August 1967, KFYA, Y.USA.9-2-37, YMCA International Work in Ethiopia Box 2, correspondence 1967.

performed 'very well'. Thus, it became 'a very hard job to sell the World Service workers to the Ethiopian YMCA'.[59]

It goes without saying that official sources, such as administrative reports, often distort the overall picture by foregrounding foreign agency. In 1967, Marvin Ludwig himself reflected on this issue and remarked:

> Many times, while I was on home leave I had the impression that the YMCA Fraternal Secretary was treated and looked upon as some sort of a hero. This is really unfortunate ... The real heroes in this business are men like Ato Desta, Ato Teffera, Ato Yehdego, Ato Teklehaimanot, Asmara YMCA, Ato Mengisha, Dire Dawa YMCA and the other one-man-shows – the guys that are lone rangers, the dedicated pioneers who are challenged to work out of traditional patterns and customs to build their own culture. These are the men who seem to go unrecognised, unsung and yet they are the very persons who are making World Service what it is.[60]

In September 1967, one of the above-mentioned heroes assumed leadership of the Ethiopian YMCA.

Desta Girma: Sports under the Ethiopian Secretarial Leadership

Following a decision already made in 1963, Desta Girma became the first Ethiopian general secretary.[61] In order to guarantee a smooth transition, including the further use of his networks at institutions such as the Ethiopian Sports Confederation, the School of Social Work at the University College or the Rotary Club,[62] Ludwig continued as fraternal secretary until 1969.[63]

---

[59] Lee Houser to Cody S. Moffat, 23 January 1973, KFYA, Y.USA.9-2-37, YMCA International Work in Ethiopia Box 3, correspondence 1973. According to Norris Lineweaver, in the late 1960s a World Service worker was compensated $50 per month paid by the US YMCA International Committee whereas Peace Corps Volunteers were receiving $250 per month paid by the US government. Neither was a cost to the Ethiopian YMCA (e-mail conversation Norris Lineweaver, 8 January 2020).

[60] YMCA of Ethiopia, no date, KFYA, Y.USA.9-2-37, YMCA International Work in Ethiopia Box 2, correspondence 1967.

[61] Marvin Ludwig to Joel Nystrom, 16 August 1963, Y.USA.9-2-37, KFYA, YMCA International Work in Ethiopia Box 6, correspondence 1962–63.

[62] In 1963, Marvin Ludwig served as board member of the School of Social Work at the University College, at the Social Service Society, the Society of the Disabled, and the Rotary Club in Addis Ababa. He was a member of the Ethiopian Sports Confederation and president of the National Basketball Federation for Ethiopia. Marvin Ludwig, End of Term Report, May 1959 through July 1962, Organizational Chart, KFYA, Y.USA.9-2-37, YMCA International Work in Ethiopia Box 6, correspondence 1962–63.

[63] In 1965, Marvin Ludwig had raised doubts about his further presence at the Ethiopian YMCA, since this might split the loyalties of staff and laymen. End

Born in 1936 in the town of Dessie, Desta had attended the prestigious Tafari Makonnen School in Addis Ababa. He studied at the Commercial College and, later, worked for the MoE. Desta became an enthusiastic member of the 'Y'. Starting as a layman in physical education, he became a staff member in 1957. Between 1960 and 1967, he spent longer periods at YMCA training institutions in the United States. His training abroad began in September 1960 with an International Visitation Fellowship at the YMCA in Middleton, Ohio. During his stay, Desta Girma inquired about studying for a degree at Springfield (Massachusetts) or Sir George Williams College (Wisconsin). Despite his experience in physical education – Desta was secretary of the Ethiopian Basketball Federation and captain of the very successful YMCA basketball team – the general secretary of the Middleton 'Y' advised him to go to Sir George Williams College with its focus on community and boys work, which he did between July 1963 and June 1966.[64] In the eyes of the North American fraternal secretaries in Ethiopia as well as the Ethiopian staff members, Desta had become the 'shining light' of the movement and an able man who had 'the poise and the rapport to deal with the Board of Management'.[65]

Numerous correspondences and reports testify that Desta Girma had fulfilled the high hopes invested in his abilities. Thus, it might not come as a surprise that Marvin Ludwig was deeply concerned when Desta Girma was appointed General Manager of Rehabilitation Agencies for the Disabled under the Ministry of Community Development in 1972. This decision, which would leave him working only half-time for the YMCA until another qualified person could fill the position of general secretary, was unacceptable to the YMCA board and hard to bear for Desta Girma himself. Thus, after a personal conversation, Marvin Ludwig proposed taking Desta out of Ethiopia, either for further training in the US or to work within a World Alliance or International Division staff position.[66]

In July 1968, the headquarters of the International Committee in New York asked Marvin Ludwig and his family to finish his work in Ethiopia and to return to the United States. His extensive correspondence with of the International Committee reveals his great concern about the further development of the Ethiopian YMCA, but also his

---

of Term Report, Marvin Ludwig to Joel Nystrom, 15 November 1965, 4, KFYA, Y.USA.9-2-37, YMCA International Work in Ethiopia Box 1, correspondence 1965.
[64] Ralph S. Knight to Garrett B. Douwsma, 17 October 1960, Personal File Desta Girma, KFYA, Y.USA.35, International Visitation Fellowship/Fellowship Training Program, Reports 1948–71, Box 2.
[65] Annual Administrative Report, Marvin Ludwig to Joel Nystrom, 28 July 1966, KFYA, Y.USA.9-2-37, YMCA International Work in Ethiopia Box 1, correspondence.
[66] Marvin Ludwig, Confidential Report, 26 March 1973, KFYA, Y.USA.9-2-37, YMCA International Work in Ethiopia Box 4, correspondence 1970–71.

conviction that the movement stood on firm ground. With regard to sports in general, Ludwig strongly advised additional involvement of the YMCA in the national confederation. Concerning basketball in particular, he recommended including the military in the organization of tournaments as well as in the training of PE leadership and coaching.[67] After his return to North America, where he took up the position of the associate executive director of the International Division of YMCAs in New York, Ludwig maintained close contact with the Ethiopian YMCA. Regular correspondence with Jarso Desta, physical education director of YMCA Ethiopia, kept him up to date on the further development of sports, especially the national federations operated by the YMCA.

Given his engagement in sports at the Ethiopian 'Y', Ludwig's absence might have created difficulties for the YMCA in continuing to fulfil the role it had achieved in physical education and the systematic training of local personnel in that field. In 1970, Jarso Desta openly spoke about weaknesses in the physical education department and asked the International Committee for support by a fraternal secretary. The choice fell on Lee Houser, who had already worked for twenty-two years as a YMCA director in several towns in the US.[68] He counted sports amongst the most important issues and highlighted the improvement of 'youth and physical education at Addis Ababa central branch' in his action plan for 1972. However, his relations to YMCA staff and committee members were described as strained. The already mentioned Aberra Jembere, who had made an impressive career as a lawyer and high-ranking administrator and served as chairman of the YMCA reorganization and policy study committee, complained that Lee Houser 'did not credit other staff members'.[69]

In 1970, Jarso Desta was selected for further training in the US. There was an agreement with both Springfield and Sir George Williams College that he should first complete undergraduate studies at Haile

---

[67] Future Concerns and Plan, 26 August 1968, KFYA, Y.USA.9-2-37, YMCA International Work in Ethiopia Box 2, correspondence 1968.

[68] Lee Houser had worked as a director in Columbus (Ohio) and Sacramento (California). An International Committee of YMCAs' Project for U.S. Partnership Support, Ethiopia, March 1972, KFYA, Y.USA.9-2-37, YMCA International Work in Ethiopia Box 3, correspondence 1972.

[69] Marvin Ludwig, Confidential Report, Conversation with Desta Girma, 26 March 1973, KFYA, Y.USA.9-2-37, YMCA International Work in Ethiopia Box 4, correspondence 1970–71. After a conversation with Lee Houser, Marvin Ludwig was concerned about what Houser 'is really achieving and fulfilling for the Ethiopian YMCA'. Marvin Ludwig, Confidential Report, Conversation with Lee Houser, 23 March 1973, KFYA, Y.USA.9-2-37, YMCA International Work in Ethiopia Box 4, correspondence 1970–71. For an extensive account of Aberra Jembere's life, see Jon Abbink, 'In memoriam Aberra Jembere (1928–2004)', *Aethiopica*, 7 (2004), 190.

Selassie I University (HSIU).[70] However, his first training took place as a six month exchange programme between the Dayton (Ohio) and the Ethiopian YMCAs.[71] Apart from improving his skills in administration, staff training, coaching, and organization of tournaments, the training objectives included 'the study of U.S. culture and the role of the Y.M.C.A. in it'.[72] In 1972–73, Jarso Desta completed two years of education at Sir George Williams College.[73]

Since Asmara had become the second most important YMCA within the empire, its general secretary, Menghisteab Teklehaimanot, received training at several YMCAs in Canada and the United States.[74] In the first half of the 1970s, Asmara YMCA Programme and Physical Education Secretary Mengesha Beyene also attended courses in the United States of between two months and two years. Applicants from YMCAs in smaller Ethiopian towns rarely had the chance to train abroad. Furthermore, earlier ideas about using possibilities in India did not materialize since 'going to India for study does not have the prestige that one would have returning from the United States or England. There is a strong feeling among Ethiopians that they are as much advanced as India'.[75] Thus, the close relationship between the Ethiopian and the North American YMCAs as well as the high prestige of degrees from the United States seem to have left no room for training institutions in other countries.

The fundamental changes in Ethiopia in 1974 also affected the YMCA. Earlier plans for getting general secretary Desta Girma out of the country were implemented by giving him a post in the International Division of YMCAs in New York. Tsegaw Ayele, executive secretary of the Addis Ababa Central Branch and formerly assistant general secretary, took up the position of national general secretary. Since he never had the in-depth secretarial training that Desta Girma had received in the US, Tsegaw was overwhelmed and very much felt left alone when fraternal secretary Lee Houser also announced his final return to the US

[70] Marvin Ludwig to Desta Girma, 10 February 10, 1970, KFYA, Y.USA.9-2-37, YMCA International Work in Ethiopia Box 4, correspondence 1970–71.
[71] Dayton YMCA Physical Director Luis Cox came to Addis Ababa during Jarso Desta's absence.
[72] Cal Sutliff to Desta Girma, 11 February 1971. KFYA, Y.USA.9-2-37, YMCA International Work in Ethiopia Box 4, correspondence 1970–71. Luis Cox had no such 'cultural' training in his schedule.
[73] Correspondence between Jarso Desta and Marvin Ludwig KFYA, Y.USA.9-2-37, YMCA International Work in Ethiopia Box 3; Correspondence with Marvin Ludwig 1970–73.
[74] Fellowship Training Program, no date, Personal File Teklehaimanot Menghisteab, KFYA, Y.USA.35, International Visitation Fellowship/Fellowship Training Program, Reports 1948–71, Box 2.
[75] Merlin A. Bishop to Lennig Sweet, 9 April 1955, KFYA, Y.USA.9-2-37, YMCA International Work in Ethiopia Box 1, correspondence 1955.

as of July 1974.[76] Even the explicit protest of the Ethiopian YMCA Vice President Dr. Emanuel Gebre Selassie[77] against this step did not change the situation to the better. Apologies from the International Division referred to problems in financing work abroad. Even the election of the Ethiopian YMCA president *Lij* Endalkachew Makonnen[78] as the president of the World Alliance of YMCAs, i.e. the highest position on the international level, did not ease the situation on the ground, especially with a shortage of administrative staff and the organization of the YMCA drought relief programme in Wollo province. In a conversation with the International Division about sending a young professional YMCA 'director' from North America to work in Dessie (Wollo province), Tsegaw Ayele also expressed his hopes that 'this person should have physical education skills'.[79]

Leadership in Transition

Documents are silent as to whether such a person ever arrived in Ethiopia at the time when the Ethiopian revolution turned violent and the YMCA was hit at the international level, when *Lij* Endalkachew Makonnen was detained and executed along with fifty-nine other high-ranking officials on 24 November 1974. What archival sources reveal is that the YMCA was not immediately dismantled, because it had always given 'service to the needy and the masses in general', as the Dire Dawa town officer expressed it, and was, thus, in line with

---

[76] Tsegaw Ayele to Frank Kiehne (Executive Director International Division), 7 March 1974, KFYA, Y.USA.9-2-37, YMCA International Work in Ethiopia Box 3, correspondence 1974. Tsegaw also expressed bitter feelings of being left alone in the face of the revolution and its aftermath in an interview (interview, Addis Ababa, 22 June 2011).

[77] The YMCA president also complained that the International Division had taken Desta Girma away from the Ethiopian YMCA. Emanuel Gebre Selassie to Frank Kiehne, 21 May 1974, KFYA, Y.USA.9-2-37, YMCA International Work in Ethiopia Box 3, correspondence 1974.

[78] Eldelkachew Makonnen (1926–74) belonged to an important aristocratic family. He studied in Oxford and, after his return to Ethiopia, worked in the highest governmental and diplomatic positions. He represented Ethiopia at the Bandung Conference (1955) and Suez Conference (1956). From 1966 to 1968, Endelkachew Makonnen was Ethiopia's Representative at the United Nations. Because of his remarkable abilities as a diplomat, he was suggested as a possible candidate for the position of the UN Secretary General. In February 1974, Endelkachew Makonnen was appointed Prime Minister. He was executed in November of the same year (Seltene Seyoum, 'Ǝndalkaččäw Mäkʷännlkaččäw Mäkakonnen (1926–74)', *Encyclopaedia Aethiopica*, 2 (Wiesbaden, 2005), pp. 296–7).

[79] Frank Kiehne, Memorandum of Record on Conference with Tsegaw Ayele on 18 July 1974, 4 September 1974, KFYA, Y.USA.9-2-37, YMCA International Work in Ethiopia Box 3, correspondence 1974.

the Ethio-Socialist approach.[80] It also continued to cooperate with the International Division and tried to raise the finances for running well-established programmes when nationalization of local enterprises reduced the possibilities for fund raising. The National Council's appeal to the Member Movements of 1975 explicitly stated that sports had been the most popular activity of the YMCA. Through its systematic training programmes, 80–100 per cent of the members of national basketball, volleyball, and table tennis teams came from the Ethiopian YMCA. In order to continue with these and other sports such as karate, judo, boxing, weightlifting, trampoline, and swimming, the Association asked for financial help to meet the 58,524 Eth$ (equivalent to 29,262 US$ at the time) budgeted for 1975.[81]

From 1976 onwards, the Ethiopian YMCA was no longer allowed to approach local companies for donations and, thus, had to use its financial reserves. In contrast, the military government paid and, in fact, increased the salaries of the YMCA staff from 1975 onwards.[82] Although the YMCA was fully functioning at the time, its transition into the new structures of the Ethiopian government had already started. In the field of sports, 'the Permanent Secretary of the Ministry of Youth, Culture, and Sports was brought up in the Y.M.C.A'.[83] In 1976, Tsegaw Ayele took up the position of Deputy Commissioner of Sports within the Ethiopian government. Kifle Wolde Mariam became YMCA national general secretary and Emmanuel Gebre Selassie remained in his position as its president. Following a meeting between the YMCA Board and the President of the Provisional Military Government in 1977, the Ministry of Culture and Sports was instructed to study the possibility of including the YMCA into its budget.[84] Despite all local attempts and the substantial financial help of the international YMCA community, the Ethiopian YMCA could not continue. On 12 September 1977, Kifle Wolde Mariam had to inform the World Alliance that the Ethiopian YMCA had been nationalized. After a five-

[80] Provisional Military Government of Ethiopia, Municipality of Dire Dawa, 4 June 1975, KFYA, Y.USA.9-2-37, YMCA International Work in Ethiopia Box 4, correspondence 1975.
[81] Tsegaw Ayele, Ethiopian YMCA, National Council Appeal to Member Movements, August 1975, KFYA, Y.USA.9-2-37, YMCA International Work in Ethiopia Box 4, correspondence 1975. In the 1960s, 1 Eth$ / Birr equalled US$ 0.40. At that time, a sub-professional civil servant received a monthly salary between 75 and 525 Eth$.
[82] Visitation Report #4, Frank C. Kiehne, African Trip, Addis, Ethiopia, 24-25 November 1975, KFYA, Y.USA.9-2-37, YMCA International Work in Ethiopia Box 4, correspondence 1975.
[83] Ibid.
[84] Field Report by Daniel Tyler, Liaison Representative in East Africa, to Ethiopia, 24–30 January 1977, KFYA, Y.USA.9-2-37, YMCA International Work in Ethiopia Box 4, correspondence 1976–77.

day visit of the World Alliance, staff member Ofori Akyea reported not only on possible reasons for this step, but also that the YMCA's main components had been integrated into the respective ministries. Thus, all sports and recreational programmes were continued under the Sports Commission of the Ministry of Culture and Sports.[85]

The Ethiopian YMCAs as Athletic Hot Spots

Sports Programmes and Facilities

Before the inauguration of the new YMCA building in Arat Kilo in May 1955, the facilities had not allowed for much systematic promotion of sports. The Association's headquarters were located in a small government-owned building. It formerly belonged to the Patriot Association with an office for the general secretary and a main room measuring twenty by sixty feet that served as a meeting place, library, and recreational centre.[86] Obviously, such a place did not attract the initial main target group (bank clerks and low-level government officials) because of the lack of facilities, which according to Merlin Bishop 'give them a FACE which is very important here'.[87] With physical training as one of the major emphases of the YMCA's philosophy, but limited spaces available in the first Ethiopian branch, the Addis Ababa YMCA needed help broadening its range of sports beyond basketball, hiking, and table tennis. In 1950, it came from the Ethiopian Athletic Association, which sponsored tennis and football.[88] The overall situation did not change much until the YMCA had its own building. The emperor had already granted land in Arat Kilo quarter. Raising the necessary funds and organizing the construction of the new headquarters became one of Bishop's main pre-occupations over the next four years until its inauguration on 5 May 1955.[89]

---

[85] Hector Caselli to Members of the Executive Committee, National General Secretaries, 7 October 1977, KFYA, Y.USA.9-2-37, YMCA International Work in Ethiopia Box 4, correspondence 1976–77.

[86] W.H. Denison, 'Expansion of the Y.M.C.A work in Ethiopia (report)', May 1950, KFYA Y.USA.9-2-37, YMCA International Work in Ethiopia Box 1, correspondence 1950–51, 4.

[87] Merlin Bishop to Dalton McClelland, 7 October 1951, KFYA, Y.USA.9-2-37, YMCA International Work in Ethiopia Box 1, correspondence 1951–52; (capitalized) emphasis in the original.

[88] Questionnaire (Progress 1951), KFYA, Y.USA.9-2-37, YMCA International Work in Ethiopia Box 1, correspondence 1951–52.

[89] The new building was to a large part financed by the International Committee, i.e. North America. Smaller sums came from Egypt, Geneva, and Ethiopia itself.

Although the strategic location of the building was opposite the University College and near secondary schools that also had sports facilities, the largest share of activities took place inside the YMCA compound, but with external help.[90] According to the 1955 report,

> organized classes were developed in Fencing, Boxing, Wrestling, Tumbling, Body-Building, Judo, Basketball, and Volleyball. In addition to organized classes we have teams in Softball, Football, Weight Lifting, Shot-Put and Discus Throwing. This has been possible because of the large number of laymen who have given their time and experience for developing these phases of our program. Laymen helping in these programs are Dutch, French, English, Greek, Ethiopian, American, Canadian and Armenian. Regular classes of instruction are being held for most of these athletics, where theory is taught and principles of good sportsmanship are discussed. These are put into practice in the actual playing sessions of each group.[91]

From 1956 onwards, annual reports distinguished between physical education/athletic/gymnastics classes or programmes (*yesewinet matenkerīya timhirt/yeatlētīk program/jīmnastīkina liyu liyu sport*) and athletic events (*yesport agelgilot*), team events (*yesport budin zigijitoch*), and games for strengthening the body (*yesewinet mat'enkerīya chewatawoch*). Programme schedules indicate systematic training in technical disciplines. From 1957 onwards, various YMCA teams entered local and national competitions. Despite them not being very successful at the beginning, they earned themselves a good reputation for 'sportsmanship' and 'clean play'. Whereas the prime interest of the YMCA secretaries lay in social and moral conduct, they were also keen to know why approximately three thousand young sports enthusiasts showed interest in YMCA physical education activities. A certain Zegeya Getachew, for example, felt that there was 'much difference in [himself] physically',[92] since he had joined the organization. Being a great sports enthusiast in general, he singled out the bodybuilding club, which already included twenty-five athletes in 1956. He hoped that the YMCA club would be the champion in the city.

---

[90] However, the 1956 report highlighted that the Addis Ababa YMCA owned a playing ground, but had no access to the other forty-one in the city. It could use only one of the six football fields. Apart from its own basketball court, YMCA members could use two additional facilities. The cricket field, the nine tennis courts, as well as the only swimming pool in town were out of reach: Merlin Bishop, Study on the Community and the Needs of Youth, KFYA, Y.USA.9-2-37, YMCA International Work in Ethiopia Box 5, correspondence 1958.

[91] Report 1955 to International Committee, KFYA, Y.USA.9-2-37, YMCA International Work in Ethiopia Box 1, correspondence 1951–52.

[92] Marvin Ludwig to Herbert P. Lansdale, 25 August 1956, KFYA, Y.USA.9-2-37, YMCA International Work in Ethiopia Box 1, correspondence 1956.

Furthermore, due to the sheer number of sports activities resulting from an explicit sports-for-all policy – 'many young men enjoy the regular Friday evening open hour in the gym which consists of wrestling, boxing, trampoline and basketball'[93] – more money was allocated to sports in the overall budget. Summer vacation schedules and monthly programmes indicate a great variety of sports practised at the 'Y' as well as a systematic approach to physical education. The Business Men's Club classes offered activities that were 'both instructional and recreational' as well as 'special skill classes'. Every club member had to attend a course in 'general physical education'.[94] Participation in such activities was reserved for members only. With membership fees of 15 Eth$ for adults and 2.50 Eth$ for students in 1959, the YMCA gyms were out of reach to most young men in the capital.[95] The same holds true for Asmara, where the second YMCA branch opened in 1960. During his visit, Marvin Ludwig noticed the existence of many private sports clubs in the Eritrean capital as well as a 'greater interest in sports and games than ... in Addis Ababa', but also their limited accessibility. He concluded that the 'first emphasis in Y.M.C.A. work should be towards group work and club development'.[96]

Access to YMCA Sports

The question of access to the 'Y' became a recurrent issue. Merlin Bishop argued as early as 1951 that 'boys who are wandering in the streets homeless cannot pay the membership fee but they desperately need the YMCA'.[97] From 1954 onwards, some of them participated in the work of 'unorganized clubs'[98] or detached work programmes. However, systematic initiatives finally began in 1967. Operation Better Boys – a detached youth work project launched in Addis Ababa

---

[93] Marvin Ludwig to Joel Nystrom, 9 June 1958, KFYA Y.USA.9-2-37, YMCA International Work in Ethiopia Box 1, correspondence 1958. Only adult education and literacy courses received a higher budget.
[94] This description appeared regularly on advertisements for the Summer Program and monthly schedules. See for example Summer Program Schedule 1960, KFYA, Y.USA.9-2-37, YMCA International Work in Ethiopia Box 1, correspondence 1960.
[95] For monetary comparisons fn. 81. In the late 1960s, youth could apply to through YMCA secretaries for a scholarship membership. Young Men's Christian Association. Vacation Program 1968, IES 267.3YOU.
[96] Marvin Ludwig to Joel Nystrom, 17 September 1960, KFYA, Y.USA.9-2-37, YMCA International Work in Ethiopia Box 1, correspondence 1960.
[97] Merlin Bishop to Dalton McClelland, 7 October 1951, 3; KFYA, Y.USA.9-2-37, YMCA International Work in Ethiopia Box 1, correspondence 1951–52; emphasis in the original.
[98] Draft letter Merlin Bishop, summer 1954, KFYA, Y.USA.9-2-37, YMCA International Work in Ethiopia Box 1, correspondence 1953–54.

– targeted street children and communities in three neighbourhoods with the primary aim of reducing juvenile delinquency.[99] The programme designed 'organized recreation', including sports, i.e. football, as antidotes to 'aimless, antisocial activities'.[100] This, of course, did not automatically mean that these youths had access to the YMCA gyms or became members of the sports teams. Sports rather had a utilitarian function of keeping street children busy, or even a 'clandestine purpose' of saving them from deportation to Shola camps outside Addis Ababa to which beggars and vagrants were customarily deported to keep Addis 'clean' during state visits.[101] Norris D. Lineweaver, a World Service worker who, amongst other important projects, co-organized Operation Better Boys, remembered:

> In a meeting with our detached worker team, we mapped a strategy to organize 'sand lot' football games to give the homeless boys a break from the corners targeting the three areas we were known to be. We took nice soccer balls and makeshift goals to these locations. We had colored over shirts to make them look like organized teams. Homeless boys never had sanctioned equipment to play with. They improvised make believe balls with scrap material when on their own. During the sweeps, the police ignored our participants (spectators and team players) and they were saved from imprisonment at 'detention camps' from which frequently, the homeless never returned.[102]

Sports also served the purpose of outreach to the community. One prominent example was the YMCA centre at Ambo. There, the Association organized an annual parents' field day; i.e. an annual track and field meet combined with basketball and volleyball matches for the community.[103] In Addis Ababa, a mobile YMCA operated on playing grounds provided by the municipality to expand its sports activities in the capital from 1965 onwards.[104]

---

[99] For an extensive discussion of 'Operation Better Boys' see Bromber, 'Make Them Better Citizens', 35–9.
[100] Asfaha Bemnet and Norris D. Lineweaver, no date, Operation Better Boys. A Detached Youth Work Project, 7, KFYA, Y.USA.35, Marvin Ludwig papers, Box 5.
[101] The fact that YMCA documents did not mention the camp at all does not mean the absence of critical voices or action to prevent the deportation of street children.
[102] E-mail conversation with Norris D. Lineweaver, 4 September 2017.
[103] Report about last four months, Marvin Ludwig to Millard Collins, 21 May 1964, KFYA, Y.USA.9-2-37, YMCA International Work in Ethiopia Box 1, correspondence 1964.
[104] Annual Administrative Report, Marvin Ludwig to Joel Nystrom, 16 November 1965, KFYA, Y.USA.9-2-37, YMCA International Work in Ethiopia Box 1, correspondence 1965.

The sheer number of young sports enthusiasts might have caused access to be strictly regulated. When Dennis Brown, retired director of the Danforth Foundation, visited the Addis Ababa YMCA in 1961, he reported that the small gym was so crowded that 'there was scarcely any room to move. During the rainy season the auditorium when not needed for large meetings, houses a series of ping pong tables, and [he] saw vigorous and acrobatic ping pong that recalled memories of Wimbledon tennis'.[105]

Whereas the YMCA restricted its sports facilities to young males with membership, it extended its activities to girls of elementary and high school levels and young women who exercised in separate physical education classes from the early 1960s onwards. Furthermore, YMCA sports reached out to handicapped people with a special programme implemented at the Kolfe Rehabilitation Centre.[106]

With the growing number of technical disciplines (e.g. boxing, weight lifting, and wrestling), participation in national tournaments, and even sponsoring of sports leagues (e.g. softball), sports equipment became an urgent issue. Marvin Ludwig used diverse channels and networks to provide the YMCA teams and others[107] with dresses and equipment. In Asmara, for example, he made sure that Kagnew Station, a US military outpost, provided help in kind, including table tennis and game tables.[108] For the first YMCA Boxing Championships in 1960, Ludwig ordered not only gloves and sportswear but also satin jackets in scarlet and white for the champions.[109] As a highlight, he organized a show of young men from the American Olympic Boxing Team on a cultural tour throughout Africa, which also served to generate additional income.[110] Donations from various YMCAs in the US and Canada in the 1960s and 1970s provided equipment for basketball, boxing, weight lifting, and table tennis.

[105] Report by Kenneth I. Brown, Executive Director, The Danforth Foundation (retired), 30 August 1961, KFYA, Y.USA.9-2-37, YMCA International Work in Ethiopia Box 6, correspondence 1961.
[106] Marvin Ludwig, End of Term Report, May 1959 through July 1962, KFYA, Y.USA.9-2-37, YMCA International Work in Ethiopia Box 6, correspondence 1962–63.
[107] In 1960, for example, he ordered uniforms for the Olympiacos basketball team through the International Committee that reached Addis Ababa through the US Military Advisory Assistance Group to Ethiopia. Marvin Ludwig to Charles Lewis, 25 June 1960 KFYA, Y.USA.9-2-37, YMCA International Work in Ethiopia Box 1, correspondence 1960.
[108] Marvin Ludwig to Joel Nystrom, 17 September 1960, KFYA, Y.USA.9-2-37, YMCA International Work in Ethiopia Box 1, correspondence 1960.
[109] Marvin Ludwig to Alma Dughi, 16 March 1960, KFYA, Y.USA.9-2-37, YMCA International Work in Ethiopia Box 1, correspondence 1960.
[110] Marvin Ludwig to Joel Nystrom, 5 June 1961, KFYA, Y.USA.9-2-37, YMCA International Work in Ethiopia Box 6, correspondence 1961.

Reaching the Next Level

By the early 1960s, the importance of the Ethiopian YMCA for sports had reached the national level. It participated in organizing and preparing national teams and operated the National Table Tennis Federation, the Boxing Federation,[111] the National Volleyball Federation, and the National Basketball Federation for Ethiopia.[112] In his capacity as the president of the National Basketball Federation, Marvin Ludwig became the motor behind re-writing its rules and regulations and, more importantly, establishing a policy for a competitive basketball programme.[113] Reports on YMCA branches in other cities confirm the existence of basketball and volleyball teams, which allowed intra-YMCA competitions. Often, Marvin Ludwig gave extra lessons and training in these branches in order to make the YMCA team the national champion.[114] Through the already mentioned skills classes for volleyball, basketball, tetherball, weight training, wrestling, boxing, badminton, lawn tennis, and table tennis, YMCA athletes improved their level of performance within the national leagues.[115]

In the early 1970s, Ethiopian YMCA athletes and teams started to go abroad.[116] In October 1971, for example, a table tennis team of five players consisting entirely of YMCA athletes and lead by Jarso Desta[117] went to China in order to participate in the Afro-Asian Table Tennis Tournament. They had won in a nationwide competition with

---

[111] The Ethiopian YMCA Progress 1969, KFYA, Y.USA.35, Marvin Ludwig papers, Box 4.
[112] Marvin Ludwig, End of Term Report, May 1959 through July 1962, KFYA, Y.USA.9-2-37, YMCA International Work in Ethiopia Box 6, correspondence 1962–63.
[113] Ludwig to Alma Dughi, 21 April 1964, and Alma Dughi to Marvin Ludwig, 28 April 1964, KFYA Y.USA.9-2-37, YMCA International Work in Ethiopia Box 1, correspondence 1964.
[114] 'The Basketball season has begun here so that this has kept me going some extra time in the evenings, the YMCA should be the national Champs again'. Marvin Ludwig to Millard Collins, 31 January 1968, KFYA, Y.USA.9-2-37, YMCA International Work in Ethiopia Box 2, correspondence 1968.
[115] YMCA of Ethiopia, no date, KFYA, Y.USA.9-2-37, YMCA International Work in Ethiopia Box 2, correspondence 1967.
[116] In 1973, the YMCA basketball team went to Nairobi and placed first in a tournament against the Kenya National Team and the All-Star Team, which consisted of the settlers. Ludwig to Jarso Desta, 11 September 1970, KFYA, Y.USA.9-2-37, YMCA International Work in Ethiopia Box 3, correspondence with Marvin Ludwig 1970–73.
[117] Personal conversation with Jarso Desta, 25 August 2021.

243 participants[118] and hoped to see 'up to date table tennis skills'.[119] The visit happened exactly as table tennis had become a diplomatic door-opener in Sino-American relations (Ping-pong diplomacy). For Marvin Ludwig, such an invitation was proof of the YMCA's importance in setting up the Nation Table Tennis Federation and establishing a nation-wide competition.[120]

Beyond Sports Proper

Apart from sports as a physical activity, the YMCA also became a hot spot for chess enthusiasts. From the early 1950s onwards, beginners and advanced players met three times a week for training. In addition to these regular chess meetings and in-house tournaments, talented players received intensive training in chess classes during the summer vacation programmes at Addis Ababa Central Branch in Arat Kilo. The close proximity to the Jolly Bar – one of the famous places to compete against local chess masters – offered direct possibilities for testing YMCA talent outside the associational frame. Chess had a long tradition in Ethiopia and a local style known as *shent'erej* developed. According to Richard Pankhurst, this variant was 'virtually dead' at the time when YMCA players enjoyed the game at Jolly Bar, Gennet Hotel, and other places in the capital.[121]

Furthermore, hiking and camping had become an important YMCA activity. It started in Asmara in 1963, but began fully developing around Lake Lagano from 1967 onwards. Integrated into the YMCA programme, the camp was to develop into 'a place where boys of our nation [Ethiopia] can grow into manhood in a wholesome outdoor setting'.[122] Amongst the physical activities, boys learned swimming, water safety, and reed boat handling.[123] The programme built on

---

[118] An International Committee of YMCAs' Project for U.S. Partnership Support, Ethiopia, March 1972, KFYA, Y.USA.9-2-37, YMCA International Work in Ethiopia Box 3, correspondence 1972.
[119] Jarso Desta to Marvin Ludwig, 14 October 1971, KFYA, Y.USA.9-2-37, YMCA International Work in Ethiopia Box 3, correspondence with Marvin Ludwig 1970–73.
[120] Marvin Ludwig to Desta Girma, 1 November 1971, KFYA, Y.USA.9-2-37, YMCA International Work in Ethiopia Box 3, correspondence with Marvin Ludwig 1970–73.
[121] Richard Pankhurst, 'History and Principles of Ethiopian Chess', *Journal of Ethiopian Studies*, 9:2 (1971), 170.
[122] Special Report, Camp Langano, 3 May 1971 and 12 May 1971, KFYA, Y.USA.9-2-37, YMCA International Work in Ethiopia Box 3, correspondence with Marvin Ludwig 1970–73.
[123] According to Alemayehu Kidanu, president of the Asmara YMCA, swimming classes were also part of the physical education programme, making it a rare exception within the overall PE programme of the Ethiopian YMCA.

3. Norris Lineweaver (World Service worker) with a group of children at the YMCA Sahle Selassie Camp, late 1960s (Kautz Family YMCA Archives, University of Minnesota Libraries, Minneapolis, USA).

the initiative of the American Peace Corps volunteer Philipp Lilienthal, who had already set up a camp on the northern shores of Lake Langano in 1966.[124] Through close cooperation between YMCA Managing Board members (first of all Desta Girma), the emperor, who granted the land, Princess Mahts'ente Gebre Mariam (wife of the late Prince Sahle Selassie), and others,[125] the YMCA was able to establish a permanent camp on the southern shores two years later.

Apart from its outdoor activities for boys, the Sahle Selassie camp, as it was now called, became another site for leadership training, with the result that Seyoum Habte became the camp director in 1968 and the camp came to be fully run 'by qualified and concerned YMCA youth

---

Alemayehu Kidanu to International Committee 20 September 1973, KFYA, Y.USA.9-2-37, YMCA International Work in Ethiopia Box 3, correspondence 1973.
[124] In line with general rhetoric about the enlightenment of the imperial family, the *Ethiopian Herald* emphasized that the camp was set up at 'the suggestion and encouragement of Princess Seble Desta': 'All Men Once Were Campers', *Ethiopian Herald*, 28 May 1969, 3.
[125] The *Ethiopian Herald*'s article mentions the Ministry of National Community Development, the Imperial Ethiopian Armed Forces, Mobil Oil, Darmar Company, Economy Supermarket and the American Women's Community.

leaders' in 1970.[126] Throughout this process, members of the American Peace Corps such as Philipp Lilienthal, the World Service workers – John Eveland, Norris Lineweaver (seen in Illustration 3), Carl McClure, and many others – shared their knowledge with Ethiopian staff members and volunteers in a camp-in-training programme (CIT). In summer 1969, ten young YMCA camp leaders from Addis Ababa, Asmara, Dire Dawa, Bahir Dar, and Debre Birhan went to the US for further training at the KON-O-KWEE camp located in Beaver County, Pennsylvania. Operated by the Pittsburgh YMCA, the camp programme provided camp counsellor training as well as international exchange about cultural specificities and camp experience.[127] The objective was to be a part of the camp leadership for a few weeks and observe the operations and programme of a residential youth camp in the traditions of the YMCA.[128] Upon their return, the group could put the newly acquired knowledge directly into practice in the upcoming Sahle Selassie camp programme for September 1969.

Besides its activities acquainting boys with modern forms of experiencing outdoor life and training YMCA leaders, the camp provides just another case of close cooperation between a volunteer organization and the American and Ethiopian militaries. Quite similar to what happened within the scout movement, the armed forces assisted with equipment and transport. Through its contacts to the US Embassy, equipment was also solicited from USAID.[129] Financial and material support, numerous individual as well as collective initiatives, and a tuition fee equivalent to US $10 for a fifteen-day period for Ethiopian nationals, did not solve all the emerging problems concerning hygiene or run-down equipment. However, the 1971 report stressed the high potential the camp had for keeping 'pace with the ever-changing needs and wants' of the Ethiopian youth.[130] Since camping and hiking were already popular through the Boy Scouts and some officials, such as Aberra Jembere, worked in both associations, collaboration existed.

---

[126] Special Report, Camp Langano, 3 May 1971 and 12 May 1971, KFYA, Y.USA.9-2-37, YMCA International Work in Ethiopia Box 3, correspondence with Marvin Ludwig 1970–73. The report, however, also mentions lack of qualified staff.

[127] 'Ethiopian "Y" Leaders Arrive in Pittsburgh', *Ethiopian Herald,* 25 June 1969, 4.

[128] I am grateful to Norris Lineweaver, who worked at the Ethiopian YMCA from 1966 to 1969 and was heavily involved in setting up Sahle Selassie camp, for this information (e-mail conversation 4 April 2019).

[129] Marvin Ludwig to Carl W. McClure, 12 May 1971, KFYA, Y.USA.9-2-37, YMCA International Work in Ethiopia Box 3, correspondence with Marvin Ludwig 1970–73.

[130] Special Report, Camp Langano, 3 May 1971 and 12 May 1971, KFYA, Y.USA.9-2-37, YMCA International Work in Ethiopia Box 3, correspondence with Marvin Ludwig 1970–73.

In 1971, fraternal secretary Lee Houser even mentioned a 'YMCA Boy Scout Troop [that] put on a demonstration of bridge-building, semaphore and first aid' during the YMCA Day in Asmara.[131] Despite such overlaps, cooperation seems to have been very limited and the Ethiopian YMCA camping activities never assumed the character and role that they had in the scout movement.[132]

Muscling In

Through the YMCA's philosophy that emphasized healthy bodies through sports, the Association helped to develop a new type of masculinity that displayed the fruits of bodywork. In Ethiopia, boxing, freestyle wrestling and, most importantly, bodybuilding became symbols of YMCA sports. Photographs of young boys with boxing gloves or young sparsely dressed men posing in front of the camera were regular visuals in annual reports and even made their way into the most important newspapers. Arguably, through its emphasis on sports as an educational as well as moral tool, the YMCA was able to become the motor of making almost nude male bodies with muscles acceptable in public. It bridged ideas of athletic performance with Orthodox Christianity's negative ideas about nudity[133] as well as regulatory principles about 'awra in Muslim contexts.[134] Thus, based on the YMCA's personnel and material capacities as well as on its institutional philosophy, the Ethiopian YMCA found a way of producing the muscular and at the same time acceptable young man.[135]

Presenting the Muscular YMCA Man through Bodybuilding

During Marvin Ludwig's term of office, the YMCA became a first-class address for bodybuilding. In contrast to the Central Branch in the Ethiopian capital, which had imported weightlifting sets from the US, young men in other branches were very creative in producing

---

[131] Lee Houser to Cody S. Moffat, 19 November 1971, KFYA, Y.USA.9-2-37, YMCA International Work in Ethiopia Box 3, correspondence 1970–71.
[132] According to Norris Lineweaver, there was less contact with the Boy Scouts Association but very good cooperation with the Ethiopian Red Cross Society (e-mail conversation 4 April 2019).
[133] I am grateful to Stefan Weninger and his colleagues from the University of Marburg for drawing my attention to the fact that, in the Ethiopian Orthodox Church, nudity has a negative connotation. In iconography, only bad figures such as demons, devils, or heathens do not wear clothes.
[134] Here, the basic rule for a man is to cover from navel to knee.
[135] For a discussion of the concept and its diverse interpretations, see John J. MacAloon, 'Introduction: Muscular Christianity after 150 Years', *International Journal of the History of Sport,* 23:5 (2006), 687–700.

the necessary equipment. In the 'railway town' of Dire Dawa, with its numerous workshops to maintain railway carriages, youth used shafts for training.

Three Ethiopians seem to have been the main drivers behind the systematic development of bodybuilding at the 'Y'. Most important, of course, was Girma Cheru, whom people inside and outside the country still celebrate as the 'father of Ethiopian bodybuilding'. Together with Alemayehu Woldetensae, who belonged to the Ethiopian navy,[136] and Abebe Terefe, an active YMCA member, he coached young athletes on the premises of the Central Branch.[137] Apart from the two branches in the capital, the YMCA served as a bodybuilding centre in Jimma, Wolayta, Nazaret, Dire Dawa, Harar, Gondar, Bahir Dar, Dessie, Nekemte, Mek'ele, and Asmara.

The daily weight training sessions and physical conditioning classes advertised in monthly programme schedules and summer vacation programmes indicate a great demand amongst the urban youth. In contrast to other sites, where landlords expelled bodybuilders from their premises out of fear, the YMCA provided safe spaces for building muscles. To counter the negative image of this muscularity, Girma Cheru organized shows that became quite popular in the 1960s. In the vicinity of churches in the capital, immediately after religious services, groups of young athletes demonstrated weightlifting and acrobatics and, thus, presented their 'beautiful bodies'.[138] Later, he also included musical performances and shifted the shows from open-air sites to the Hager Fikir Theatre, the Cinema Ras, and other halls. Bodybuilders from the YMCA even made it into the Imperial Palace, when they performed during the reception of the Ethiopian National Football Team after its victory in the Africa Cup of Nations in 1962.[139] Arguably, such performances had become acceptable because an

---

[136] It is still an open question as to the extent to which bodybuilding and weightlifting was systematically pursued in the navy. This military branch has been mentioned as one of the key promoters of the sport in information material by the Ministry of Youth and Sports ('Ye kibdet mansatinna sewinnet megenbat sport' [Weightlifting and bodybuilding], in *Yewet'atochin sport mīnīster, Huletenyaw yemelaw Ītyop'ya ch'ewatawoch* [Ministry of Youth and Sports, Second All Ethiopian Championships (Addis Ababa, 2002 EC, 2009/10), p. 57.

[137] Similar to YMCA annual reports, the current Ethiopian Weightlifting and Bodybuilding Federation emphasizes that bodybuilding and weightlifting became very fashionable amongst young men in the 1960s. *Yeītyop'ya kibdet mansatina sewinet megenbat fēdērēshin ametawī mets'hēt liyu 'ittim* [Annual Journal of the Ethiopian Weightlifting and Bodybuilding Federation (Addis Ababa, 1999 EC, 2007), p. 6.

[138] Wendimu Negash Desta, 'Girma Cheru – g^wolmasaw sportenya I' [Girma Cheru – a fully accomplished athlete], *Yekatīt,* hidar 1974 [November 1981], p. 32.

[139] *Menen,* January 1963, 9.

athletic male physique was associated with ethical behaviour through the institutional philosophy of the YMCA.

The public display of the YMCA muscular man was not reserved to places in the Ethiopian capital. Famous weightlifters such as Alemayehu Feyisa, who trained at the Mek'ele YMCA, participated in sports shows at Baloni Stadium[140] and performed with other athletes in the old town hall of Tigray province's capital.[141] Young YMCA sportsmen of the Abebe Bikila Bodybuilding Club in Addis Ababa demonstrated bodybuilding and weightlifting in smaller settlements while en route to the town of Nazaret. In doing so, they not only raised the funds for their travels, but also 'educated' the rural population about 'muscular male beauty'.[142]

In November 1970, the Amharic daily *Addīs Zemen* announced the establishment of the Ethiopian Weightlifting Federation with sixteen registered clubs as its members, and Girma Cheru as its general secretary.[143] Exactly one year later, on 1 November 1971, the YMCA branch in Addis Ketema quarter opened its gym for the first weightlifting competition in Ethiopia – the Addis Ababa Championships. Thirty athletes from seven clubs from the Shoa province were registered as participants.[144] Girma Cheru considered the competition as a way to measure the position of Ethiopian weightlifting in relation to its African neighbour states and the international scene.[145] Despite the initial emphasis on weightlifting only, the contest included performances in acrobatics and, most importantly, bodybuilding. Girma told *Addīs Zemen* that although future events will strictly follow international standards of weightlifting, the inclusion

---

[140] I am grateful to Surafiel Photo Studio in Mek'ele for giving me access to their collection of historical photography, which contains a picture of Alemayehu Feyisa performing at Baloni. Without Mulugeta Hagos and Abreham Tewelde, I would not have identified the athlete in the picture.

[141] Mek'ele's Old Town Hall was built in the 1960s as a multipurpose centre. It contained a big hall that became one of the town's first cinemas. Beneath the stage, in the cellar, there was a bodybuilding club, whose members regularly performed in the hall. I am grateful to Mulugeta Hagos, who researched the place with me on 21 March 2013.

[142] 'Benazrēt 30 wet'atoch yekibdet mansat tir'īt asayu' [In Nazareth thirty youngsters demonstrate weightlifting], *Addīs Zemen,* 17 meskerem 1963 [27 September 1970], 4.

[143] 'Yekibdet anshī shampyona wididir līzegaj new' [Weightlifting championships in preparation], *Addīs Zemen,* 23 hidar 1963 [2 December 1970], 4.

[144] 'Zarē Yemejemerīyaw yekibdet mansat wididir yideregal' [Today the first weightlifting competition will be conducted], *Addīs Zemen,* 20 t'ik'imt 1964 [31 October 1971], 4.

[145] Ethiopia's bodybuilders were approached by the South African physical culturalist Coomerasamy Causea (Milo) Pillay as early as 1951 for form a Pan-African Federation of Physical Education: Francois Cleophas, 'Black Physical Culture and Weight Lifting in South Africa', in Todd Cleveland, Tarminder Kaur, and Gerard Akindes (eds), *Sports in Africa: Past and Present* (Athens OH, 2020), p. 214.

of evaluating posture and walk, measuring the shape of the muscles, and assessing the overall aesthetics of the body were highly likely.[146]

After the initial phase in which weightlifting became a recognized sport at the national level, the YMCA remained its motor. Similar to the Ethiopian volleyball and basketball federations, the 'Y' had the means, the organizational potential and, most importantly, the institutional philosophy to run a national sports federation that explicitly displayed strength through visible muscularity. Sports teachers such as Girma Cheru as well as volunteers from the United States trained young Ethiopians in how to form their bodies. The long-lasting impact of the strong bodies' cult is substantiated by the fact that weightlifting and bodybuilding continued under the umbrella of the YMCA after the political change in 1974. A provisional federation organized the sport from 1976 to 1978, when the Ethiopian Weightlifting and Bodybuilding Federation was established and incorporated into a socialist sports structure.[147]

Wrestling at the 'Y' as Style Alternative

In contrast to weightlifting, which was a new sport in Ethiopia, wrestling was well established and highly diversified all over the empire. Wrestling was part of religious festivals as well as an integral part of becoming an adult.[148] In Orthodox religious instruction, it served to let steam off in a coordinated way during breaks.[149] Urban leisure spaces such as the YMCA and especially migrant community institutions created, however, pockets for Greco-Roman and freestyle wrestling (both called *nets'a tigil*), which also gained importance within the urban amusement industry from the 1950s onwards.[150] Egyptian, Sudanese, and Greek wrestlers entertained the public in Addis Ababa and other towns in bouts with local wrestlers. Arguably, its 'non-Ethiopian' style also made freestyle wrestling acceptable as a modern form of leisure within the YMCA.

---

[146] BeĪtyop'ya yemejemerīyaw yekibdet mansat wididir t'ik'imt 15 yideregal [First weightlifting competition will take place on 26 October], *Addīs Zemen*, 22 meskerem 1964 [3 October 1971], 4.

[147] *YeĪtyop'ya kibdet mansatina sewinet megenbat fēdērēshin*, 9.

[148] Katrin Bromber, '"Ethiopian" Wrestling between Sportization of National Heritage and Dynamic Youth Culture', *ITYOPIS: Northeast African Journal of Social Sciences and Humanities*, 2 (2013a), 38.

[149] *Resedebri* Gebreanenia Gebremedhin (78-year-old inhabitant from Mariam P'ap'aseti) revealed to me that he started wrestling at the religious school in Chala (near Hawzien) in the 1960s. During the breaks, it was quite common that pupils wrestled. Priests acted as referees: interview with Alemnesh Gessesew and Resedebri Gebreanenia Gebremedhin, Mariam P'ap'aseti Village, 18 July 2012.

[150] Katrin Bromber, 'Muscularity, Heavy Athletics and Urban Leisure in Ethiopia, 1950s–1970s', *The International Journal of the History of Sport*, 30:16 (2013b), 1922.

4. Freestyle wrestling at the YMCA, probably early 1960s (Kautz Family YMCA Archives, University of Minnesota Libraries, Minneapolis, USA).

The inclusion of wrestling in the YMCA sports programmes began after Marvin Ludwig's arrival. His personal interest in technical disciplines such as wrestling, boxing, and fencing made these sports visible in the various reports, letters, and orders for sports equipment. Illustration 4 shows him in the background observing a freestyle wrestling match.

Interestingly, the first report located wrestling in an 'all boxing and wrestling show' performed in May 1958, in which 'twelve ... rugged fisted boys put on a demonstration of their agility and endurance. Following boxing the audience enjoyed three wrestling matches, the last was an Australian Tag Match'.[151] Interestingly, the Australian tag matches come very close to the there-can-only-be-one-champion principle of local Ethiopian wrestling practices.[152] Furthermore, photographs from this period and visuals reproduced in *Addīs Zemen* about wrestling at the 'Y' show that the young wrestlers were dressed in shorts and shirts and not in wrestling suits. Given the fact that the representation of uncovered male bodies was not a taboo – as we have seen in connection with bodybuilding and weightlifting – such an outfit

---

[151] Marvin Ludwig to Joel Nystrom, 9 June 1958, KFYA Y.USA.9-2-37, YMCA International Work in Ethiopia Box 1, correspondence 1958.
[152] Bromber, '"Ethiopian" Wrestling', 27.

might indicate a bridge between YMCA freestyle and acceptable dress codes for Ethiopian highland wrestlers.

In the beginning, Marvin Ludwig held wrestling classes once a week. Later, when he had assumed full responsibility as general secretary, local staff, World Service workers and American Peace Corps volunteers took over. John Eveland's job description, for example, explicitly stated that he 'will be expected to conduct one wrestling class per week under the auspices of Ato Admus, [the] Physical Education Secretary'.[153]

In the early 1970s, the Addis Ababa YMCA initiated a further systematic attempt to promote freestyle wrestling. The summer programme of 1971 offered a basic course for thirty participants to learn the sport according to international rules. Those who showed talent continued to train twice a week for another two months and publicly competed in November.[154] David Wayding, an American Peace Corps volunteer from Pennsylvania, was in charge of the training. He checked the physical state of the Ethiopian applicants before he started to work with them. It is not quite clear whether the Addis Ababa YMCA continued with the programme after the young coach left for the Wollega YMCA, where he was responsible for physical fitness.[155]

The perception that wrestling was traditional later resulted in the organization of the sport in a standardized local form under the Ethiopian Cultural Sports Federation. Thus, in contrast to weightlifting and bodybuilding, no Ethiopian wrestling federation has emerged.

The development of sports and physical education at the Ethiopian YMCA was highly dependent on the engagement of the Ethiopian and fraternal secretaries. They facilitated the necessary links inside and outside the country to integrate YMCA sports into the national sports scene, to raise the funds for the necessary equipment, and to gain access to playing fields. Most importantly, the YMCA contributed to an overall attempt to develop leadership in physical education, which coincided with the leadership training necessary to put the Association on firm local ground. This included training abroad in the US, where all those concerned with physical education went to Sir George Williams College and not to Springfield, which was famous for the subject. The YMCA's clear mission to help those in need, its well-trained staff, and

---

[153] Job Description for John Eveland, Junior World Service Worker, Ethiopian YMCA, no date, KFYA Y.USA.9-2-37, YMCA International Work in Ethiopia Box 1, correspondence 1965. As a Junior World Service worker, John Eveland served the 'Y' from 1965 to 1967.

[154] 'Lemejemerīya gīzē: Wewekima nets'a tigil timhirt līseṭ' new' [For the first time: YMCA offers freestyle wrestling classes], *Addīs Zemen*, 6 t'ik'imt' 1964 [17 October 1971], 4.

[155] 'Wet'atoch benets'a tigil yiselet'inalu' [Youth exercises freestyle wrestling], *Addīs Zemen*, 18 hidar 1964 [28 November 1971], 4.

its long experience in leadership training qualified the Association for a transition into post-revolutionary Ethiopia. Since general secretary Tsegaw Ayele had worked in the YMCA's physical education sector from the early 1960 onwards, it did not come as a surprise that he transferred YMCA sports to the Sports Commission, where he made a career as the Commissioner for Sports and Physical Culture and, later, National Olympic Committee President. Such a personal advancement was by no means a straightforward process. It would only be fair to quote him on his situation in September 1975, when he asked the International Committee for help with a scholarship:

> To my deep regret, things are now changing tremendously in Ethiopia. With disappointment, reluctance and broken heart I am obliged to change my personal plans. I have fought situation [sic] very bravely like a committed soldier to perpetuate the Philosophy of the YMCA in everybody's mind over the last 17 years ... But now I have felt and it is high time for me to widen my horizon of thinking and experience. So, I have decided to continue my post-graduate study in America.[156]

The lack of any assistance in this respect, combined with the fact that International Committee officials had stopped accepting any invitations to Ethiopia, made Tsegaw Ayele feel left without international support. Thus, he chose the option offered to him within the new political system.

By 1972, the Ethiopian YMCA had twenty-two branches in eighteen cities.[157] The YMCA's philosophy about the importance of strong bodies and the means to achieve them through regular training had spread across the country. Its stress on following rules, being systematic and, most importantly, playing fair within a competitive system merged with other efforts in the same direction such as physical education at schools, colleges, and universities, and within established initiatives of the foreign communities. As the second section of this chapter shows, close cooperation facilitated the joint use of facilities and coaches as well as the acquisition of sports equipment through various channels. A regular budget for physical education as well as coaching expertise allowed the YMCA to host national sports federations and to compete on an international level. Conditions were best in the capital due to a new building (the Central Branch), which included a gym. Here, the YMCA offered an impressive range of sports. However, as the chapter discusses, access to these facilities was highly regulated, primarily through membership fees, which became a recurrent issue.

---

[156] Tsegaw Ayele to Frank Kiehne, 15 September 1975, KFYA, Y.USA.9-2-37, YMCA International Work in Ethiopia Box 4, correspondence 1975.
[157] An International Committee of YMCAs' Project for U.S. Partnership Support, Ethiopia, March 1972, KFYA, Y.USA.9-2-37, YMCA International Work in Ethiopia Box 3, correspondence 1972.

With its emphasis on a healthy and strong physique, the YMCA provided the ideal conditions to promote male muscularity. In doing so, it furthered an existing trend towards integrating the muscular body into public performances in urban and rural entertainment. As the final part of this chapter shows, the YMCA became the ideal site to establish weightlifting within Ethiopian sports through an Ethiopian weightlifting and, later, bodybuilding federation. In contrast, (freestyle) wrestling did not reach such a level of formalization. Despite all attempts within and outside the YMCA, it remained to be perceived as a traditional sport, which later resulted in its standardization under the auspices of the Cultural Sports Federation of Ethiopia.

5
Sports' Material Infrastructure and the Production of Space (1910s–1970s)

Where did the urban population do sports? Although briefly touched upon in previous chapters, this chapter looks more systematically at infrastructural and spatial aspects. Looking specifically at educational institutions, mostly located in Addis Ababa, the first part shows the different situations at schools and how creative teachers and pupils tackled the problems they faced. At institutions of higher learning; i.e. universities and colleges, which were established from the 1950s onwards with the help of a broad international spectrum of agents, sports continued to be a compulsory activity. Arguably, the success in intercollegiate competitions greatly depended on the (international) donor. The universities had to provide the necessary facilities not only for their students, but also as a service for the national and, most importantly, international staff members.

The vicinity of schools and colleges to playing fields and, more importantly, the first stadiums, created sports nuclei in Ethiopian urban centres. Especially during big competitions, opening ceremonies, athletic performances, the presentation of trophies by politicians, and other forms of ritual produced social spaces that served sports both as a physical activity in competition and as a spectacle for political power. Whether located in the capital or the provincial towns, stadiums fulfilled this double role in an exceptional way. Stadiums in newly independent African states that were built around the same time and often by the same foreign companies, signalled the new era with names such as Independence Stadium (Accra, Lusaka) or Stadium of the Revolution (Brazzaville).[1] In contrast, stadiums in Ethiopia and annexed Eritrea bore names of important personalities such as Ras Alula[2] and the Queen of Sheba in Asmara, Asfa Wossen in Dire Dawa or Haile Selassie I in

---

[1] Michelle Sikes, 'Sport History and Historiography', *Oxford Research Encyclopedia of African History* (2018) DOI: 10.1093/acrefore/9780190277734.013.232, p. 11.
[2] *Ras* Alula (1827–97) was an important Tigrayan military and political figure.

Addis Ababa. The stadium in the provincial capital Mek'ele was named *Kagnew Astadium* – after *Ras* Makonnen's war horse.[3]

In a similar vein, places of entertainment, tourism or work included sports in a number of ways. Cinemas and theatres became venues for boxing bouts and bodybuilding shows; sports facilities in hotels served for the recreation of guests, city-dwellers who could afford a membership card, as well as (college) sports clubs that had managed to negotiate access. Lobbies of public buildings such as the Addis Ababa and Mek'ele municipalities hosted table tennis matches. Even if the work place (especially hotels) did not allow the staff members to use facilities such as swimming pools or tennis courts, the work context increasingly provided the organizational framework for doing sports. Similar to colonial and post-colonial contexts in other African states and beyond, government departments saw sports as a means 'to create social cohesion, camaraderie, and fealty to the ... state'.[4]

From their offices in the United Nations Economic Commission for Africa, or from the rooms of the Hilton Hotel, people (staff and guests) had a direct view of the starting line of Ethiopia's most famous motor sports event – the Ethiopian Highland Rally. Organized from 1964 to 1974, the rally connected towns within the imperial territory. It symbolized technological and urban progress through a sport that included the most important symbol of modern life – including on an individual level – the motor car. For those schoolchildren and youth who witnessed the race or heard about it on the radio or from other people, it was certainly a topic that shaped their ideas of personal success. Some of them might have discussed the scene, the noise, the speed, and the results with their (foreign) physical education teachers on the sports fields or in the gymnasiums, which I will discuss now.

Educational Institutions as Sports Grounds

One of the first photographs depicting sports in a modern educational context seems, at first glance, to have nothing to do with modern sports. The picture shows how pupils of the first French Mission School of the Brothers of Saint Gabriel (established in 1907) in Addis Ababa played *genna* – the Ethiopian version of hockey.[5] A typical *genna* playing field in rural areas measured the distance between two villages and, thus, could extend to one kilometre or more. In contrast, the field at the school

---

[3] *Ras* Makonnen (1852–**1906**) was appointed ruler of Harar; he was cousin to Menelik II and father of Haile Selassie.
[4] Sikes, 'Sport History and Historiography', p. 7.
[5] Fasil Giorgis and Denis Gérard, *Addis Ababa 1886–1941: The City and its Architectural Heritage* (Addis Ababa, 2007), p. 286.

was determined by the comparatively small size of the compound. Likewise, the number of players, which normally included half a village, was confined to carefully selected pupils. The brothers were not even required to move because they could monitor the game from an elevated position. What is modern about this scene is the attempt by an educational institution to turn a 'traditional' game into a modern sport (i.e. sportization). The picture is reminiscent of Michel Foucault's microphysics of power. 'Discipline worked through a system of surveillance and did not need arms, physical violence, material constraints. Just a gaze. An expecting gaze'.[6]

It might not be an overstatement to argue that the modern schools in the Ethiopia of the 1920s and 1930s contained the first facilities for doing the kind of sports that became part of physical education, as I described in Chapter 1, *The Emergence of Ethiopia's Modern Sports Scene (1900–1935)*. This does not mean that they were the first places for regularly doing sports in Ethiopia, which were very much linked to agrarian, religious, or other life cycles, and had their specific locations:[7] most probably, there were a high number of overlaps. However, by increasingly making physical education a compulsory subject, schools had to provide specific areas or convert places such as school courtyards into places for doing gymnastics or drills. Thus, the provision of suitable places was never solely a spatial issue, but also a temporal one.

With the closure of schools during the Fascist occupation, these sporting facilities within the educational system disappeared. In contrast, the schools for the few children from noble families promoted sports via coordinated activities of the Sports Bureau for the Natives. Although the sources analysed in Chapter 2, *Sports and Propaganda during the Fascist Occupation (1935–1941)*, do not disclose much about the facilities at these schools, they reveal that children used existing places, such as the Jan Mēda racing grounds, for competition and the display of athletic talent.

After the liberation in 1941, sports continued in its role of moulding the minds and bodies of the intellectual elite and serving as an antidote to social vices amongst youth. This recognition resulted in the establishment of the Department of Physical Education and Boy Scouting within the Ministry of Education and Fine Arts (MoE) in 1950. With the help of the Executive Committee of the Inter-School Athletic Association (established in September 1948), 'a survey of sports facilities and

---

[6] Michel Foucault, *Discipline and Punish: The Birth of the Prison* (London, 1977), p. 215.
[7] For the case of wrestling see Katrin Bromber, '"Ethiopian" Wrestling between Sportization of National Heritage and Dynamic Youth Culture', *ITYOPIS: Northeast African Journal of Social Sciences and Humanities*, 2 (2013a), 27.

equipment [and] a test to assess the best equipment for Ethiopian conditions' was carried out in Addis Ababa schools.[8] Based on this report, the MoE distributed equipment for football, volleyball, basketball, croquet, badminton, weights for shot put, and trapeze equipment in 1953 – all imported directly from abroad or through French, Swedish, Yugoslav, and Armenian sports shops.[9]

However, the distribution of equipment did not ease the situation in terms of cramped facilities. In terms of space, it mattered where the school was located, because the location often determined the size of allocated land for schools and playing fields. The Commercial School may serve as an example of schools in the fast-growing capital. It was and still is located in the city centre with little physical space around it for expansion. Thus, sports had to be taught within the school compound, i.e. in a rather small area. Since the school had financially powerful alumni, it was otherwise well equipped for doing sports. In 1952, they donated sufficient funds to buy badminton, tennis, football, volleyball, basketball, table tennis, and horseshoe pitching equipment. They also 'secured pole-vaulting stands, big jumping stands, and putting shots for track and field practice'.[10] Given the lack of space, the school arranged to use volleyball and basketball facilities at the Armenian Club and organized 'friendly games of football with other teams on their fields'.[11]

The Teacher Training College was less fortunate, with a small playing field and only one volleyball court. Often, the sheer will to participate in the competitions of the Ethiopian Inter-School Athletic Association (EISAA) motivated educational institutions such as the Beyene Merid School to invest in physical education without the necessary space and equipment.[12] In contrast, Tafari Makonnen School was allocated enough land for six large playing fields (football, volleyball, basketball, softball) and facilities for tumbling, horseshoe pitching, parallel bars, and athletics.[13] In other cases, students and staff members built their own facilities. Amha Desta School may serve as an example. Each class was assigned its share of ground to level. A competition amongst the

---

[8] First Annual Track & Field Meet 1950, 4; 'Sile sport mesarīyawoch' [About the sports organizations], Second Annual Track & Field Meet, 1951, 20, IES 796 ADD ETH. All issues of the journal are catalogued under the same reference number.
[9] Third Annual Track & Field Meet 1952, 31.
[10] Third Annual Track & Field Meet 1952, 6.
[11] Ibid.
[12] Fourth Annual Track & Field Meet 1952–53, 31. Located near Meskel Square, the school is named after Beyene Merid (1897–37). He was a major-general, a patriot during the Italian occupation, and married to Haile Selassie's eldest daughter.
[13] Ibid., 11.

classes finding which one first finished ground-levelling ensured that the playground was completed in 1953.[14] In the same year, students of Asfa Wossen School built their own basketball court. However, this initiative could not ease the situation in which the school 'had not enough playing space for the growing needs'.[15] At General Wingate School, staff members provided the means to construct a tennis court and it was hoped that 'certain boys ... will soon become proficient in this game as well'.[16] By the mid-1960s, EISAA finals on the provincial level were being conducted either in 'school stadiums' such as the sports ground at Haile Selassie I School in Nekemte (Wollega Province) or in nearby stadiums such as *Kagnew Astadium* in Mek'ele (Tigray Province). Sources are silent about the fact that, apart from athletic talent, good coaching, and equipment, athletic performance also depended on pupils being used to the exact measures of the track, jumping bar, or basketball court. In contrast to the EISAA journals of the 1950s, there is no information about sports facilities, including playgrounds, in provincial towns.

However, the epicentre of school sports was, at least once a year, the Haile Selassie I Stadium in Addis Ababa. In 1955, on the Silver Jubilee of Haile Selassie's Coronation, 1,700 children from Addis Ababa schools displayed mass gymnastics, presenting fit and disciplined youth to the imperial family and thousands of people who had come to watch.[17] These performances became the template for replicas on the provincial level.[18] Thus, the EISAA journal increasingly reported in detail about procedures as well as the involvement of high-ranking officials such as provincial governors.

By the late 1960s, thirteen to fourteen provinces participated in athletic competitions under the umbrella of the EISAA.[19] Parents' committees were formed to increase acceptance of modern competitive sports amongst pupils' families, but more importantly to improve the facilities and guarantee equal opportunities. In Wollega Province, for example, eleven parents' committees worked to achieve this aim by monitoring the development of physical education and raising funds for, or even individually buying, sports equipment for the schools.[20] However, the EISAA journal and other sources do not reveal if they

[14] Ibid., 19.
[15] Ibid., 21.
[16] Ibid., 20.
[17] Seventh Annual Track & Field Meet 1955–56, 7.
[18] The description of the Tigray province finals held in Mek'ele on 8 February 1967 is a good example. Yetigrē t'/gizat t/bētoch yeruzina yesewinet mat'enkerīya wididir [Athletic and sports competition of the Tigray Province schools], Eighteenth Annual Track & Field Meet 1967–68, 24–25.
[19] Twenty-fourth Annual Track & Field Meet, 1972–73, 16.
[20] Ibid., 25.

also participated in building the necessary material structures, such as playing fields and gymnasiums.

Athletic Facilities and Higher Education

There is no doubt that sports facilities at the university and colleges primarily served to keep the student population fit and disciplined. A systematic approach that made sports a compulsory extra-curricular activity or even part of the curriculum served to put the motto *mens sana in corpore sano* (a healthy mind in a healthy body) into practice as early as the 1950s. Freshmen and sophomores had to take part in at least one sports activity. Facilities and coaching in Addis Ababa allowed for football, basketball, volleyball, softball, tennis, badminton, field hockey, archery, fencing, boxing, weight lifting, track and field sports,[21] and wrestling.[22] A daily time slot from 5.00–6.15 p.m. was reserved for athletic activities.[23] From 1962 onwards (except 1970), students from the University College of Addis Ababa (UCAA), renamed Haile Selassie I University (HSIU) in 1962, the Health College and Training Centre in Gondar, the Imperial Ethiopian College of Agricultural and Mechanical Arts in Haremaya, and the Debre Zeit Veterinary College met for the Intercollegiate Sports Competitions at the University Sports Day.[24] Students were recurrently asked to do sports, to use the facilities, and to take part in intercollegiate meets. 'There is the man-power, what we lack is adequate participation'.[25] From 1968/69, these sports meets also served to identify student athletes who would represent HSIU at the International University Sports Federation.[26]

According to Shiferaw Agonafir, who, as Director of Sports at HSIU was in charge of organizing the University Sports Days, the university had a football field with a track around it on the premises of today's

---

[21] The University College of Addis Ababa, *Ethiopia Observer*, 2: 6, July 1958, 206.
[22] Sports Day, University College of Addis Ababa, March 1956, 10, IES 796.378 HSU.
[23] 'Sport', *Journal of the University College of Addis Ababa Sports Day*, March 1952, 16. IES 796.378 HSU.
[24] Teams from Haremaya and Gondar could not participate in 1970 for financial reasons. Addis Ababa Colleges Sports Day, 6 June 1970, 1, IES 796 HSU.
[25] Gebru Tareke (President of Sports Office, UCAA), 'Sports for Unity', *News & Views*, 15 November 1963, 10:5, 11.
[26] 'Ye'alem ak'ef yunīversītī sport federēshin' [International University Sports Federation], Addis Ababa Colleges Sports Day, 6 June 1970, 9, IES 796 HSU. In 19664/65, HSIU had become a member of the federation. In 1970, Abera Asres, Boru Taetcha, Yemane Yayinu, and Tilahun Assefa represented HSIU in medium and long-distance running.

Technical College at Arat Kilo. Volleyball courts were constructed[27] and an indoor gymnasium invited enthusiasts to watch boxing bouts or even to get training in the art of fist fighting. College Days as well as the University Sports Days not only provided the stage for demonstrating the students' fitness but also for the 'Grand Opening of the Basketball Season' by the emperor.[28] The close proximity of Menelik II Secondary School and the YMCA Central Branch with its excellent sports facilities made the area a sports hub.

Other institutions of higher learning also invested in their students' fitness. In the early 1960s, the Health College and Training Centre in Gondar (established in 1954) advertised to both students and (mostly foreign) staff its 'playground [sic] for out-door sports and volleyball, basket-ball and tennis courts as well as recreational rooms'.[29] Improvements most likely came after the student magazine *The Health Pioneer* had complained about the bad conditions for sports.[30] Despite these difficulties, Gondar students competed not only in the annual Intercollegiate Sports Competitions or against staff members, but also against an 'Amateur Team [that] was composed of Peace Corps members and teachers and other workmen from Gondar and its vicinity'.[31]

The Imperial Ethiopian College of Agricultural and Mechanical Arts in Haremaya as well as the Jimma Agricultural Technical School (JATS) – both founded in the early 1950s – received substantial support from the United States through an agreement under the Point Four Program.[32] They were thus able to develop their sports facilities and athletic performance accordingly.[33] Growing athletic success, especially in volleyball, is well documented in the *JATS Year Books* and the monthly bulletin *The Farmer*, later *The Farmer's Voice*. Amongst other areas, Cold War politics with its soft power ambitions especially played out in the field of education and Ethiopia profited from it. Based on an agreement between the Soviet Union and Ethiopia, the Soviet Union provided the financing, teachers, and technical

---

[27] Interview with Shiferaw Agonafir (8 June 2011); also see 'Sports', *The University Reporter*, 1: 2, 24 February 1967, IES 378 HSU PER.
[28] College Day, 7 December 1958, University College Addis Ababa, ENA 1.2.80.03.
[29] *Information Bulletin* 1961–62, Haile Selassie I Health College & Training Centre, Gondar, 4. IES 371.805 HSU GON.
[30] *The Health Pioneer*, 2, 1960, 8. IES 371.805 HSU GON.
[31] *Health Mirror*, May 1963, 5. IES 371.805 HSU GON.
[32] The agreement between the Ethiopian government and the Technical Cooperation Administration of the government of the United States of America was signed on 16 March 1952 and mandated Oklahoma State University to build and, at least initially, run the college. It received the first students in 1954.
[33] Both journals are located at the Institute of Ethiopian Studies, Addis Ababa (*JATS Year Books*, IES 371.805 JIM AGR and *The Farmer*, later *The Farmer's Voice*, IES 371.805 JIM TEC).

support for the Polytechnic Institute in Bahir Dar. Inaugurated and opened on 11 June 1963, the school had sports facilities that allowed for all kinds of ball games, and opened its own boxing club.[34] The yearbooks of these and other institutions of higher learning mention facilities for volleyball, basketball, and football, but also show initiatives such as the construction of parallel bars for gymnastics.[35] The Technical School in Addis Ababa was proud of its table tennis team and the equipment in its recreation room. Its swimming club trained on Saturdays and Sundays at the Ghion Hotel.[36] In 1968, the student journal *Target* revealed that the school had its own set of weights and could, thus, form its own bodybuilding club.[37] In line with the bodybuilding hype in urban Ethiopia of the late 1960s, yearbooks regularly included photographs of muscular students' bodies.

Despite a multitude of sports activities being compulsory, a critical evaluation of the physical condition of university students in 1973 concluded:

> If we try to assess the situation in our institution of higher learning as related to the matter of sports, it seems that we are under-exercised; we have become onlookers rather than participants in this noble effort. The age of mechanization has brought with it so many elements of comfort that people have lost some of their physical strength. The unenthusiastic attitude we hold towards sports deprives us of even the minimal physical activity essential for healthy living, and the only way out of this is through broad programs ... that shall produce new standards of excellence in the field of sports, for it is through mass active participation that better standards can be achieved.[38]

The assessment shows that the provision of the material infrastructure and coaching personnel did not guarantee 'successful' subject formation. If their financial situation allowed, students might also have preferred to meet at the stadium to watch a football match or to enjoy dancing at one of the clubs.

[34] *Year Books of the Polytechnic Institute in Bahir Dar*, 1968, 48, IES 373 BAH POL.
[35] *Bulletin* Teacher Training Institute, Debre Berhan, 1970, 44, IES, 371.805 DAB TEA.
[36] *Technical School Year Book* 1964–65, 77, IES 371.805ADD TEC.
[37] TARGET, Fourth Year Student Association of the Technical School, Addis Ababa, 1968, IES 371.805 ADD TEC.
[38] 'The Value of Student Participation in Sports in Institutions of Higher Learning', *Journal of the University College of Addis Ababa Sports Day*, February 1973, 13, IES 796.378 HSU.

Of Stadiums and Night Clubs

For athletes and their families, the imperial family and high-ranking officials, as well as all lovers of sports in the city, the stadium became the place to be. In Ethiopia as elsewhere, stadiums developed into stages for athletic talent, for the display of consent (as well dissent) to political power,[39] and for leisure and entertainment. They symbolized modernity and national pride. Since stadiums in Ethiopia were owned by the municipalities, they became signifiers of nation-building. In terms of gender, they offer spaces for a male sociability – especially through the game of football. They are what Christopher Gaffney and John Bale describe as 'unique container[s] of collective emotion which [produce] experiences that are as varied and complex as the individuals who periodically visit them'.[40] Their architectural structure and immediate surroundings provide possibilities for commerce as well as activities of legal and illegal nature. Stadiums are urban landmarks, symbols of modernity, and nodal points in the international athletic network.

Prince regent *Ras* Tafari may already have sensed the fascination of a stadium on his tour to Europe. He and the entire Ethiopian delegation were invited by Baron Pierre de Coubertin to visit the opening ceremony of the 1924 Summer Olympics at the Stade Olympique Yves-du-Manoir, in the north-western suburbs of Paris.[41] Although the construction of the first stadium in Ethiopia had to wait until after the liberation from the Italian occupation, it was exactly during this period and within the occupation context that early plans were drawn.

On a global scale, stadiums became important elements of modern urban centres. This also applied to colonial modernity in general, and

---

[39] The fact that Ethiopia's victory at the 1962 African Cup of Nations was achieved by a team that included nine players from Eritrea spoke to Eritrean nationalism and the independence struggle, especially after the annexation as the fourteenth province later in the same year. The following political conflict was regularly expressed in battles on the football pitch, in the stands, and in after-match-fights between fans, especially when the *Hamasēn* team from Asmara played against teams from Ethiopian provinces (Bahru Zewde, individual statement, 22 March 2014). More details in Alex Last, 'Containment and Counter-Attack: A History of Eritrean Football', in Gary Armstrong and Richard Giulianotti (eds), *Football in Africa: Conflict, Conciliation and Community* (Basingstoke, 2004), pp. 27–40.
[40] Christopher Gaffney and John Bale, 'Sensing the Stadium', in Patricia Vertinsky and John Bale (eds), *Sites of Sport: Space, Place and Experience* (London, 2004), p. 47.
[41] Daniel Abebe Kifle, 'The Infant Stage of Olympism in Ethiopia versus Ethiopian-NOC Governance', in Konstantinus Georgiadis (ed.), *Olympic Studies: 23rd International Seminar on Olympic Studies for Post-graduate Students* (Athens Gr.), p. 153; Boris Monin, 'The Visit of Rās Tafari in Europe (1924): Between Hopes of Independence and Colonial Realities', *Annales d'Éthiopie*, 28 (2013), p. 386.

Italian colonial modernity in the Horn of Africa in particular. In Italy, the *Foro Mussolini*, which was built between 1928 and 1938, became the pre-eminent example of Fascist sports architecture. The Fascist propaganda material in Amharic portrayed the *foro* as a venue for sports as well as a place to display youthful militarized manliness.[42] Arguably, Le Corbusier produced the first image of Addis Ababa as a modern (colonial) city. Number 16 in his sketch of 'a city for modern times',[43] which conceptualized the Ethiopian capital in a tabula rasa manner, resembles a stadium structure. However, Mussolini relied on Italy's modern architects and urban planners. Thus, Ignazio Guidi and Cesare Valle drew the first master plan of the city that included a *zona sportiva* in the form of a stadium.[44] Similarly, suggestions for urban development by the Office for General Town Plan and the Technical Office for the Use of Buildings in Addis Ababa show the *centro sportivo* as a central element of urban planning. As the master plans for the provincial town of Jimma reveals, the idea for stadiums was not restricted to the capital of the *Africa Orientale Italiana*.[45]

Although no stadium was built during the occupation, the concept of an Olympic-sized stadium in the capital, as well as the idea of where to build it, continued in the post-liberation period. Thus, it might not come as a surprise that the suggested location for the *centro sportivo* matched the location of Ethiopia's first stadium. The flatter topography compared to its surroundings, as well as the fact that people already used to play football in *Campo Alogo*, as the area was called, might have suggested the place. The emperor granted the building plot as *rist* land.[46] Responsibility for constructing the stadium was in the hands of

---

[42] *YeK'ēsar Mengist Mel'iktenya*, 6 tirr 1931 [15 January 1939], 4.

[43] Le Corbusier to Roberto Cantalupo, Paris, 19 August 1936, cited in Giuliano Gresleri, *Architecture in the Italian Colonies in Africa* (Bologna, 1992), p. 37. For Le Corbusier's intellectual involvement in Italian city planning of Addis Ababa during the Fascist occupation, see Rixt Woudstra, 'Designing the Town of the Future: Le Corbusier's Sketch of Addis Ababa', *Simulacrum*, 21:1 (2012), 6–10 and Rixt Woudstra, 'Le Corbusier's Vision for Fascist Addis Ababa' Failed Architecture (9 October 2014), https://failedarchitecture.com/le-corbusiers-visions-for-fascist-addis-ababa [accessed 15 September 2021].

[44] Ignazio Guidi and Cesare Valle became famous in inter-war Italy by experimenting not unlike Le Corbusier from a tabula rasa perspective that was typical for modern urban planning of the period.

[45] For reproductions of these plans see Giuliano Gresleri and Pier Giorgio Massaretti (eds), *Italian Architecture Overseas: An Iconographic Atlas* (Bologna, 2008), pp. 359, 360, 367, 401.

[46] Ethiopian Football Federation, *25 Years of Football in Ethiopia* (Addis Ababa, 1968), p. 60. *Rist* is a form of land tenure system in which a person inherits land by descent. Although this tenure system does not allow the alienation of land outside the kinship group, it became increasingly common that the emperor allocated land for specific purposes such as the YMCA central branch and the stadium.

Addis Ababa municipality,⁴⁷ which awarded the tender to the engineer Alexander Myriallis and his company.⁴⁸

On 2 November 1947, the emperor laid the foundation stone for the stadium, which later took his name. The first shape of Haile Selassie I Stadium was a wooden structure with a football pitch measuring 68 x 110 metres, a running track of 400 metres, other athletic facilities, and a seating capacity of 5,000. A wooden grandstand covered with corrugated iron included the imperial loge, separated by a beautifully forged metal fence. Parking space outside served various purposes in addition to parking.⁴⁹ In the 1950s, the area was developed according to ideas of the park system. The Filwoha Group – named after the hot springs – included the new Imperial Guest House, the baths, the enlarged Ghion Hotel, and the Filwoha Park.⁵⁰

With the growing number of sports enthusiasts as well as the development of the area into Filwoha Park, it soon became clear that the stadium was too small. It was torn down and replaced by a concrete structure with a seating capacity of 16,000 in 1954/55. Facilities such as changing rooms for teams and referees were included. Six 250-flux floodlights allowed for night matches.⁵¹ This time, the tender had gone to Solel Boneh – an Israeli firm that was very active in breaking the diplomatic isolation of Israel by exporting architecture to Africa and Asia. Golda Meir, Foreign Minister and later Prime Minister of Israel, considered the construction and civil engineering company a 'national tool of highest degree'.⁵² In Addis Ababa alone, Solel Boneh built the new airport terminal and hangars, the Ministry of Foreign Affairs, part of the HSIU, military camps, and the new Filwoha Baths.⁵³

Thus, when the imperial couple celebrated the Silver Jubilee (1955), the new stadium fulfilled its role beyond sports – namely as a space for what Guy Debord called '*la société du spectacle*'.⁵⁴ The stadium became the perfect place to produce and consume images that linked the sporting body to ideas of imperial modernity. Thousands of people came to watch the 1,700 children from Addis Ababa schools' gymnastics displays, presenting fit and disciplined youth to the emperor.⁵⁵ When Ethi-

---

47 Interview with Tibebu Gorfu (14 May 2014).
48 Michel B. Lentakis, *Ethiopia: A View from Within* (London, 2005), p. 175.
49 Ethiopian Football Federation, *25 Years of Football in Ethiopia*, p. 123.
50 Getachew Mahiteme Selassie, The Master Plan for Addis Ababa, 1956, IES 711.4 GET, p. 2.
51 Interview with Tibebu Gorfu (14 May 2014).
52 Cited in Haim Yacobi, *Israel and Africa: A Genealogy of Moral Geography* (New York, 2016) p. 39.
53 Steven Carol, *From Jerusalem to the Lion of Judah and Beyond: Israel's Foreign Policy in Africa* (Bloomington IN, 2012), p. 80.
54 Guy Debord, *La société du spectacle* (Paris, 1967).
55 Eighth Annual Track & Field Meet, 1955–56, IES 796 ADD ETH, 7.

opia won the Africa Cup of Nations against Egypt in 1962, the Haile Selassie I Stadium became the place where the '"Father of the Nation" [sanctioned one of] Ethiopia's greatest sporting victor[ies] in the capital stadium bearing his name'.[56]

In his opening speech in 1947, Haile Selassie had already emphasized his expectations about the location: the stadium will be the place where young Ethiopian athletes reveal to the world the physical strength of the empire. For him, the building was a signifier of sports as a moral force for overcoming human weakness.[57] The stadium was a space of expectations and imaginaries. Whereas the Ethiopian Football Federation dreamed of ownership, as well as winning the African Cup of Nations, the EISAA saw the Haile Selassie I Stadium as a place to host a civilian sports club giving young promising athletes the possibility of training after leaving school.[58] Sports fans anticipated victory for their local team and street vendors around the stadium hoped for brisk business.

The finished stadium gave way to international meets. In 1962, Ethiopia hosted the Africa Cup of Nations. Apart from Addis, stadiums in Asmara and Dire Dawa were built or completely overhauled to meet international standards. The existing stadium in Dire Dawa, for example, had no grass pitch and was located in an extremely hot and arid part of the country. Thus, officials asked Haremaya Agricultural College for help. Further improvements to Addis Ababa's main stadium and the one in Dire Dawa took place under new political conditions. In 1976, when Ethiopia hosted the tenth Africa Cup, the seating capacity of the Addis Ababa Stadium (former Haile Selassie I Stadium), was increased to thirty-six thousand. Under the Agency for Government Houses, the area around the stadium was cleaned up by installing shops in the outer basement structure. An additional incentive might have been to generate extra income.

By the 1960s, nearly every provincial capital had a small stadium or a playing field in line with FIFA (Fédération Internationale de Football Association) regulations, often surrounded by a 400-metre athletic track. The seating capacity varied greatly. An outer wall fenced in some of these playing fields. Others, such as *Kagnew Astadium* in Mek'ele,

---

[56] Peter Alegi, *African Soccerscapes: How a Continent Changed the World's Game* (London, 2010), p. 68. In contrast to Peter Alegi, I would argue that the greatest sporting victory of that time was Abebe Bikila's marathon victory in the Summer Olympics in Rome 1960.
[57] Haile Selassie, YeGirmawī Niguse Negest K'edamawī Hayle Sillasēn yeliyu liyu ch'ewatawoch malaya (stadiyem) yemeseret dingay līyanoru yetenagerut k'al [Speech by His Majesty Emperor Haile Selassie on the occasion of laying the foundation stone at the place where various games will be shown], *Addīs Zemen*, 28 tik'imt 1940 [8 November 1947], 3.
[58] Ninth Annual Track & Field Meet, 1958–59, 20.

also used the natural surroundings for this purpose.[59] The financing of these smaller stadiums and playing fields seems to have been a mix of government investment and local initiative.[60] In Mek'ele, stadium development received substantial support from *Ras* Mengesha, the provincial governor, who was an active football player himself. In Gondar, the committee for the improvement of sports in Begemder Province raised funds for a new stadium by organizing a gala dinner.[61] In other cases, communal work levelling the ground resulted in a playing field. In contrast to the stadium as a landmark in the city centre (e.g. Addis Ababa, Awassa), the *Kagnew Astadium* and sports fields of the nearby Atse Yohannes Preparatory School (established in 1952) formed a sports nucleus on the margins of Mek'ele.[62] On Sundays, however, football fans watching a match in the stadium or from elevated places (hills or electricity poles) turned the city's margins into its centre.

As shown in Chapter 2, *Sports and Propaganda during the Fascist Occupation (1935–1941)*, mass media not only served to promote sports as a means to build the civilized colonial subject but also captured excitement on the sports venues through linguistic creativity. After the liberation, sports news often consumed two or more pages in *Addīs Zemen* or the *Ethiopian Herald*, which reported about stadium construction projects in great detail. By the late 1960s, the press had its own facilities called 'Little Berlin' in Haile Selassie I Stadium.[63]

However, stadiums were not only places of athletic competition or political spectacle, but also spaces of entertainment such as athletic shows. These ranged from wrestling performances to raise money for charity to performances of strength by pulling cars. On the other hand, places of entertainment also became athletic venues. According to Girma Cheru, bodybuilding shows took place in Hager Fikir Theatre, the

---

[59] Under the name *Baloni* (meaning ball made of used cloths, and now the formal name of the stadium), it served the Italian community with a small football field and a tennis court in the 1930s.
[60] Tibebu Gorfu, *Yesport mazewterīya sifrawochinna mabelts'egīya standard* [Sports places and development standards], Addis Ababa, 1990 EC, 1997/8, 24. MS., Library of the Ethiopian Sports Commission.
[61] BeGonder ketema wist' stadiyum līsera tak'idwal [Plan to build a stadium in the city of Gondar], *Addīs Zemen*, 14 meskerem 1964 [5 September 1971]. According to the master plan of the Ministry of Interior (1967, p. 10 and p. 38), Gondar already had a municipal stadium near the Fasilidas Bath: Ministry of Interior, Municipalities Department (1967), General analysis and the report on the Master Plan for Gondar. Consultants: Barucci – Di Gaddo – Sacco, 20, 38, IES 711.4 IN.
[62] I am deeply indebted to Abraham Tewelde, athlete, referee, and sports enthusiast, for showing and explaining these localities to me. He generously shared his time to compare historical photographs of the Surafiel Photo Studio with the current structure of the place in March and July 2013.
[63] 'Little Berlin', *Addis Reporter*, 1:4 (1969), 1.

Cinema Ras, and other halls, often including musical performances.[64] Display of strength, e.g. lifting heavy tables, having cars rolled over one's body, or breaking stones with the chest, were in demand from the mid-1960s onwards and were thus reported upon in the media.[65] Girma Cheru featured as the 'sports teacher of the nation' through regular sports programmess on the radio and, more importantly, on Ethiopian television (established in 1964). People still remember him for his instructions as part of a children's show when they 'used to follow his instructions … while doing the exercises on the living room carpet'.[66] From the late 1940s, boxing bouts took place at the Cinema Ethiopia and, sometimes, even the emperor followed the match.

Although there is no evidence yet that boxing or bodybuilding shows were part of Addis Ababa's nightlife scene, dancing definitely was. This refers not only to the many restaurants where local dancing companies performed Ethiopian dances, but also to the numerous nightclubs. 'Swinging Addis' refers to Ethio-Jazz music, while dancing was definitely a part of the whole trend.

> In the 1960s and early 70s … Addis Ababa's nightlife was electrified by a blend of traditional folk music, jazz, swing, rhythm and blues. Clubs were full, dance floors packed with young people moved by the music of a new generation of Ethiopian pop stars who were inspired by Elvis and James Brown but gave their sound a unique twist.[67]

Live bands such as Addis Ababa Club, Wallia Band, Omedla Band, Ibex, Ayalew's Band, Venus Band, and Zerai Deres played at least once a week at the Ghion Hotel, Ras Hotel, Wabe Shebelle Hotel, the Hilton, Omedla, Venus, and Stereo Night Club. Hotel d'Afrique, Osibissa, and Sheba Night Club played recorded music every night. No less than twelve nightclubs offered dancing facilities in the Nefas Silk area on the way to Debre Zeit.[68] The interchangeable use of places for sports, leisure, and entertainment constructed unique social spaces that always served more than one purpose. This is even truer for places and buildings that were part of the emerging tourism industry.

---

[64] Wendimu Negash Desta, 'Girma Cheru – gʷolmasaw sportenya I' [Girma Cheru – a fully accomplished athlete], *Yekatit,* hidar 1974 [November 1981], p. 32.
[65] Katrin Bromber, 'Muscularity, Heavy Athletics and Urban Leisure in Ethiopia, 1950s–1970s', *The International Journal of the History of Sport,* 30:16 (2013b), 1922–3.
[66] Nolawi, 'Abebayoosh!' bernos, 10 September 2006, www.bernos.com/blog/2006/09/10/abebayoosh [accessed 15 September 2021].
[67] 'Swinging Addis', BBC Radio, www.bbc.co.uk/programmes/b03ynfpl [accessed 15 September 2021].
[68] Tadesse Negash, 'Night Clubs in Addis Ababa', no date, IES 839a.

Useful Recreation and Fitness for Work

A look at Filwoha Park shows that Haile Selassie I Stadium is only a stone's throw away from Ghion Hotel.[69] The hotel not only had a spacious garden for recreation, but also provided an Olympic-sized swimming pool with five-, three-, and one-metre diving platforms. In contrast to armed forces facilities, educational institutions, or the premises of factories such as the cement factory in Dire Dawa, the Ghion pool was open to the public and, from 1968/69 onwards, home to the ten female and male athletes of Ethiopia's first swimming team outside of the armed forces.[70] Access to the facilities was restricted to those who could pay. Tickets cost 3 Ethiopian dollar (Eth$) for adults and 1 Eth$ for children and students (with a 1 Eth$ increase on weekends). For 45 Eth$ a person could buy a monthly ticket, and for 180 Eth$ an annual ticket. Access to the Hilton Hotel swimming pools was even more restricted. Apart from entrance fees, users had to be members. A weekday membership for adults cost 175 Eth$. An annual ticket of 275 Eth$ allowed use of the facilities on all days.[71] This might not have been expensive for somebody in a higher administrative position earning 1,000 Eth$ per month, but would definitely have been for a sub-professional civil servant who received a monthly salary between 75 and 525 Eth$.[72]

It goes without saying that only a minority of the urban population could afford such recreational luxury. However, hotels did not only provide sports facilities for guests and club members. They were also the frame for employees to do sports in an organized way. As early as 1969, the Hilton Hotel had five workers' football teams who regularly com-

---

[69] As we have already seen in the previous chapters, sports facilities had become an integral part of hotels from the early twentieth century onwards, with billiards taking the lead. By the 1960s, the situation had changed to such an extent that hotels became venues for major sports meets. Ground tennis facilities could be found in many hotels. Itege Hotel in Addis Ababa, for example, provided the necessary space for Ethiopian championships. In the basement of Gennet Hotel, bowling enthusiasts could, and can still today, enjoy their sport.
[70] '20 wet'atoch yewana budin ak'ʷak'ʷamu' [Swimming team of 20 youth founded], *Addīs Zemen*, 15 meskerem 1965 [25 September 1972]. Swimming competitions started within the armed forces from 1958/59 onwards. The Ethiopian Swimming Federation, founded in 1978/79, developed within the military framework: Mekonnen Sintayehu, 'Swimming in Ethiopia', (Unpublished BE thesis Kotebe College of Teacher Education, 1995), p. 10.
[71] Tadesse Negash, 'Swimming Pools in Addis Ababa', not dated, IES 192.05 HAG Per. In the 1960s 1 Eth$ equalled US$ 0.40.
[72] Irvin Kaplan, Mark Farber, Barbara Marvin, James McLaughlin, Harold D. Nelson, and Donald Whitaker (eds), Area Handbook for Ethiopia (Washington, 1971), p. 396.

peted against the teams from the Economic Commission for Africa.[73] It is highly doubtful whether workers also had access to facilities such as tennis courts or if the hotel lobby occasionally served as a table tennis venue for them, as had the YMCA Central Branch lobby and the lobby in the Municipality Hall. From the early 1950s onwards, boxing and freestyle wrestling bouts took place in the capital's administrative centre.[74] Furthermore, the Workers' Help and Saving Association (*seratenyoch meredajana k'ot'eba mahber*), working for the Addis Ababa municipality in 1963/64, ran a modern club that included facilities for table tennis, badminton, chess, and other games. Similar to Addis Ababa, Mek'ele Town Hall also included facilities for doing sports. However, there is no indication that employees used the bodybuilding facilities in the basement for their own athletic ambitions. However, they were closest to the place where cinema and athletic performance merged into entertainment. In Jimma, outdoor films, which included documentaries about sports (mostly by the US Information Service), were shown in front of the Municipal Hall.[75]

Organized sports events that included workers or employees were not restricted to the capital, but also took place as part of sports festivals in other towns. In June 1972, for example, civil servants of the Wollega Province competed against the traders' football team, and employees of St. Maryam Hospital played against the farmer's team on the football field in Axum.[76] In contrast to other Ethiopian provincial capitals at that time, Dire Dawa was an industrial town with a cotton factory, a cement factory, and diverse railway workshops. A labour union was already formed in 1947 (Railroad Workers Syndicate), and was responsible for welfare. Whether this also included sports and recreation is not clear. Probably, the enthusiasm of the Italian owners of the cement and cotton factories led to the establishment of their football teams with good financial support. By 1947, Dire Dawa already had its own league and the *Taffari* team, which represented the province, entered the Ethiopian Championships series in the same year.[77] Whereas Boy Scouts and secondary school children received permission to use the cement

---

[73] 'Hīltenina Ī.Si.Ē. keseratenya budin gar wididir līk'et'il new' [Competition between employees of the Hilton and the ECA continues], *Addīs Zemen*, 3 tir 1962 [11 January 1970], 2.

[74] 'Bemazegaja bēt adarash yetederegu bogsina tigil' [Boxing and wrestling in the Municipality hall], *Addīs Zemen*, 27 meskerem 1943 [7 October 1950]; for continuation see for example 'Boxing', *Ethiopian Herald*, 13 January 1960, 2.

[75] *The Framer's Voice*, 2:4 (February 1959), p. 4, IES 371.805 JIM AGR.

[76] 'Negadē seratenyan begemed guteta reta' [Traders won against civil servants in tug-of war], *Addīs Zemen*, 20 ginbot 1964 [28 May 1972], 2.

[77] Local history in Ethiopia, compiled by Bernhard Lindahl, https://nai.uu.se/library/resources/thematic-resources/local-history-of-ethiopia.html [accessed 15 September 2021].

factory's swimming pool, this might not automatically have been the case for the workers.[78] Unfortunately, works by Ethiopian labour historians, who conducted intensive research on various companies in the 1980s, do not reveal anything about the workers' spare time activities, except drinking.

It definitely made a difference if expatriates were staff members. Haile Selassie I University of the mid-1960s might serve as an example. Foreign staff members received the information that the university campuses are 'equipped with softball, soccer, and basketball fields. Tennis courts are available and are very popular with foreign staff (once they become used to the altitude)' along with their work contract.[79] Apart from sports on or around the campus, the universities also advertised leisure activities that coupled sports and tourism, mountaineering, hunting, or simply driving out of Addis in order to experience marvellous landscapes. However, these landscapes were also transformed into testing grounds for man and machine in a competitive context – motorsports. By the 1960s, 'long distance' had become a topic in Ethiopia's sports scene.

A Race that Constructs the Nation: The Ethiopian Highland Rally

By the 1950s, long-distance races became a regular feature of Ethiopia's sports scene. Bicycle races, which continued after the Italian occupation, were gradually opened even to female athletes. On 15 May 1954, Haile Selassie personally gave the starting signal for the first marathon in Ethiopia from Haile Selassie I Stadium along Bishoftu Road and back.[80] Two years later, fifteen athletes, trained in the armed forces, completed the 42.195 km from the Imperial Ethiopian Army's Field via Akaki to the army grounds near the civilian airport. The result of 2.45 hrs for a race at high altitude inspired the *Ethiopian Herald* to anticipate that 'with some appropriate training and more experience in Road Races, we can certainly look forward to international Marathon victory'.[81] Although muscular strength and athletic success were promoted amongst the (young) Ethiopians by various sports federations, physical education, and volunteer organizations such as the YMCA and the Boy Scouts ranked very high on the agenda, 'the great appeal of cycling could also be interpreted as part

---

[78] Onni Niskanen, The Boy Scout Camp in Dire*Dawa [sic] and Harar during August 1949, 15 September 1949, RNT TWU, 3.
[79] Haile Selassie I University AA, 1966, Information for Foreign Staff, IES, 369.43 Misc. papers.
[80] 'Field Athletic Championships is to be Held soon', *Ethiopian Herald*, 9 May 1954, 1.
[81] 'Fourth Track Field Meet at Army Stadium', *Ethiopian Herald*, 14 May 1956, 1.

Sports' Material Infrastructure and the Production of Space (1910s–1970s) 171

of the fascination with modern machines'.[82] Arguably, this fascination grew even stronger with motor racing.

With the increasing number of cars in the capital, motor sports enthusiasts already started to organize races in 1953. Due to its growing popularity, the National Ethiopian Sports Confederation (NESC) decided to form the Imperial Ethiopian Automobile Club. Right from the beginning, two representatives of the Eritrean Automobile Club participated in the project. Coming from the centre of car mechanics in the Horn of Africa, where the Italians had already established a *Reale Automobile Club d'Italia* (Head Office of the Royal Automobile Club of Italy) in 1937, Eritrean expertise was very welcome in creating institutional structures as well as in organizing rallies. A first idea was, of course, to hold a race as part of the Silver Jubilee celebrations.[83]

In October 1964, the tourism development enterprise Oasis Ltd. Share Company asked Crown Prince Asfa Wossen for support in organizing the first Ethiopian Highland Rally on the occasion of the royal visit by the British queen to Ethiopia in 1965. They argued that such an event would provide 'worldwide publicity for Ethiopia'[84] and special attraction to the royal visitors. In fact, reports about the planned event even made it into *The New York Times*.[85] Oasis Ltd. further suggested that the emperor might act as patron of the event and, if possible, one of the royal couple may present the victory cup.[86] Despite the support of the crown prince, the race was not included in the royal tour, which, instead, resorted to allegedly more appropriate mass gymnastic performances in Haile Selassie I Stadium and *feres gugs* (horse race with shield and lance) at the Jan Mēda racing grounds.[87]

However, the rally itself took place a month earlier, and a small number of motor sports enthusiasts raced out of the Ethiopian capital on 30 January 1965. *The New York Times* reported about the organizers' hopes 'to make this rally an annual event' on a route that 'would cover about 700 miles, about 50 per cent good and the rest, mediocre to terrible' on a terrain 'well suited to a thorough testing of all types of motor

---

[82] Jakob Krais, 'Mastering the Wheel of Chance Motor Racing in French Algeria and Italian Libya', *Comparative Studies of South Asia, Africa and the Middle East*, 39:1 (2019), 147.
[83] 'Automobile Club is to be Formed [sic] in the City', *Ethiopian Herald*, 22 October 1955, 2.
[84] Oasis Ltd. Share Company to Crown Prince Asfa Wossen, 7 October 1964, ENA 1.2.54.08.
[85] 'About Motorcar Sports: Ethiopia Planning Rally in the Highlands', *The New York Times*, December 1964, 31.
[86] Oasis Ltd. Share Company to Crown Prince Asfa Wossen, 7 October 1964, ENA 1.2.54.08.
[87] 'Royal Tour of Ethiopia (1965)', 3 April 2014, www.youtube.com/watch?v=oA3u8JzcO2Y [accessed 15 September 2021].

5. Onni Niskanen and Per-Arne Thyberg with their Saab V4 at the Ethiopian Highland Rally 1966 (Onni Niskanen Private Collection, courtesy of Ulf Niskanen).

vehicles'.[88] With forty-one cars flagged off at the start, the first Ethiopian Highland Rally had its highest number of participants, who had not really anticipated the requirements for man and machine at what later was described as 'Africa's toughest car race'.[89] Car companies such as Renault, Peugeot, Fiat, and Volkswagen sponsored the teams. As shown in Illustration 5, Onni Niskanen – who was among the founders of the Ethiopian Highland Rally – and his co-driver Per-Arne Thyberg participated, of course, in a Saab from Sweden.[90]

In the following years, the number of participants decreased, but also became more and more international. In 1967, six Soviet teams participated driving Volga and Moskvitch vehicles.[91] From neighbouring

[88] 'About Motorcar Sports', p. 31.
[89] 'Ethiopia: Cars Start Gruelling Three Thousand Mile Rally. Despite World Petrol Shortage, 1973', British Pathé www.britishpathe.com/video/VLVACVOBOHRQ371LZQB7IS89NBKKA-ETHIOPIA-CARS-START-GRUELLING-THREE-THOUSAND-MILE-RALLY-DESPITE/query/MILE [accessed 15 September 2021].
[90] 'Ethiopian Highland Rally 1965–1974', 3 January 2013, https://ulfniskanen.wordpress.com/2013/01/03/ethiopian-highland-rally-1965-1974 [accessed 15 September 2021].
[91] 'Ethiopian Highland Rally 1967', Raw21 http://raw21.com/2017/03/02/iv-ethiopian-highland-rally-1967 [accessed 15 September 2021].

Kenya, champions such as Joginder Singh – 'The Flying Sikh' or *Simba wa Kenya* [Lion of Kenya] – and Edgar Hermann competed for the title.[92] The race also attracted teams from Germany and Great Britain. By the early 1970s, the Ethiopian Highland Rally had become as important as the Rallye du Maroc or East Africa Safari Rally and gained entry into the *Yearbook of Automobile Sport* – the international racing calendar.

Organization and sponsorship changed from the already mentioned Oasis Ltd. Share Company (1965) to being co-organized by Ethiopian Airlines and the Ethiopian Tourism Organization (1966). In 1968, the Addis Ababa-based Italian Sports Club Juventus took over the organization and sponsorship of over thirty local motor races of smaller size.[93] Apart from the Ethiopian Highland Rally, regular races took place in and around Dire Dawa, Jimma, and Awassa.[94] The strong involvement of the Italian community comes as no surprise. They had already gained experience in the former Libyan colony, where they had organized rallies to mark 'Fascist power in the desert'.[95] Inspired by the success of the Tripoli Grand Prix, car races also took place in colonial Eritrea.[96] In 1938, the 'Primo Circuito di Asmara' 'enjoyed widespread popularity among the Italian and Eritrean public'.[97] Steffano Belucci and Massimo Zaccaria convincingly argue that Eritrea's urban centres were not only centres for training African mechanics, but also hubs for cultivating use of the car and the motorbike amongst Eritreans.

The Ethiopian Highland Rally was, at least as far as the teams were concerned, the business of the foreign and expatriate communities. However, Ethiopians were involved in a number of ways: as members of the honorary committee or as stewards of meetings.[98] They were in charge of public relations and advertising.[99] During the race, they

---

[92] *Yearbook of Automobile Sport* http://doczz.cz/doc/66669/1---prohistoric.cz [accessed 15 September 2021].

[93] Eighth Ethiopian Highland Rally, Programme, 9–12 December 1971, IES 796.72 ETH, 21–2.

[94] Second Awasa Rally, 5 April 1970, IES 796.73 ETH.

[95] Mussolini, 'Ai Camerati di Tripoli'; 'Solenne inaugurazione della Fiera di Tripoli, sagra del lavoro italiano nelle colonie dell'Impero. Il chiaro e fiero discorso pronunciato dal DUCE', Il Littoriale, 18 March 1937, cited in Krais, 'Mastering the Wheel of Chance', 147.

[96] Mahamad Kheir Omer et al., *Asmara: Pictorial View, 1890–1938* (Asmara, 2012), p. 56.

[97] Steffano Belucci and Massimo Zaccaria, 'Engine of Change: A Social History of the Car-Mechanics Sector in the Horn of Africa', in Jan-Bart Gewald, André Liviveld, and Iva Peša (eds), *Transforming Innovations in Africa: Explorative Studies on Appropriation in African Societies* (Leiden, 2012), p. 243.

[98] In 1970, YMCA Chairman Desta Girma was in this position.

[99] Eighth Ethiopian Highland Rally, Programme, 9–12 December 1971, IES 796.72 ETH, 3.

acted as controllers and radio operators.[100] They were consumers of the sport by personally watching and cheering, by listening through the radio broadcasts in English, French, or Amharic or by watching the daily 'TV progress report'.[101] Arguably, by conquering vast distances of several thousand kilometres by car – a powerful symbol of modernity in general and individual advancement in particular – the Ethiopian Highland Rally constructed several overlapping and interpenetrating spaces through a specific sporting practice, the involvement of imperial political symbolism, and historical links between Ethiopia and Eritrea.

The distance, which increased each year,[102] was raced in three circuits on three days. These circuits extended to the south, east, and north-east of Addis Ababa and included stops in urban centres such as Jimma, Debre Zeit, Nazareth, and Dire Dawa. Although the Ethiopian Highland Rally never went as far north as Asmara, motorsports enthusiasts remember it that way. Looking at motorsports from the perspective that Ethiopia had annexed Eritrea, and that the student movement had made the issue of Eritrean self-determination one of its major political demands, this challenge for man and machine gains a political dimension. Programmes always included maps that included Eritrea while making the Ethiopian capital the centre. They 'conceived space', as the French philosopher Henri Lefebvre argued, as a social and political act by following a logic that aimed at long-term effects.[103] It was yet another attempt to construct imperial space.

The power of the map was coupled with other symbolic practices. Crown Prince Asfa Wossen was the patron of the Ethiopian Highland Rally and, thus, presented the trophies. In 1971, the programme informed its readers that he 'will start the first car'.[104] The honorary committee consisted of high-ranking personalities such as ministers, governors, and commanders of the armed forces, who had in the case of Col. Tamrat Yegezu (for many years, the very active president of the Ethiopian YMCA) long-standing experience of what kind of support was needed.[105] Similar to other athletic events, the imperial family and

[100] Ibid., 52.
[101] Ibid., 17.
[102] 2,688 km; 1966: 2,987 km; 1967: 3,000 km; 1968: 3,450 km; 1969: 4,000 km; 1970: 4,200 km (Eighth Ethiopian Highland Rally, Programme, 52.)
[103] Henri Lefebvre, *The Production of Space*, trans. Donald Nicholson-Smith (Oxford, 1991), p. 39.
[104] Eighth Ethiopian Highland Rally, Programme, 18.
[105] In 1971, for example, the committee included ministers such as Ketema Yifru (Minister of Commerce, Industry, and Tourism), *Lij* Endalkachew Makonnen (Minister of Communication, Telecommunication, and Posts), Dr. Seyoum Heregot (Minister in the Prime Minister's Office), Salih Henit (Minister of Public Works), Seifu Mahteme Selassie (Minister of Education), and Habte Selassie Taffesse (Minister of State of Tourism). It also incorporated high-

the aristocratic elite were deeply involved in modern sports on a symbolic level. In contrast to motor sports in colonial Eritrea or Libya, where car races served to symbolically integrate colonial territory, to demonstrate technological progress, and to establish colonial possessions as 'laboratories of modernity and experimentation',[106] the Ethiopian Highland Rally followed the logic that Ethiopia was part of technological progress through guidance from the imperial government or family.

The third overlapping space was that of the foreign or expatriate communities. The close cooperation with the Eritrean Automobile Club went hand in hand with the numerous formal and informal relations between mechanics and motorsports fans in Ethiopia and Eritrea through family and other relationships. Sports enthusiasm met economic networks that included the Greek community and blurred territorial boundaries. Whereas the foreign communities strengthened spatial practice within an Ethiopia that included Eritrea, the expatriate communities linked the event to the international racing scene. Thus, by becoming a part of the international racing calendar, the Ethiopian Highland Rally mapped itself in the global competitive arena.

The Highland Races stopped after 1974, and motorsports decreased in importance for a number of reasons. The athletic space that it had produced vanished. In contrast, stadiums, gymnasiums, and swimming pools are material traces built to last. Arguably, they provide access to study the continuities entailed in dreams and plans, which might need decades of implementation. Gulele Stadium, later renamed Abebe Bikila Stadium, in Addis Ababa is a good case in point. The emperor had granted the land to the Ethiopian Sports Confederation in the 1960s. In spring 1972, *Addīs Zemen* reported on the work to level the ground, published plans of how the sports and recreation complex should look, and presented ideas about its use in the future.[107] Dreams to open the stadium in November 1972 did not come true. The area remained a football field until 1990, when Addis Ababa City administration commissioned the stadium's construction with funds provided by FIFA.[108] Two years later, the *Ethiopian Herald* wrote that Chinese contract workers would soon begin construction.[109]

---

ranking members of the armed forces such as Major General Kebede Worku (Commander of the Fourth Army Division), and Yilma Shibeshi (Commander of the Imperial Police Force).
[106] Krais, 'Mastering the Wheel of Chance', 143.
[107] 'Yegulelē stadium sira behidar wer yit'enak'ek'al' [Work on Gulele Stadium starts in November], *Addīs Zemen*, 13 megabīt 1964 [22 March 1972], 2.
[108] Interview by Edlawit Hirpa and Emnet Woubishet with Genet Werkenhe, general manager of the Abebe Bikila complex on 6 June 2014.
[109] 'New Stadium for Addis', *Ethiopian Herald*, 17 December 1992, 2.

However, the most revealing document signalling changes in the quality and quantity of places for doing sports was Yidnek'achew Tesemma's *Pilot Study to Re-Organize and Promote Sport in Ethiopia*. Finished in November 1973, it was a constructive response to the proposed inclusion of the Ethiopian Sports Confederation (established 1948) in the Ministry of Community Development and Social Affairs, and formulated sports-related aspects for the country's fourth Five-Year Plan. The author proposed that the 'Planning & Programming and Engineering Sections' of the confederation should provide detailed studies 'about the country's main problems regarding facilities for sport activities [including] the availability of stadiums, sports arena, [and] gymnasiums'.[110] Apart from service to the public, the section was to also study and plan for private organizations 'which are interested in building their own sport facilities'.[111] This assistance, however, shifted the responsibility for building and maintaining sporting places from the municipalities. Yidnek'achew emphasized that a town needs a minimum of buildings for the public: 'a spiritual centre (church, mosque, etc.), a school, one town hall (theatre), one public park and one stadium'.[112] This demand clearly clashed with the scarcity of vacant plots of land and the already soaring real estate prices in the urban areas. Giving sports and healthy recreation a chance in the city, 'the government would declare ... public property areas, [and] remove the private owners by providing them with the proper re-location options'.[113]

Even such radical measures did not ease the situation much, especially in the capital. In 1990, the *Ethiopian Herald* complained that playgrounds in the capital were disappearing because of the construction boom and commented that if 'the absence of adequate large sports complexes and gymnasiums can rightly be attributed to [the] lack of adequate financing ... the growing scarcity of playgrounds cannot be justified'.[114] The main argument for providing enough inner-city facilities remained the same as in the 1940s: sports as 'the' antidote to the spread of social vices amongst the youth.

The *Pilot Study* also stressed the importance of sports for the working masses. It envisaged that 'factories and other large business or agricultural establishments would provide such facilities for their employees'.[115] Such declared aims of regular sports for employees to keep workers healthy and provide space for socializing was well in line with

[110] Yidnek'achew Tesemma, *Pilot Study to Re-Organize and Promote Sport in Ethiopia* (Unpublished MS.) November 1973, IES 796.332YED, p. 6.
[111] Yidnek'achew Tesemma, *Pilot Study*, p. 6
[112] Ibid., p. 12.
[113] Ibid., p. 13.
[114] 'Children's Playgrounds Vanishing beneath Works of Construction', *Ethiopian Herald*, 6 June 1990, p. 2.
[115] Yidnek'achew, *Pilot Study*, p. 12.

post-1974 sports within a socialist context and thus continued accordingly. In 1978, *Addīs Zemen* provided information that, of the ten Hilton Hotel football teams, three would register with the Ethiopian Football Federation. A professional coach would train the best players before competing against other Hilton teams in Egypt, Kenya, Madagascar, Iran, and Kuwait. Female employees were encouraged to join the volleyball team.[116] Two years earlier, in 1976, *Addīs Zemen* reported on athletic and football finals at which different male and female teams of the Ministry of Information competed for the trophies.[117] Arguably, such sports competitions have to be seen as a continuation of earlier developments and attempts to link healthy recreation and socializing within a competitive framework to the working environment. It also shows that sports was increasingly conceptualized in terms of a mass movement that was to serve as a broad basis for identifying talent and countering the tendency of spectator rather than active sports. Both aspects were also discussed in the MoE and notably in the Ethiopian Sports Confederation, so that we can speak of a shift in the overall conception of sports in the early 1970s.

This shift also included the proposed substitution of expensive imports by locally manufactured equipment. Yidnek'achew suggested waiving taxes as an incentive to invest in local athletic shoe production.[118] The turn to the local also resulted in an in-depth study of local-cum-traditional sports practices in terms of regulations as well as spatial specificities. Following a proclamation in 1975 to establish sporting competition with a view to promoting and coordinating traditional sports in Ethiopia, as well as to scientifically and systematically registering and studying traditional sports, a group of sports experts went to all provinces. By 1978 they had registered 293 traditional sports, identified locally specific rules, dress, and equipment and described the time and places for practising them.[119] This study laid the basis for selecting and further developing (regulating) a limited number of 'cultural' sports practices – including their spatial regimes – within the socialist and post-socialist context.[120] The explicit promotion and

---

[116] 'K'wamī aselt'any bek'irbu yik'et'eral: Hīlten 3 budin ak'ʷak'ʷame' [Permanent coach will be employed: Hilton founded three teams], *Addīs Zemen*, 10 hamlē 1971 [17 July 1979], 2.
[117] 'Yeprēs budin tek'lala ashenafī hono tesheleme' [Press team excelled as winner], *Addīs Zemen*, 29 hamlē 1967 [5 August 1975], 2.
[118] Yidnek'achew, *Pilot Study*, 15.
[119] Teferi Mekonnen, *Nebbar sport* [Traditional sports], Addis Ababa, 1973 EC, 1980/81, MS, Library of the Ethiopian Sports Commission.
[120] *Bahilawī sportochachinin besir'at inawek'achew/inich'awetachew* [Let us know our cultural sports in a correct way / Let us practice them]. Be'Ītyop'ya bahilawī sport fēdērēshin [By the Ethiopian Cultural Sports Federation], Addis Ababa, ginbot 1992 [May 1999], MS, Library of the Ethiopian Sports Commis-

sportization[121] of local sports practices in the late 1970s leaves ample space for speculation. It might not be wrong to expect a government that had proclaimed the rule of the working masses (i.e. farmers) to be interested in their local sports practices. An emphasis on local sports with low costs offered a way to solve the tension between the promotion of sports in general and the high financial investments associated with it. Thus, it could serve as a way to implement the slogan: 'Sports for all!'

---

sion. For the case of wrestling, see Katrin Bromber, '"Ethiopian" Wrestling', 23–40.
[121] Norbert Elias' term 'sportization' refers to the transformation of folk games into modern sports. This process includes codifying rules, writing them down, and strictly enforcing them in an effective manner.

6
Conclusion and Outlook

Modern sports in Ethiopia during the late imperial period, especially during Haile Selassie's rule, was part of a larger attempt to modernize the empire as well as a way to appropriate new athletic practices and forms of leisure. It left an imprint on the educational system, urban development, and a youth training undergirded by conceptions of useful recreation and the fit human body for the Ethiopian 'New Man'. During the period I have looked at, sports also functioned as a political propaganda tool at home and abroad. This especially holds true for the occupation and post-liberation periods. Sports became a way to stage or contest loyalty to the emperor and to demonstrate Ethiopia's road to progress. In educational institutions as well as in volunteer organizations such as the YMCA and the Boy Scouts, sports offered multiple entry points for foreign soft power from diverse, often conflicting, ends of the political spectrum during the Cold War. In this final chapter, I return to the thematic gateways to study *zemenawīnet* that I described in the *Introduction*. I conclude by suggesting further fields for exploring social transformation through sports in the Ethiopia of the twentieth century.

Zemenawīnet through the Lens of Sports

What does the perspective of modern sports contribute to recent discussions on *Zemenawīnet* (Ethiopian modernity) that have brought to the fore new perspectives on coloniality, the relation of the religious and the modern, urban developments, and specific forms of subject formation? As this book has shown, sports cannot be viewed in isolation, but has an important part to play in a nation's identity formation and politics. This book has focused on Ethiopia, but also argues to look at the multiplicity of athletic developments beyond the framework of the empire – especially in its relationship to the Middle East. Thus, it contributes to a scholarship which emphasize 'South–South' relations in sports, which cannot be easily subsumed under geographical labels such as 'African' or 'Middle Eastern' sports history. Although Ethiopia could successfully resist long-term colonization, the book contributes to the historical scholarship about sports, coloniality and modernity in Africa and beyond.

Ethiopian Modernity and Coloniality

The lens of sports in Ethiopian modernity reveals the epistemic legacy of globally circulating projects of linear development mediated by coloniality. From the early twentieth century onwards, engagement in modern sports served as a symbol of Ethiopia's path to overcoming its perceived backwardness that stood in the way of being accepted as an equal partner vis-à-vis the surrounding colonial powers. As part of international diplomacy, participation in international sporting meets such as the Olympic Games was on the agenda from early on. The price for global recognition in sports was not only the acceptance of rules and regulations formulated by sporting organizations dominated by European and North American agents. It was the dismissal of local athletic techniques of the body in favour of internationally regulated competitive sports. Despite the occasional reference to so-called 'traditional' sports as a proof that physical exercise and competition was nothing new to Ethiopians, local athletic practices evidently did not fit the narrative of progress. Thus, Ethiopia sought expert knowledge on modern sports in the global North or (former) European colonial possessions – such as India – where British ideas of physical education in ministries and schools were spread throughout the empire.

During the Italian occupation, sports became a means of direct domination and racial segregation through what Partha Chatterjee has called the 'rule of colonial difference'.[1] It found its expression in promoting Eritrean athletes in competitions, establishing segregated sporting venues for the 'natives', renaming football clubs, and enforcing ideas of the Italian 'civilizing mission' by emphasizing moral conduct in sports. Athletic competitions became a stage for performing colonially induced progress as well as claiming the loyalty of athletes, fans, and local notables. The newly established system of local and regional competitions and the translation and enforcement of internationally valid rules and regulations were not peculiar to Italian colonialism or Fascism at all, but this did push the idea that the athletic practices of the 'natives' simply had no rules. Forty years later, this attitude led to the sportization of selected 'traditional' sports such as wrestling (*tigil*), horse racing (*feres gugs*), or mind games such as *gebeta* on a national level.[2]

The emphasis on regulating sports and athletic behaviour in accordance with international standards continued after the liberation. Within the educational sector, it found its expression in the introduction of adapted regulations for athletics and football by the Ethiopian Inter-School Athletic Association (EISAA). The competition board sep-

---

[1] Partha Chatterjee, *The Nation and Its Fragments* (Princeton NJ, 1993), p. 10.
[2] *Sportization*, a term coined by Norbert Elias, refers to the transformation of folk games into modern sport by codifying rules, writing them down, and strictly enforcing them in an effective manner.

arately assessed and rewarded school teams for playing according to rules. The EISAA pamphlets and YMCA reports recurrently emphasized the mantra of 'fair play' and the value of cooperation over harsh competition in sports. Modesty in victory became a marker of the morally acceptable athlete – at least in the official documents of these organizations. In contrast, the aggressive style of play favoured by army football teams led to stark criticism of their 'uncivilized' behaviour on the pitch and the withdrawal of the civilian teams Ararat and Olympiacos from the national league.

With the decline of British influence after 1951 (the end of the British Military Mission in Ethiopia), sports developed as one gateway for the United States' soft power in Ethiopia. This does not only refer to the very successful sports programmes of the YMCA, the exclusive training of its Ethiopian physical education secretaries in the US, and inclusion of Peace Corps volunteers as sports instructors. The influence through sports also reached institutions of higher learning that were part of the Point Four Program. Arguably, more than twenty-five years of continuous work in the Ethiopian sports sector (which, for the YMCA, continued until 1978) were sufficient to transfer American YMCA ideas about physical fitness to the (socialist) Sports Commission of Ethiopia.

Modern Sports, the Spiritual, and the Religious in Ethiopian Modernity

Another point of the debate about what studies on *zemenawīnet* should include revolves around the question of the extent to which the spiritual and the religious shaped both narratives and practices of Ethiopian modernity. Religious figures, often of high rank, became involved in decisions and processes of legitimizing power. Following the demand of the Coptic Church, the first (physical education) teachers at modern schools in Ethiopia came from Egypt. During the occupation, local religious figures, who regularly participated as guests of honour in major sporting events, praised the Fascist sports policy in speeches that were reproduced in the Amharic press. At the same time, sports officers of the occupation government enforced the division of sports teams along religious lines. Thus, religion was part of colonial athletic modernity in Ethiopia.

After the liberation, the sports pages of YMCA pamphlets as well as Haile Selassie's speeches during athletic events recurrently emphasized ideas about the human body as a sacred temple. Care for the body through physical training came close to worship that led, for example, to the favouring of bodybuilding amongst YMCA members. The spiritual side of football deserves its own study. Most probably, players and fans hoped and prayed for victory. Stories of players burying religious objects under goal posts to increase their chances for victory hint at the materiality of religion in sports. Furthermore, naming practices and club paraphernalia point to the divine. Club names such as Ararat (sacred mountain of the Armenians and the mythical resting place of Noah's Ark) and St. George (patron Saint of Ethiopia) are telling examples.

Modern Sports' Influence on Urban Development

Infrastructure development and urbanization in early twentieth-century Ethiopia shaped and were shaped by spaces for doing and consuming modern sports. The integration of the empire into global economic and political networks accelerated the immigration of foreign labour and the establishment of diplomatic missions in Ethiopian urban centres. Workers and experts from abroad came with diverse ideas about physical fitness. Hotels provided athletic entertainment for both travellers from abroad as well as the local nobility. Members of the so-called foreign communities and legations opened clubs that provided facilities and programmes for modern sports. In contrast to these exclusive spaces, multipurpose locations such as Jan Mēda became hot spots for modern athletic practices and their consumption by the urban population. Since Jan Mēda also served as a venue for competitions of the 'cultural' or 'traditional' sports during religious festivals, local competitive practices increasingly blended with internationally regulated ones. During the Italian occupation, the venue increased its function as an athletic competition ground. Thus, one might have expected the first stadium to be constructed there. However, master plans for the development of the Ethiopian capital as the colonial and, later, imperial centre integrated the stadium into the city centre as a representation of a modern state.

From the 1940s onwards, stadiums became markers of modern urban-ness in Ethiopia. The fact that both public and private investment went into building them shows that stadium construction was not an exclusively top-down process. The development of open fields into enclosed and properly measured sports grounds, the conversion of grandstands from traditional tents for the nobility into corrugated iron constructions, the reduced visibility of sporting events after the introduction of ticket boxes, as well as the inclusion of changing rooms and press offices produced spaces for experiencing modernity in sports and its monetization.

Modern educational institutions did not only subscribe to ideas about physical fitness. They invested in them by expanding the physical space of schools and colleges via the construction of sports fields and gymnasiums. Addis Ababa's rapid urban growth did not always allow the physical expansion of schools for athletic purposes. In such cases, diverse networks facilitated access to other institutions. Furthermore, the initial unacceptability of sports such as football or heavy athletics also determined their spatial configuration.

The temporality of urban athletic space, especially in city centres, was also expressed in public athletic performances, acrobatic shows, and diverse races. From the 1930s onwards, the combinations of man and machine in bicycle and motor races performed accelerated time as an aspect of modern city life. Urban rhythms changed through the reservation of time slots for practising and consuming sports. For sports enthusiasts and their families, competition schedules increasingly determined the week and especially the weekend. Those who could afford it went to nearby recreation hot spots that offered water sports such as Debre Zeit, Lake Langano, or Ambo. Arguably, the weekends of many urban dwellers became athletic in a number of ways – formal and informal, in town and out of town. Furthermore, races of all sorts as well as walking tours arranged by volunteer organizations – such as the Ethiopian Boy Scouts and the YMCA – linked urban spaces to national territory in a very perceptible way.

Modern Sports and the Ethiopian 'New Man'

Attempts to transform Ethiopia into a modern state, shaped ideas of the Ethiopian 'New Man' as well as practices for forming him or her into a 'torchbearer of progress'. I have argued that the 'new' did not only refer to the intellect but also to the human body as the site where ideas of progress could be inscribed. From the early twentieth century onwards, modern sports served as a marker of the progressive subject. I have demonstrated that modern sports as a means of subject formation did not only apply to young members of the nobility, i.e. students who were sent abroad for study or the emperor's most-favoured son. It was also true for those Boy Scouts who came from the lowest stratum of society and were supposed to form the human material for building a powerful imperial army.

During the Fascist occupation, sports served to form the 'New Ethiopian' along the lines of the fit colonial subject and became instrumental to the colonial civilizing mission. According to the new context, competitions served as a stage to perform new loyalties and, in a few cases, to contest them. The performance of modern sports through publicly visible cycling competitions transformed local ideas of athletic heroism. The new athletic subject was a disciplined master of the machine.

After the liberation, modern sports increasingly helped to propagate a healthy national body consisting of 'New Men' as athletic citizens in the making. The underlying ideas were by no means consistent, but ranged on a spectrum from the loyal subject to the citizen as bearer of rights and duties. On the one hand, the personal involvement of Haile Selassie, members of his family, and the nobility in sports-promoting institutions led to the performance of loyalty as a ritual on the sports ground. On the other hand, leadership training in volunteer organizations and educational institutions instilled ideas of individuality, creativity, and responsibility. The promotion of diligence in training and fairness in competition made sports a suitable means to inculcate these ideas.

The Ethiopian 'New Man' that I portrayed in my book lived in urban centres (most notably in the capital) that offered facilities for practising modern sports and/or consuming it. This does not mean that the lives of the highly diverse rural population were static. I fully acknowledge the fact that Ethiopian modernity is multiple as modernity is in general. In terms of sports as social capital and local practices of physical education, I will now make some suggestions for further research.

Further Research Perspectives

Sports in the Reformed Armed Forces

Sports in the Imperial Ethiopian Army, the Imperial Body Guard, and the police forces definitely deserves its own study. Relying on a high degree of discipline and physical fitness, the armed forces were an ideal testing ground for any kind of modern sports. From the 1920s onwards, contracted military personnel from abroad brought with them their ideas about which physical exercise served best.[3] Furthermore, Ethiopian army and police officers who had served or studied abroad returned to Ethiopia with their own sports-related experiences. Some had served in the King's African Rifles in Kenya or in Italian contingents in Tripoli (Libya) prior to the Second World War. In the 1920s, Ethiopian cadets studied at the Ecole Spéciale Militaire de Saint-Cyr in France. During the war, thirty-two Ethiopians received training at St. George's Military School in Khartoum (Sudan).[4] In all these military institutions, sports was a compulsory part of everyday life as well as a suitable pastime. After their return to Ethiopia, the soldiers most probably did not want to miss their sports anymore.

Apart from the usual suspects such as football and boxing, equestrian sports, which could rely on a widespread practice in Ethiopia, became an essential training feature of the military institutions' cadets at the

---

[3] Richard Pankhurst mentions officers from Russia, Switzerland, Belgium, Great Britain, and Israel as well as Swedish, American, German, French, Romanian, and Armenian personnel who served in Air Force training centres: 'An Introduction to the History of the Ethiopian Army' (Unpublished MS., Archives of the Debre Zeit Imperial Ethiopian Air Force 101st Training Centre, 1967), p. 52. Norwegians trained the marines, while Japanese officers instructed the members of the special security forces (Ernest W. Lefever, *Spear and Scepter: Army, Police, and Politics in Tropical Africa* (Washington DC, 1970), p. 139.

[4] Mamo Eshetu H. Mariam, *The History of the Haile Selassie I Military Academy from Its Foundation to 1977* (Unpublished senior paper, Addis Ababa University, 1990), p. 8.

Guenet Military Training Centre (established in 1934), at Haile Selassie I Military Academy (established in 1954), and at institutions of the (mounted) police forces. Arguably, sports such as riding, boxing, and ground tennis were in part forming the 'Ethiopian Gentleman Officer'. Newspapers such as the *Ethiopian Herald* and *Addīs Zemen*, as well as an annual pamphlet, regularly reported on the Armed Forces Sports Day. Apart from documents located in various Ethiopian archives, files on the British Military Mission to Ethiopia (BMME, 1941–51) at The National Archives in Kew, London, provide valuable insights into the development of sports in the Imperial Ethiopian Army. The documents not only reveal that the BMME was an important player in the post-liberation athletic scene. They also show how it changed their system of competitions to reduce 'the pressure on Addis Ababa sports grounds'.[5] Private archives should be sought out in a more systematic way. Apart from the numerous memoirs by Ethiopian armed forces officers in Amharic that have appeared in past two decades, Onni Niskanen's private collection is also largely under-researched. The documents of the armed forces sports clubs are certainly a major source, and oral history interviews with coaches and athletes are still possible.

Sports and Cold War Politics

The focus on sports during the Cold War shifts the political, geographical as well as the temporal foci. It brings to the fore Ethiopia's increasing role in sports policy decisions at the continental level and beyond. Ethiopia's active involvement in the exclusion of South Africa from the Olympic Games before and after 1974 is but one example. Given the high symbolic value of first order sports events such as the Olympic Games or the World Cup, the participation of Ethiopian athletes in the Melbourne Summer Olympics of 1956 as well as Abebe Bikila's victory in Rome 1960 influenced African self-esteem. Further research could clarify where exactly and in what way.

Research on Indian-Ethiopian relations through the lens of sports and physical education offers a potential opening for including sports in the study of the non-aligned movement. This refers to the numerous teachers who played an important role in expanding modern educational facilities from the post-liberation period onwards. It also refers to their role in planning and implementing physical education and specialized sports training in military institutions such as Haile Selassie I Military Academy, which was operated largely by Indian officers.

Research on Ethiopia, sports, and Cold War politics shifts the temporal focus into the 1980s. I have argued at several points in this book

---

[5] Quarterly Historical Reports British Military Mission to Ethiopia (January–December 1947) NA, WO 202/940, p. 1.

that, viewed through the lens of sports, 1974 was not a total break. Turning sports from elite participation into a mass phenomenon had already begun in the 1960s. The same is true for including sports-related activities in workplaces. Further research should clarify the extent to which trade unions became active players in promoting mass sports through organization within the work context. Furthermore, a study on athletic competitions within the educational sector that spans from the early 1950s to the early 1990s could clarify the knowledge transfer from the EISAA to the *Spartakiade* movement. What exactly did athletic officials gain from participating in the three-month courses at the Deutsche Hochschule für Sport und Körperkultur (German University for Sports and Physical Culture, DHfK) in Leipzig (German Democratic Republic) to organize the *Spartakiade* in Ethiopia? Which experiences did athletes, PE teachers, coaches, and athletic officials have in the various places abroad where they studied – before and after 1974? It is not only time to include sports as a genuine field in *New Cold War Studies*. It is high time to collect the voices and memories of Ethiopians who studied sports abroad – especially at Sport Studies Departments in Kiev, Bratislava, Warsaw, or Leipzig.

Women in Sports

The whole complex of sports and gender, which I have primarily looked at in terms of masculinity – or, to be precise, male youth – needs more historical depth. Furthermore, I can only agree with Michelle Sikes and John Bale that 'new perspectives to studies of gender, sport and Africa, and African sportswomen offer a promising new approach for studying sport in society'.[6] The fact that women in contexts of modern sports during the late imperial period are less visible in the media obscures the fact that they both formally and informally contributed to the development of the Ethiopian athletic scene. Visual material from the IES, the Kautz Family Archives, and Surafiel Photo Studio shows women teams in ball games, athletics, and cycling competitions. From the early 1950s onwards, the annual journal of the EISAA documented female success in sports. There is still the possibility of interviewing Ethiopian women who formally engaged in modern sports at schools, colleges, and in sports clubs as well as in informal contexts during the late imperial period and beyond. Apart from the valuable historical details, a systematic study of the female athletic body in the context of *Zemenawīnet* provides the chance to shift academic scholarship about moral issues away from the notorious 'mini-skirt' to other aspirations and dreams that girls and young women had during this period. Furthermore, sports

---

6   Michelle Sikes and John Bale, 'Introduction: Women's Sport and Gender in Sub-Saharan Africa', *Sport in Society*, 17:4 (2013), 449.

would provide a suitable gateway to discuss issues of morality and the dominant masculine gaze on the female sporting body. How did female athletes, sometimes performing in mixed teams, perceive themselves? How did they cope with allegations of immoral behaviour? Directing the historical research on Ethiopian female athletism would enrich the global studies on the 'masculine domination' in sports.[7]

My last suggestion refers to the study of sportization processes, i.e. the transformation of local athletic practices into highly regulated sports.[8] Such research should not only refer to modern sports such as football, boxing, or athletics according to spatial and temporal regimes after their appearance in Ethiopia and their adaptation to Ethiopian realities, as I briefly mentioned in Chapter 3, *Muscular Reconstruction: Urban Leisure, Institutionalized Physical Education, and the Re-establishment of Boy Scouting (1940s–1960s)*. It should also give 'traditional' sports a true place in the history of athletic modernity in Ethiopia. For the period before 1974, for example, a first glance at the documents of Haile Selassie I Military Academy reveals that field hockey became a part of the systematic athletic training. Could players build on earlier experiences in playing *genna*? Did athletes who had already gained experience, if not fame, in 'traditional wrestling' have greater chances to enter the freestyle wrestling classes offered by the YMCA, especially in smaller towns. What exactly led to the selection of the six to eight Ethiopian 'traditional' sports after an extensive survey in the late 1970s? To what extent did 'traditional' sports provide a channel to transfer existing notions of masculinity and femininity to sports practices that were conceived and perceived as modern?

I put forward these ideas to encourage future research that goes beyond the narrow focus on long-distance running that has distorted our perception of the multiplicity of modern sports in Ethiopia (and East Africa) long enough. While the 2021 Summer Olympics in Tokyo have indeed demonstrated the strength of Ethiopian sports in athletics, I hope what my book has shown is not only that sports in Ethiopia was and is more than running, but how sports is entwined with politics, urban development, and the formation of modern subjectivities.

---

[7] Here I refer to Pierre Bourdieu, *Masculine Domination* (Stanford CA, 2001), which deeply influences studies about sport and gender.
[8] This would be an excellent opportunity to engage critically with Allan Gutman's book, *From Ritual to Record: The Nature of Modern Sport* (New York, 1978) and the literature that followed in this vein.

Bibliography

Ethiopian authors' names remain in the original order of the referenced manuscript or publication.

Primary Sources

Interviews

The semi-structured interviews of different length were not recorded. The author provided questionnaires to the chairpersons of different Ethiopian Sports Federations. All interviewed individuals agreed to have their real names mentioned in the book.

Interview with Paulos N. Donikian, Addis Ababa, 5 March 2014.
Interview with Vartkes Nalbandian, President of the Armenian Community in Ethiopia, Addis Ababa, 27 February 2014.
Interview with Shiferaw Agonafir, Addis Ababa, 8 June 2011.
Interview with Shiferaw Agonafir, Alemu Miteku, Zora Yarsu, and Telahun Woldehana, Addis Ababa, 18 June 2011.
Interview with Alemnesh Gessesew and Resedebrī Gebreanenia Gebremedhin, Mariam P'ap'aseti, 18 July 2012.
Interview with Tsegaw Ayele, Addis Ababa, 22 June 2011.
Interview by Edlawit Hirpa and Emnet Woubishet with Genet Werkeneh, general manager of the Abebe Bikila complex, Addis Ababa, 6 June 2014.
Interview with Tibebu Gorfu, Addis Ababa 14 May 2014.

E-mail Conversation

E-mail conversation with Norris Lineweaver, 4 September 2017, 4 April 2019, and 8 January 2020.

Archival Sources

Archiv des Auswärtigen Amts, Berlin (Germany)
AA R 77868: Errichtung einer deutschen Schule in Addis-Abeba, no date.
AA R 77868: Uebersicht ueber den gegenwaertigen Stand des Schulwesens in Addis-Abeba, no date.
AA RAV 89: Schulgesetz für Italienisch-Ostafrika, 26 July 1937, Georg-Haccius-Schule.

Centre français d'études éthiopiennes, Addis Ababa
EDU 370.063.SIL: The History of the Empress Menen School, 1931–1956 in Commemoration of the Silver Jubilee, Addis Ababa 1956.
EDU 370.063 BEF: Befek'ade Sillasē Fantaye, Sile boy iskawt agelgilot ach'ch'ir meglech'a [On the Boy Scout service: A short explanation] (Addis Ababa, 1947 EC, 1954/5).

Ethiopian National Archives, Addis Ababa
ENA 1.2.18.13, 17: Anglo-Ethiopian Club, British Institute and Anglo-Ethiopian Club, Report 1 January–31 December 1945.
ENA 1.2.18.13, 57: Second Annual Red Cross Gymkhana 1944.
ENA 1.2.80.03: College Day, University College Addis Ababa 7 December 1958.
ENA 1.2.52.03: Honorary Membership H.S.I., 1971.
ENA 1.2.43.09: Indian Community Sports Tournaments, Prize Distribution, 1959, Indian Community Addis Ababa.
ENA 1.2.67.05: The Yugoslav Club in Addis Ababa, no date.
ENA 1.2.54.08: Oasis Ltd. Share Company to Crown Prince Asfa Wossen, 7 October 1964.
ENA 1.2.18.13: E. F. Collier (Peace Corps), 1 June 1946.

Institute of Ethiopian Studies, Addis Ababa
Annual Sports Events
IES 796 ADD ETH: Annual Track & Field Meet (First 1950, Second 1951, Third 1952, Fourth 1952–53, Sixth 1954–55, Seventh 1955–56, Eighth 1956–57, Ninth 1957–58, Tenth 1958–59, Thirteenth 1961–62, Eighteenth 1966–67, Twenty-fourth 1972–73).
IES 796.72 ETH: Eighth Ethiopian Highland Rally, Programme, 9–12 December 1971.
IES 796.73 ETH: Second Awasa Rally, 5 April 1970.
IES 796.378 HSU: *Journal of the University College of Addis Ababa Sports Day,* March 1952.
IES 796.378 HSU: Sports Day: University College of Addis Ababa, March 10, 1956.

IES 796 HSU: Addis Ababa Colleges Sports Day, 6 June 1970.
Sports Magazines
IES, 796 AWA PER: *Awet. Sportawī mets'hēt* [Success. *Sport Magazine*], 6, 1960 EC [1968].
Annual and Monthly School Bulletins and Yearbooks
IES 371.805 HSU GON: *The Health Pioneer,* 2, 1960; *Health Mirror,* May 1963.
IES 371.805 HSU GON: *Information Bulletin,* 1961–62, Haile Selassie I Health College & Training Centre, Gondar.
IES 371.805 DIR PRI: *School Bulletin,* Prince Mekonnen Haile Selassie Comprehensive Secondary School, Dire Dawa, May 1971.
IES 371.805ADD TEC: *Technical School Year Book,* 1964–65; TARGET, Fourth Year Student Association of the Technical School, Addis Ababa, 1968.
IES 371.805 JIM TEC: *The Farmer.*
IES 371.805 JIM AGR: *The Farmer's Voice,* 2:4 (February 1959).
IES 373 BAH POL: *Year Book of the Polytechnic Institute in Bahir Dar,* 1966–67, 1968
IES YB JATS: *Year Book of the Jimma Agricultural Technical School* (1958, 1959).
IES 371.805 DAB HAI: *Yearbook of the Haile Mariam Mamo Secondary School* 1958 EC (1965/66).
IES 371.805 NAZ ATS: *Year Books of the Atse Gelawdeos Comprehensive School*, Nazareth, 1970–72.
IES 371.805 DAB TEA: *Bulletin Teacher Training Institute*, Debre Berhan, 1970.

University Publications
IES 378 HSU PER: The University Reporter, 1:2 (24 February 1967).

Misc. papers
IES 711.4 IN: Consultants: Barucci – Di Gaddo – Sacco, no date.
IES 711.4 GET: Getachew Mahiteme Selassie, The Master Plan for Addis Ababa, 1956.
IES 369.43: Information for Foreign Staff, Haile Selassie I University AA, 1966.
IES 378.006 GEN: Department of Health and Physical Education, Haile Selassie I University Catalogue, May 1965.
IES 267.3YOU: Vacation Program, 1968.
IES 796.332YED: Yidnek'achew Tesemma, Pilot Study to Re-Organize and Promote Sport in Ethiopia (Unpublished MS.), November 1973.
IES 192.05 HAG Per: Tadesse Negash, 'Swimming Pools in Addis Ababa', no date,
IES 839a: Tadesse Negash, 'Night Clubs in Addis Ababa', no date.

Kautz Family YMCA Archives, University of Minnesota Libraries, Minneapolis, USA

KFYA, Y.USA.9-2-37 YMCA International Work in Ethiopia, 1947–78

Box 1:

Correspondence 1946–49

James K. Quay to Dalton F. McClelland, 6 May 1946.

James K. Quay to Eugene Barnett, 1 January 1947.

Minutes of the First Meeting to Plan the Establishment of a YMCA, Addis Ababa, 8 February 1947.

Memorandum about the Extension Project into Ethiopia, Naguib Kelada, February 1947.

The Ethiopian Project: The Field, Its Opportunities, Handicaps and Immediate Needs, Naguib Kelada, Mainau, 4 July 1949.

Tracy Strong, World Alliance, to Dalton F. McClelland, 9 August 1949.

Tamrat Yegezu to Dalton McLealand [sic], 7 November 1949.

Correspondence 1950–51

Ryder Dittmann to Barnett, 24 March 1950.

W.H. Denison, Expansion of the Y.M.C.A work in Ethiopia (report), May 1950.

Dalton McClelland to Tamrat Yegezu and Michel Wassef, 21 March 1951.

Merlin Bishop to Dalton McClelland, 7 October 1951.

Telegram from Dalton McClelland to Naguib Kelada, 21 December 1951.

Correspondence 1951–52

Merlin A. Bishop to Eugene Barnett, 22 January 1952.

Merlin Bishop to Dalton McClelland, 7 October 1951.

Report Dalton McClelland to Herbert P. Lansdale about his visit to Ethiopia, 13 November 1952.

Questionnaire (Progress 1951), no date.

Correspondence 1953–54

Merlin Bishop to Floyd A. Wilson, YMCA Bangkok (Thailand), 6 October 1953.

Merlin Bishop, Summer 1954.

General Secretary Merlin Bishop and Lenning Sweet, 21 September 1954.

New York and Addis Ababa, no date.

Correspondence 1955

Dalton McClelland to Herbert P. Lansdale, 18 January 1955.

Tamrat Yegezu to Lennig Sweet, 14 February 1955.

Lennig Sweet to Merlin Bishop, 7 March 1955.

Merlin A. Bishop to Lennig Sweet, 9 April 1955.

Report 1955 to International Committee, no date.

Correspondence 1956

Marvin Ludwig to Herbert P. Lansdale, 25 August 1956.

Correspondence 1958
Marvin Ludwig to Joel Nystrom, 9 June 1958.
Correspondence 1959
Merlin Bishop to Emmett Gissenaas (Executive Secretary YMCA, St. Louis), 16 March 1959.
Hugo Cedergreen to Joel Nystrom, 23 April 1959.
Correspondence 1960
Marvin Ludwig to Alma Dughi, 16 March 1960.
Marvin Ludwig to Charles Lewis, 25 June 1960.
Marvin Ludwig to Joel Nystrom, 17 September 1960.
Marvin Ludwig to Joel Nystrom, 22 December 1960.
Summer Program Schedule 1960, no date.
Correspondence 1964
Marvin Ludwig to Joel Nystrom, 24 March 1964.
Marvin Ludwig to Alma Dughi, 21 April 1964.
Alma Dughi to Marvin Ludwig, 28 April 1964.
Marvin Ludwig to Millard Collins, 21 May 1964.
Marvin Ludwig to Millard Collins, Report about Last Four Months, 21 May 1964.
Correspondence 1965
Marvin Ludwig to Joel Nystrom, 15 November 1965.
Marvin Ludwig to Joel Nystrom, 16 November 1965.
Job Description for John Eveland, Junior World Service Worker, Ethiopian YMCA, no date.
Correspondence 1966
Marvin Ludwig to Joel Nystrom, 28 July 1966.
Box 2:
Correspondence 1967
Marvin Ludwig to Millard Collins, 7 August 1967.
Marvin Ludwig to Joel Nystrom, 5 September 1967.
YMCA of Ethiopia, no date.
Correspondence 1968
Marvin Ludwig to Millard Collins, 31 January 1968.
Marvin Ludwig to Millard Collins, 6 August 1968.
Owen R. Manchester to Millard Collins, 6 June 1968.
Future Concerns and Plan, 26 August 1968.
Information for the new staff from US, 1968.
Box 3:
Correspondence 1970–71
Marvin Ludwig, Confidential Report, 26 March 1973.
Lee Houser to Cody S. Moffat, 19 November 1971.
Correspondence 1972
International Committee of YMCAs' Project for U.S. Partnership Support, Ethiopia, March 1972.

International Committee of YMCAs' Project for U.S. Partnership Support, Ethiopia, March 1972.
Correspondence 1973
Lee Houser to Cody S. Moffat, 23 January 1973.
Alemayehu Kidanu to International Committee 20 September 1973.
Correspondence 1974
Emanuel Gebre Selassie to Frank Kiehne, 21 May 1974.
Tsegaw Ayele to Frank Kiehne (Executive Director International Division), 7 March 1974.
Frank Kiehne, Memorandum of Record on Conference with Tsegaw Ayele on 18 July 1974, 4 September 1974.
Correspondence with Marvin Ludwig 1970–73
Marvin Ludwig to Jarso Desta, 11 September 1970.
Darso Desta to Marvin Ludwig, 14 October 1971.
Special Report, Camp Langano, 3 May 1971 and 12 May 1971.
Box 4:
Correspondence 1970–73
Marvin Ludwig to Desta Girma, 10 February 1970.
Carl Sutliff to Desta Girma, 11 February 1971.
Marvin Ludwig to Carl W. McClure, 12 May 1971
Marvin Ludwig to Desta Girma, 1 November 1971.
Marvin Ludwig, Confidential Report, Conversation with Lee Houser, 23 March 1973.
Marvin Ludwig, Confidential Report, Conversation with Desta Girma, 26 March 1973.
Correspondence 1975
Provisional Military Government of Ethiopia, Municipality of Dire Dawa, 4 June 1975.
Tsegaw Ayele, Ethiopian YMCA, National Council Appeal to Member Movements, August 1975.
Tsegaw Ayele to Frank Kiehne, 15 September 1975.
Visitation Report #4, Frank Kiehne, African Trip, Addis, Ethiopia, 24–25 November 1975.
Correspondence 1976–77
Field Report by Daniel Tyler, Liaison Representative in East Africa, to Ethiopia, 24–30 January 1977.
Hector Caselli to Members of the Executive Committee, National General Secretaries, 7 October 1977.
Box 5:
Correspondence 1958
Merlin Bishop, Study on the Community and the Needs of Youth, no date.
Merlin Bishop, Summary Review of Local Situation Section IV, no date.
The 1958 Participation Report, no date.
Box 6:

Correspondence 1958
Memorandum, Emery M. Nelson to Paul B. Anderson, 17 January 1958.
Correspondence 1961
Marvin Ludwig to Joel Nystrom, 5 June 1961.
Report by Kenneth I. Brown, Executive Director, The Danforth Foundation (retired), 30 August 1961.
Correspondence 1962
Marvin Ludwig to Joel Nystrom, 11 April 1962.
Correspondence 1962–1963
Marvin Ludwig to Joel Nystrom, 16 August 1963.
Marvin Ludwig, End of Term Report, May 1959 through July 1962.
Correspondence 1963
Joel Nystrom to Marvin Ludwig, 3 April 1963.
Cody S. Moffat to Marvin Ludwig, 5 June 1963.
Leadership Training Course, September 1963.

KFYA, Y.USA.35

Marvin Ludwig Papers
Box 4:
Marvin Ludwig to Erika Stephan, SIGNAL-Verlag Baden-Baden, no date 1962.
The Ethiopian YMCA Progress 1969.
Box 5:
Asfaha Bemnet and Norris D. Lineweaver, no date, Operation Better Boys: A Detached Youth Work Project, no date.
International Visitation Fellowship/Fellowship Training Program 1948–71
Box 4:
Personal File Teklehaimanot Menghisteab, no date.
Ralph S. Knight to Garrett B. Douwsma, Personal File Desta Girma, 17 October 1960.

Library of the Ethiopian Sports Commission, Addis Ababa
Teferi Mekonnen, *Nebbar sport* [Traditional sports] (Addis Ababa, 1973 EC, 1980/81).
Tibebu Gorfu, *Yesport mazewterīya sifrawochinna mabelts'egīya standard* [Sports places and development standards] (Addis Ababa, 1990 EC, 1997/8).
—— *Yebahil sport mazewterīya sifrawoch standerd menesha t'inat* [Pilot study on the standardization of places for doing everyday cultural sports] (Addis Ababa, 1993 EC, 2000/1).
'Ye kibdet mansatinna sewinnet megenbat sport' [Weightlifting and bodybuilding], in Yewet'atochinna sport mīnīster, *Huletenyaw yemelaw Ītyop'ya ch'ewatawoch* [Ministry of Youth and Sports, Second All Ethiopian Championships] (Addis Ababa, 2002 EC, 2009/10), p. 57.

Yeĭtyop'ya kibdet mansatinna sewinnet megenbat fēdērēshin ametawī mets'hēt liyu 'ittim [*Annual Journal of the Ethiopian Weightlifting and Bodybuilding Federation*] (Addis Ababa, 1999 EC, 2007/8).
Be'ītyop'iya bahilawī sport fēdērēshin, *Bahilawī sportochachin sir'at iniwek'achew* [Ethiopian Cultural Sports Federation, Let us know our cultural sports correctly] (Addis Ababa: ginbot 1992 EC, May 1999).

Ministry of Education, Addis Ababa

MoE 371.207 MIN861: Education Planning Task Force Report, HSIU, May 15, 1973.
MoE, 378 Ac.1525 SH-32, 349, 354, 357: Report of the Education Sector Review. Education – Challenge to the Nation, Addis Ababa, August 1972, HSIU, Five Year Plan 1967–1971 (EC), Genbot 1966 (1974).
—— Report of the Education Sector Review. Education – Challenge to the Nation, Draft Revised Edition (Part C) (Technical Papers: Extracts from Task Force Reports and other Documentation), November 1973.
MoE, KCTE'S 1174, 1: Public Relations Office Addis Ababa: General Information on KCTE'S Twenty-Six Years of Training Experience (1969–1996).

Norma Alloway Library, Trinity Western University, Canada

Robert N. Thompson Collection (RNT TWU)
Crown Prince to R.N. Thompson, January 10, 1948.
R.N. Thompson to Aberra Jembere, July 27, 1949.
Meeting of Executive Board, 28 July, 1949.
Onni Niskanen, The Boy Scout Camp in Dire*Dawa [*sic*] and Harar during August 1949, 15 September 1949.
R.N. Thompson to Col. J.S. Wilson (Director, Boy Scouts International Bureau, London), 5 December 1949.
R.N. Thompson to H. Pratten, New York, November 22, 1950.

The National Archives, London (UK)

War Office (WO)
WO 202/940: Quarterly Historical Reports British Military Mission to Ethiopia (January–December 1947).

Newspapers Cited

Yekatīt, 1974 EC [1981/2].
Addīs Zemen, 1940–71 EC [1947–79].
Menen, 1961–63.
YeK'ēsar Mengist Mel'iktenya, 1931–32 EC [1938–40].
YeRoma Birhan, 1931–32 EC [1939–40].
Berhanena Selam, 1927 EC [1934/5], 1944 EC [1951/1952].
Addis Reporter, 1969.

Ethiopia Observer: Journal of Independent Opinion, Economics, History and the Arts, 1957–64.
The Ethiopian Herald, 1947–92.
The New York Times, 1964.
Olympic Review, 1987.

Secondary Sources

Ethiopian authors are given by their first name followed by their second name as usual in Ethiopia.

Published Secondary Sources

Abbink, Jon, 'In Memoriam Aberra Jembere (1928–2004)', *Aethiopica*, 7 (2004), 189–92.

Aboneh Ashagrie, 'The Role of Women on the Ethiopian Stage', *Journal of African Cultural Studies*, 24:1 (2012), 1–8.

Akalou Wolde-Michael, 'Buhe', in *Ethnological Society Bulletin*, 7 (2011), 57–63.

Akyeampong, Emmanuel and Charles Ambler, 'Leisure in African History: An Introduction', *The International Journal of African Historical Studies*, 35:1 (2002), 1–16.

Alegi, Peter, *African Soccerscapes: How a Continent Changed the World's Game* (London, 2010).

Ambler, Charles, 'Writing African Leisure History', in Paul Tiyambe Zeleza and Cassandra Rachel Veney (eds), *Leisure in Urban Africa* (Trenton NJ, Asmara, 2003), pp. 3–18.

—— 'Mass Media and Leisure in Africa', *The International Journal of African Historical Studies*, 35:1 (2002), 119–36.

Ancel, Stéphane, 'Yoḥannəs I', in Siegbert Uhlig (ed.), *Encyclopaedia Aethiopica*, 5 (Wiesbaden, 2014), p. 80.

Andreas Eshete, 'Modernity: Its Title to Uniqueness and its Advent in Ethiopia', *Northeast African Studies*, 13:1 (2013), 1–17.

Anonymous, *Das ist Abessinien* (Leipzig, 1935).

Anthony III, David Henry, 'Unwritten History: African Work in the YMCA of South Africa', *History in Africa: A Journal of Method*, 32 (2005), 435–44.

Asfa-Wossen Asserate, *Der letzte Kaiser von Afrika: Triumph und Tragödie des Haile Selassie* (Berlin, 2014).

Ashenafi Kebede, 'Zemenawi Muzika: Modern Trends in Traditional Secular Music of Ethiopia', *The Black Perspective in Music*, 4 (1976), 289–302.

Asfaw Geremew, *Ye' Ethiopia Radio Ketelant Esk Zare, 1923–1992 E.C.* [Ethiopian radio from yesterday until today, 1930/31–1999/2000] (Addis Ababa, 1992 EC, 1999/2000).

Baden-Powell, Robert, *Scouting for Boys: A Handbook for Instruction in Good Citizenship*, 7nd edn (London, 2013).

Bahru Zewde, *A History of Modern Ethiopia, 1855–1991*, 2nd edn (Oxford, 2001).

—— *Pioneers of Change in Ethiopia: The Reformist Intellectuals of the Early Twentieth Century* (Oxford, 2002).

—— 'Economic Origins of the Absolutist State in Ethiopia (1916–1935)', in Bahru Zewde (ed.), *Society, State and History: Selected Essays* (Addis Ababa, 2008), pp. 96–119.

Bale, John and Chris Philo, 'Introduction: Henning Eichberg, Space, Identity and Body Culture', in John Bale and Chris Philo (eds), *Body Cultures: Essays on Sport, Space and Identity by Henning Eichberg* (London, New York, 2002), pp. 3–21.

Baller, Susan and Scarlett Cornelissen, 'Introduction: Sport, Leisure and Consumption in Africa', *The International Journal of the History of Sport*, 30:16 (2013), 1867–76.

Balogun, Oluwakemi M. and Melissa Graboyes, 'Every Day Life in Africa: The Importance of Leisure and Fun', in Oluwakemi M. Balogun, Lisa Gilman, Melissa Graboyes, and Habib Iddrisu (eds), *Africa Every Day: Fun, Leisure, and Expressive Culture on the Continent* (Athens OH, 2019), pp. 1–17.

Bar-Yosef, Eitan, 'Fighting Pioneer Youth: Zionist Scouting and Baden-Powell's Legacy', in Nelson R. Block and Tammy M. Proctor (eds), *Scouting Frontiers: Youth and the Scout Movement's First Century* (Newcastle upon Tyne, 2009), pp. 42–55.

Batistoni, Milena and Gian Paolo Chiari, *Old Tracks in the New Flower: A Historical Guide to Addis Ababa* (Addis Ababa, 2004).

Belcher, Wendy Laura, 'Sisters Debating the Jesuits: The Role of African Women in Defeating Portuguese Proto-Colonialism in Seventeenth-Century Abyssinia', *Northeast African Studies*, 13:1 (2013), 121–66.

Belloni, Eleonora, 'The Birth of the Sport Nation: Sports and Mass Media in Fascist Italy', *Aloma Revista de Psicologia, Ciències de l'Educació i de l'Esport*, 32:2 (2014), 53–61.

Belucci, Steffano and Massimo Zaccaria, 'Engine of Change: A Social History of the Car-Mechanics Sector in the Horn of Africa', in Jan-Bart Gewald, André Liviveld, and Iva Peša (eds), *Transforming Innovations in Africa: Explorative Studies on Appropriation in African Societies* (Leiden, 2012), pp. 237–56.

Bette, Karl-Heinrich, *Sportsoziologie* (Bielefeld, 2010).

Bezabih Wolde and Benoît Gaudin, 'The Institutional Organization of Ethiopian Athletics', *Annales d' Ethiopie*, 23 (2007/08), 471–93.

Bezunesh Tamru and Amina Saïd Chiré, 'Citadinités dans les villes de la Corne de l'Afrique', *Annales d'Èthiopie,* 32 (2018/19), 11–20.

Boardman, Chris, *The Biography of the Modern Bike: The Ultimate History of Bike Design* (London, 2015).

Bonacci, Giulia, 'Back to Ethiopia: African-American and West-Indian Returnees in Ethiopia (1896–2010)', in Kwesi Kwaa Prah (ed.), *Back to Africa, 2: The Ideology and Practice of the African Returnee Phenomenon from the Caribbean and North America to Africa* (Cape Town, 2012), pp. 355–79.

Bonsa, Shimelis, 'The City as Nation: Imagining and Practicing Addis Ababa as a Modern and National Space', *Northeast African Studies,* 13:1 (2013), 167–213.

Bourdieu, Pierre, *Distinction: A Social Critique of the Judgement of Taste* (London, 1984).

—— 'Program for a Sociology of Sport', *Sociology of Sport Journal,* 5 (1988), 153–61.

——*Masculine Domination* (Stanford CA, 2001).

Bromber, Katrin, '"Ethiopian" Wrestling between Sportization of National Heritage and Dynamic Youth Culture', *ITYOPIS: Northeast African Journal of Social Sciences and Humanities,* 2 (2013a), 23–40.

—— 'Muscularity, Heavy Athletics and Urban Leisure in Ethiopia, 1950s–1970s', *The International Journal of the History of Sport,* 30:16 (2013b), 1915–28.

—— 'Improving the Physical Self: Sport, Body Politics, and Ethiopian Modernity, ca. 1920–1974', *Northeast African Studies,* 13:1 (2013c), 71–99.

——'Muscles, Dresses, and Conflicting Ideas of Progress: Ethiopia in the 1960s and 1970s', in Josep Martí (ed.), *African Realities: Body, Culture and Social Tensions* (Newcastle upon Tyne, 2014), pp. 171–90.

—— 'The Stadium and the City: Sports Infrastructure in Late Imperial Ethiopia and Beyond', *Cadernos de Estudos Africanos,* 32:1 (2017), 53–72.

——'Make Them Better Citizens: YMCA Training in Late Imperial Ethiopia (1950s–1970s)', *Annales d'Ethiopie,* 32 (2018/19), 19–40.

—— 'Scouting: Training the "New Man" in Post-Liberation Ethiopia', *Comparativ: Zeitschrift für Globalgeschichte und vergleichende Gesellschaftsforschung,* 28:5 (2019), 22–37.

—— 'Education for Leadership: The YMCA in Late Imperial Ethiopia (1940s–1970s)' in Harald Fischer-Tiné, Stefan Huebner, Ian Tyrrell (eds), *Mediating Modernity: Global Perspectives on the 'Secular' Work of the YMCA and YWCA* (c. 1870–1970) (Honolulu, 2020,), pp. 237–58.

Bussemer, Thymian, *Propaganda: Konzepte und Theorien* (Wiesbaden, 2005).

Caprotti, Federico, 'Visuality, Hybridity, and Colonialism: Imagining Ethiopia through Colonial Aviation, 1935–1940', *Annals of the Association of American Geographers*, 101:2 (2011), 380–403.

Carlson, Jon D., 'Ethiopia and the Middle East: The Red Sea Trade, Prester John, and Christians in the Muslim World', in Jon D. Carlson (ed.) *Myths, State Expansion, and the Birth of Globalization* (New York, 2012), pp. 115–43.

Carol, Steven, *From Jerusalem to the Lion of Judah and Beyond: Israel's Foreign Policy in Africa* (Bloomington IN, 2012).

Carotenuto, Matthew, 'Grappling with the Past: Wrestling and Performative Identity in Kenya', *The International Journal of the History of Sport*, 30:16 (2013), 1889–1902.

Chatterjee, Partha, *The Nation and Its Fragments* (Princeton NJ, 1993).

Cleophas, Francois, 'Black Physical Culture and Weight Lifting in South Africa', in Todd Cleveland, Tarminder Kaur, and Gerard Akindes (eds), *Sports in Africa: Past and Present* (Athens OH, 2020), pp. 207–18.

Coon, Carleton S., *Measuring Ethiopia and Flight into Arabia* (Boston MA, 1935).

Cooper, Frederick, 'Modernity', in Frederick Cooper (ed.), *Colonialism in Question: Theory, Knowledge, History* (Berkeley, Los Angeles, London, 2005), pp. 113–49.

Crotty, Martin, 'Scouts Down Under: Scouting, Militarism and "Manliness" in Australia, 1908–1920', in Nelson R. Block and Tammy M. Proctor (eds), *Scouting Frontiers: Youth and the Scout Movement's First Century* (Newcastle upon Tyne, 2009), pp. 74–88.

Crummey, Donald, 'The Politics of Modernization: Protestant and Catholic Missionaries in Ethiopia', in Getatchew Haile, Aasulv Land, and Samuel Rubenson (eds), *The Missionary Factor in Ethiopia* (Frankfurt/ M., 1998), pp. 85–99.

Daniel Abebe Kifle, 'The Infant Stage of Olympism in Ethiopia versus Ethiopian-NOC Governance', in Konstantinus Georgiadis (ed.), *Olympic Studies: 23rd International Seminar on Olympic Studies for Post-graduate Students* (Athens Gr.), pp. 56–73.

De Castro, Lincoln, *Nella terra dei negus* (Milano, 1915).

Debord, Guy, *La société du spectacle* (Paris, 1967).

Del Boca, Angelo, *Italiani, brava gente? Un mito duro a morire* (Milan, 2005).

Dietschy, Paul, 'Sport, éducation physique et fascisme sous le regard de l'historien', *Revue d'histoire moderne et contemporaine*, 55:3 (2008), 61–84.

Dogliani, Patrizia, 'Sport and Fascism', *Journal of Modern Italian Studies*, 5:3 (2000), 326–48.

Donham, Donald L. and Wendy James (eds), *The Southern Marches of Imperial Ethiopia: Essays in History and Social Anthropology* (Athens OH, 2002).

Dueck, Jennifer, 'A Muslim Jamboree: Scouting and Youth Culture in Lebanon under the French Mandate', *French Historical Studies*, 30:3 (2007), 485–516.
Elizabeth Wolde Giorgis, 'Charting Out Ethiopian Modernity and Modernism', *Callaloo*, 33:1 (2010), 82–99.
—— *What is 'Zemenawinet'? Perspectives on Ethiopian Modernity* (Friedrich-Ebert-Stiftung: Addis Ababa, 2013a).
—— 'Engaging the Image of Art, Culture, and Philosophy: Particular Perspectives on Ethiopian Modernity and Modernism', *Northeast African Studies*, 13:1 (2013b), v–xii.
—— 'The Aureal, the Visual, and Female Agency in the Mušo', *Northeast African Studies*, 13:1 (2013c), 101–19.
—— *Modernist Art in Ethiopia* (Athens OH, 2019).
Elleni Centime Zeleke, *Ethiopia in Theory: Revolution and Knowledge Production, 1964–2016* (Leiden, 2019).
Equestrian Association, *Ethiopian Riders and their Horses* (Addis Ababa, 2005).
Erlich, Haggai, *Ethiopia and the Middle East* (Boulder, London, 1994).
—— *The Cross and the River: Ethiopia, Egypt, and the Nile* (Boulder, Denver, London, 2002).
—— *Saudi Arabia and Ethiopia: Islam, Christianity and Politics Entwined* (Boulder, London, 2007).
—— 'The Egyptian Teachers of Ethiopia – Identities and Education along the Nile', in Walter Raunig and Asfa-Wossen Asserate (eds), *Äthiopien zwischen Orient und Okzident: Wissenschaftliche Tagung der Gesellschaft Orbis Aethiopicus, Köln, 9–11 October 1998* (Münster, 2004), pp. 117–38.
—— 'Ethiopia and Egypt – Ras Tafari in Cairo, 1924', *Aethiopica*, 1 (1998), 64–84.
Ethiopian Football Federation, *25 Years of Football in Ethiopia* (Addis Ababa, 1968).
Fair, Laura, *Pastimes and Politics: Culture, Community, and Identity in Post-Abolition Urban Zanzibar, 1890–1945* (Athens OH, 2007).
Falceto, Francis, *Abyssinie Swing: A Pictorial History of Modern Ethiopian Music* (Addis Ababa, 2001).
Fantahun Ayele, 'Missionary Education: An Engine for Modernization or a Vehicle towards Conversion?' *African Journal of History and Culture*, 9:7 (2017), 56–63.
Fasil Giorgis and Denis Gérard, *Addis Ababa 1886–1941: The City and its Architectural Heritage* (Addis Ababa, 2007).
Ferguson, James, 'Global Disconnect: Abjection and the Aftermath of Modernism', in Peter Geschiere, Birgit Meyer, and Peter Pels (eds), *Readings in Modernity in Africa* (Oxford, 2008), pp. 8–16.
Fik'ru Kīdane, *YePīyassa lij* [Child from Piazza] (Addis Ababa, 2009).

Fischer-Tiné, Harald, Stefan Huebner, Ian Tyrrell (eds), *Spreading Protestant Modernity: Global Perspectives on the Social Work of the YMCA and YWCA, 1889–1970* (Honolulu, 2020).

—— 'The Rise and Growth of a Global "Moral Empire": The YMCA and YWCA during the Late Nineteenth and Early Twentieth Centuries', in Harald Fischer-Tiné, Stefan Huebner, and Ian Tyrrell (eds), *Spreading Protestant Modernity: Global Perspectives on the Social Work of the YMCA and YWCA, 1889–1970* (Honolulu, 2020), pp. 1–35.

Foucault, Michel, *Discipline and Punish: The Birth of the Prison* (New York, 1977).

Gaffney, Christopher and John Bale, 'Sensing the Stadium', in Patricia Vertinsky and John Bale (eds), *Sites of Sport: Space, Place and Experience* (London, 2004), pp. 24–48.

Garretson, Peter P., *A Victorian Gentleman & Ethiopian Nationalist: The Life & Times of Hakim Wärqenäh, Dr. Charles Martin* (Woodbridge, 2012).

Gartley, John, 'Broadcasting', in Siegbert Uhlig (ed.), *Encyclopaedia Aethiopica, 1* (Wiesbaden, 2003), pp. 29–31.

Gennaro, Michael J., '"We are Building the New Nigeria": Lagos, Boy's Clubs, and Leisure, 1945–60', in Oluwakemi M. Balogun, Lisa Gilman, Melissa Graboyes, and Habib Iddrisu (eds), *Africa Every Day: Fun, Leisure, and Expressive Culture on the Continent* (Athens OH, 2019), pp. 155–64.

Germany, Elizabeth, *Ethiopia My Home: The Story of John Moraitis* (Addis Ababa, 2001).

Giannaki, Dora, 'Youth Work in Greece: An Historical Overview', *The History of Youth Work in Europe*, 4 (2014), 91–106.

Gori, Gigliola, *Italian Fascism and the Female Body: Sport, Submissive Women and Strong Mothers* (London, New York, 2004).

Gresleri, Giuliano, *Architecture in the Italian Colonies in Africa* (Bologna, 1992).

Gresleri, Giuliano and Pier Giorgio Massaretti (eds), *Italian Architecture Overseas: An Iconographic Atlas* (Bologna, 2008).

Griaule, Marcel, *Jeux et divertissements abyssins* (Paris, 1935).

Gutman, Allan, *From Ritual to Record: The Nature of Modern Sport* (New York, 1978).

Habtamu Mengiste Tegegne, 'Rethinking Property and Society in Gondärine Ethiopia', *African Studies Review*, 52:3 (2009), 89–106.

Haile Selassie I, 'Modern Ethiopianism, 2 November 1961', in The Imperial Ethiopian Ministry of Information (ed.), *Selected Speeches of His Imperial Majesty Haile Selassie First, 1918 to 1967* (Addis Ababa, 1967), pp. 448–61.

—— 'Address to the Boy Scout Movement 6 June 1959', in The Imperial Ethiopian Ministry of Information (ed.), *Selected Speeches of His*

Imperial Majesty Haile Selassie First, 1918 to 1967 (Addis Ababa, 1967), pp. 648–9.
—— *Important Utterances of H.I.M. Emperor Haile Selassie I, 1963–1972* (Addis Ababa, 1972).
—— *My Life and Ethiopia's Progress, 1892–1937*, trans. and annotated Edward Ullendorff (New York, London, 1976).
Hamouda, Sahar, 'A School is Born', in Sahar Hamouda and Clement Colin (eds), *Victoria College: A History Revealed* (Cairo, New York, 2002), pp. 15–62.
—— 'The Reed Phenomenon', in Sahar Hamouda and Clement Colin (eds), *Victoria College: A History Revealed* (Cairo, New York, 2002), pp. 63–136.
Hamouda, Sahar and ᵣClement Colin (eds), *Victoria College: A History Revealed* (Cairo, New York, 2002).
Harper, Jim C., *Western-Educated Elites in Kenya, 1900–1963: The African American Factor* (New York, 2006).
Henze, Paul B., *Layers of Time: A History of Ethiopia* (London, 2000).
Iadarola, Antoinette, 'Ethiopia's Admission into the League of Nations: An Assessment of Motives', *The International Journal of African Historical Studies*, 8:4 (1975), 601–22.
Imru Haile Selassie, *Kayehut kemastawisew* [Of what I saw and remember] (Addis Ababa, 2002 EC, 2009/2010).
Jacob, Wilson Chacko, *Working Out Egypt: Effendi Masculinity and Subject Formation in Colonial Modernity, 1870–1940* (Durham NC, London, 2011).
Junge, Peter and Silke Sybold, *Bilder aus Äthiopien: Malerei und Fotografie 1900–1935* (Bremen, 2002).
Kalb, Lothar, *Sendboten Olympias: Die Geschichte des Ausländerstudiums an der DHFK Leipzig* (Leipzig, 2008).
Kaplan, Irvin, Mark Farber, Barbara Marvin, James McLaughlin, Harold D. Nelson, and Donald Whitaker (eds), *Area Handbook for Ethiopia* (Washington DC, 1971).
Kebede Mikael, *'Ītyop'yana mi'irabawī silt'anē'* – Ethiopia and Western Civilisation
—— *L'Éthiopie et la civilisation occidentale* (Addis Abeba, 1948/49).
Keller, Edmond J., 'Constitutionalism, Citizenship and Political Transition in Ethiopia: Historic and Contemporary Processes', in Francis Mading Deng (ed.), *Self-Determination and National Unity: A Challenge for Africa* (Trenton NJ, 2010), pp. 57–90.
Khashba, Jamal, *Harakat al-Kashshafa fi 78 'Am* (Cairo, 1992).
Kheir Omer, Mahamad, Jelal Yassin, Vito Zita, Negash Asfaha, and Mauro Ghermandi, *Asmara: Pictorial View, 1890–1938* (Asmara, 2012).
Kimberlin, Cynthia Tse, 'Säggaye Däbalqe', in Siegbert Uhlig (ed.), *Enyclopaedia Aethiopica*, 4 (Wiesbaden, 2010), pp. 456–7.

Köppen, Grit, *Performative Künste in Äthiopien: Internationale Kulturbeziehungen und postkoloniale Artikulationen* (Bielefeld, 2017).
Krais, Jakob, 'Mastering the Wheel of Chance: Motor Racing in French Algeria and Italian Libya', in *Comparative Studies of South Asia, Africa and the Middle East,* 39:1 (2019), 143–58.
—— 'Muscular Muslims: Scouting in Late Colonial Algeria between Nationalism and Religion', *International Journal of Middle East Studies,* 51:4 (2019), 567–85.
Ladislas Farago, *Abyssinia on the Eve* (London, 1935).
Landor, Arnold Henry Savage, *Across the Widest Africa: An Account of the Country and the People of Eastern, Central and Western Africa as Seen During a Twelve Months' Journey from Djibuti to Cape Verde* (London, 1907).
Last, Alex, 'Containment and Counter-Attack: A History of Eritrean Football', in Gary Armstrong and Richard Giulianotti (eds), *Football in Africa: Conflict, Conciliation and Community* (Basingstoke, 2004), pp. 27–40.
Lefever, Ernest W., *Spear and Scepter: Army, Police, and Politics in Tropical Africa* (Washington DC, 1970).
Lefebvre, Henri, *The Production of Space,* trans. Donald Nicholson-Smith (Oxford, 1991).
Lentakis, Michel B., *Ethiopia: A View from Within* (London, 2005).
Levin, Ayala, 'Haile Selassie's Imperial Modernity: Expatriate Architects and the Shaping of Addis Ababa', *Journal of the Society of Architectural Historians,* 75:4 (December 2016), 447–68.
Levine, Donald, 'The Masculinity Ethic and the Spirit of Warriorhood in Ethiopian and Japanese Cultures', *International Journal of Ethiopian Studies,* 2:1/2 (Summer/Fall 2005–2006), 161–77.
Lewis, Joanna, *Empire State-Building: War & Welfare in Kenya 1925–52* (Oxford, Nairobi, Athens OH, 2000).
Lilius, Muddle Suzanne, 'Multiple Loyalty: Complex Identities in the Horn of Africa' in Muddle Suzanne Lilius (ed.), *Variations on the Theme of Somaliness* (Turku, 1998), pp. 250–61.
Lindsay, Lisa A., 'Trade Unions and Football Clubs: Gender and the "Modern" Public Sphere in Colonial Southwest Nigeria', in Paul Tiyambe Zeleza and Cassandra Rachel Veney (eds), *Leisure in Urban Africa* (Trenton NJ, Asmara, 2003), pp. 105–24.
MacAloon, John J., 'Introduction: Muscular Christianity after 150 Years', *International Journal of the History of Sport,* 23:5 (2006), 687–700.
Makki, Fouad, 'Empire and Modernity: Dynastic Centralization and Official Nationalism in Late Imperial Ethiopia', *Cambridge Review of International Affairs,* 24:2 (2011), 265–86.
Martin, Phyllis, *Leisure and Society in Colonial Brazzaville* (New York, 2002).

Martin, Simon, *Football and Fascism: The National Game under Mussolini* (Oxford, New York, 2004).

Marzagora, Sara, 'History in Twentieth-Century Ethiopia: The "Great Tradition" and the Counter-Histories of National Failure', *Journal of African History*, 58:3 (2017), 425–44.

Mazrui, Ali A., 'Boxer Muhammad Ali and Soldier Idi Amin as International Political Symbols: The Bioeconomics of Sport and War', *Comparative Studies in Society and History*, 19:2 (1977), 189–215.

Melton, J. Gordon, *Religious Celebrations: An Encyclopaedia of Holidays, Festivals, Solemn Observances, and Spiritual Commemorations*, vol. 1 (Santa Barbara, 2011).

Meseret Chekol Reta, *The Quest for Press Freedom: One Hundred Years of History of the Media in Ethiopia* (Lanham, 2013).

Messay Kebede, *Survival and Modernization: Ethiopia's Enigmatic Present* (Trenton NJ, 1999).

Miescher, Stephan F. and Lisa A. Lindsay, 'Introduction: Men and Masculinities in Modern African History', in Stephan F. Miescher and Lisa A. Lindsay (eds), *Men and Masculinities in Modern African History* (Portsmouth NH, 2003), pp. 1–29.

Mitchell, Timothy, 'The Stage of Modernity', in Timothy Mitchell (ed.), *Questions of Modernity: Contradictions of Modernity*, vol. 11 (Minneapolis, 2000), pp. 1–34.

Möller, Esther, *Orte der Zivilisierungsmission: Französische Schulen im Libanon 1909–1943* (Göttingen, 2013).

Monin, Boris, 'The Visit of Rās Tafari in Europe (1924): Between Hopes of Independence and Colonial Realities', *Annales d'Éthiopie*, 28 (2013), 383–9.

Norberg, Viveca Halldin, *Swedes in Haile Selassie's Ethiopia, 1924–1952* (Uppsala, 1977).

Oron, Yitzhak (ed.), *Middle East Record*, 1:1, for The Israel Oriental Society, Jerusalem (London 1960).

Pankhurst, Alula, 'Buhe: An Ethiopian Children's Festival', *Selamta: The Inflight Magazine of Ethiopian Airlines*, 28:3 (2011), 18–20.

Pankhurst, Richard, 'The Horsemen of Old-Time Ethiopia', *Ethiopia Observer*, 8:1 (1970), 1–7.

—— 'History and Principles of Ethiopian Chess', *Journal of Ethiopian Studies*, 9:2 (1971), 149–72.

—— 'Education in Ethiopia during the Italian Fascist Occupation (1936–1941)', *The International Journal of African Historical Studies*, 5:3 (1972), 361–96.

—— *The History of Ethiopian Towns from the Mid-Nineteenth Century to 1935* (Stuttgart, 1985).

—— *Economic History of Ethiopia, 1800–1935* (Addis Ababa, 1986).

—— 'Sports' in Siegbert Uhlig (ed.) *Encyclopaedia Aethiopica*, 4 (Wiesbaden, 2010), pp. 728–9.

Pankhurst, Sylvia, 'The Changing Face of Addis Ababa', *Ethiopia Observer*, 4:5 (1960), 134–76.

Parsons, Timothy, *Race, Resistance, and the Boy Scout Movement in British Colonial Africa* (Athens OH, 2004).

Paulos Milkias, *Haile Selassie, Western Education and Political Revolution in Ethiopia* (London, Amherst NY, 2006).

—— 'Mussolini's Civilizing Mission, and Fascist Political Socialization in Occupied Ethiopia, 1936–41', in Siegbert Uhlig (ed.), *Proceedings of the 15th International Conference of Ethiopian Studies* (Wiesbaden, July 2006), pp. 328–36.

—— *Ethiopia, Africa in Focus* (Santa Barbara, Denver, Oxford, 2011).

Putney, Clifford, *Muscular Christianity: Manhood and Sports in Protestant America, 1880–1920* (Cambridge MA, London, 2003).

Rambali, Paul, *Barefoot Runner* (London, 2008).

Rey, Charles F., *Unconquered Abyssinia* (London, 1923).

Rosenthal, Michael, *The Character Factory: Baden-Powell and the Origins of the Boy Scout Movement* (London, Collins, 1986).

Rubinkowska, Hanna, 'Ras 'Siyyum Mengesha', in Siegbert Uhlig (ed.) *Encyclopaedia Aethiopica*, 4 (Wiesbaden, 2010), pp. 746–7.

Rubinkowska-Anioł, Hanna, *Etiopia pomiędzy tradycją a nowoczesnością: Symbolika koronacji Cesarza Etiopii Hajle Syllasje I* [Ethiopia between tradition and modernity: Symbolism of the emperor of Ethiopia during Haile Selassie I's coronation] (Warszawa, 2016).

Said, Edward, *Out of Place: A Memoir* (London, 2000).

Seltene Seyoum, 'Əndalkaččäw Mäkʷännlkaččäw Mäkakonnen', in Siegbert Uhlig (ed.), *Encyclopaedia Aethiopica*, 2 (Wiesbaden, 2005), pp. 296–7.

Sikes, Michelle, 'Print Media and the History of Women's Sport in Africa: The Kenyan Case of Barriers to International Achievement', *History in Africa*, 43 (2016), 323–45.

—— 'Sport History and Historiography', *Oxford Research Encyclopedia of African History*, (2018), DOI: 10.1093/acrefore/9780190277734.013.232, 1–28.

Sikes, Michelle and John Bale, 'Introduction: Women's Sport and Gender in Sub-Saharan Africa', *Sport in Society*, 17:4 (2013), 449–65.

Sisay Zeleke, *Yebalemuyawoch silt'ena beĪtiop'ya' yeĪtyop'ya yesewinet magolmesha timhirtina yesport balemuyawoch mahber* [PE teacher training in Ethiopia, physical education classes, and the Sport Teachers Association], 1985 EC, 1992/3 and 1986 EC, 1993/4 (Addis Ababa 1987 EC, 1994/5).

Solomon Addis Getahun, 'A History of Sport in Ethiopia', in Svein Ege, Harald Aspen, Birhanu Teferra, and Shiferaw Bekele (eds), *Proceedings of the 16th International Conference of Ethiopian Studies* (Trondheim, 2009), pp. 409–19.

Tadäsä Betul Kebrät, *Azaj Hakim Wärqenäh Eshätu* [Chief Hakīm Werk'neh Eshetu] (Addis Ababa, 2009 EC, 2016/17).

Tadele Yidnek'achew Tesemma, *Yidnek'achew Tesemma, meskerem 1-1914 – nehasē 13-1973: Be'alemna besport 'alem* [Yidnek'achew Tesemma, 11 September 1921 to 19 August 1981: In the world and in the sports world] (Addis Ababa, 1989 EC, 1996/7).

Talbot, David Abner (ed.), *Imperial Ministry of Education Year Book* (Addis Ababa, 1950).

Tamirat Gebremariam and Benoît Gaudin, 'Sports and Physical Education in Ethiopia during the Italian Occupation, 1936–41', in Michael J. Gennaro and Saheed Aderinto (eds), *Sports in African History, Politics and Identity Formation* (New York, 2019), pp. 196–205.

Tekeste Negash, *Italian Colonialism in Eritrea, 1882–1941: Policies, Praxis and Impact* (Stockholm, 1987).

Tek'ewame Wolde Ts'adik', *Yesewinet magolmesha timhirt beīty-op'ya: T'inatawī ts'ihuf* [Physical education in Ethiopia: A scientific approach] (Addis Ababa, 1978 EC, 1985/86).

Tewodros Gebre, 'Period, History, and the Literary Art: Historicizing Amharic Novels', *Northeast African Studies,* 13:1 (2013), 19–51.

The Imperial Ethiopian Ministry of Information (ed.), *Selected Speeches of His Imperial Majesty Haile Selassie First, 1918 to 1967* (Addis Ababa, 1967).

Thomas, Keith, 'Work and Leisure in Pre-Industrial Societies', *Past and Present,* 29 (1962), 50–62.

Thompson, E.P., 'Time, Work-Discipline and Industrial Capitalism', *Past and Present,* 38 (1967), 57–97.

Thompson, Robert N., 'Down a Memory Lane from Ethiopia', in *World Scouting,* 4 (1965), 1–10.

Tibebu Teshale, *The Making of Modern Ethiopia: 1896–1974* (Trenton NJ 1995).

Tiyambe Zeleza, Paul, 'The Creation and Consumption of Leisure: Theoretical and Methodological Considerations', in Paul Tiyambe Zeleza and Cassandra Rachel Veney (eds), *Leisure in Urban Africa* (Trenton NJ, Asmara, 2003), vii–xii.

Tyrrell, Ian, *Reforming the World: The Creation of America's Moral Empire* (Princeton NJ, 2010).

Vallory, Eduard, 'Status Quo Keeper or Social Change Promoter? The Double Side of World Scouting's Citizenship Education', in Nelson R. Block and Tammy M. Proctor (eds), *Scouting Frontiers: Youth and the Scout Movement's First Century* (Newcastle upon Tyne, 2009), pp. 207–22.

Veblen, Thorstein, *The Theory of the Leisure Class: An Economic Study in the Evolution of Institutions* (New York, 1899).

Vivian, Herbert, *Abyssinia: Through the Lion-Land to the Court of the Lion of Judah* (London, 1901).

White, Luise, 'Separating the Men from the Boys: Constructions of Gender, Sexuality, and Terrorism in Central Kenya, 1939–1959', *The International Journal of African Historical Studies*, 13:1 (1990), 1–25.

Woudstra, Rixt, 'Designing the Town of the Future: Le Corbusier's Sketch of Addis Ababa', *Simulacrum*, 21:1 (2012), 6–10.

Yacobi, Haim, *Israel and Africa: A Genealogy of Moral Geography* (New York, 2016).

Ydlibi, May, *With Ethiopian Rulers: A Biography of Hasib Yidlibi*, edited by Bahru Zewde (Addis Ababa, 2006).

Yerevanian, Mouchegh, *The Ethiopian-Armenian Community from 1941 to 1975* (Glendale CA, 1996).

Yidnek'achchew Asefu, *Yaltenegerellet yehager balewileta – Bek'ele Alemu 'Gant'* [The man whose service for his country was not talked about – Bek'ele Alemu 'Gant'] (Addis Ababa, 2004 EC, 2011/12).

Yidnek'achew Tesemma, 'YeItyop'ya atletīks tarīkinna wit'ēt' [History and results of Ethiopian athletics], in YeItyop'ya 'atletiks federēshin (eds), *Arengwadēw gorf* [The green torrent] 5 t'ir 1977, 13 January 1985, 6–30.

Yonas Adamassu, 'Afewerk' Gebre Īyesus', in Siegbert Uhlig (ed.), *Encyclopaedia Aethiopica* 1 (Wiesbaden, 2003), p. 123.

Zervos, Adrien, *L'empire d'Ethiopie: le miroir de l'Ethiopie moderne 1906–1935* (Athènes, 1936).

Theses

Gezahhegne Beyene, 'Emergence and Development of Boxing in Ethiopia' (Unpublished BE thesis, Kotebe College of Teacher Education, 1998).

Ghantakis, John Anestis, 'The Greeks of Ethiopia, 1889–1970' (Unpublished Ph.D. dissertation, Boston University Graduate School, 1979).

Jakes, Aaron, 'Extracurricular Nationalism: Youth Culture in the Age of Egypt's Parliamentary Monarchy' (Unpublished MA thesis, University of Oxford, 2005).

Johnson, Chrystal L., 'Reshaping Urban Environments in Ethiopia: Exploring Life through the Use of Space in Four Addis Ababa Kebele' (Unpublished Ph.D. dissertation, University of Wisconsin-Milwaukee, 2008).

Lulusegged Alemayyehu, 'A Descriptive Analysis of the Administration of Education in Transition in Ethiopia' (Unpublished Ph.D. dissertation, University of Southern California, 1969).

Mamo Eshetu H. Mariam, 'The History of the Haile Selassie I Military Academy from Its Foundation to 1977' (Unpublished senior paper, Addis Ababa University, 1990).

Marzagora, Sara, 'Alterity, Coloniality and Modernity in Ethiopian Political Thought: The First Three Generations of 20th Century

Amharic-Language Intellectuals' (Unpublished Ph.D. dissertation, SOAS, University of London, 2016).

Mekonnen Sintayehu, 'Swimming in Ethiopia' (Unpublished BE thesis, Kotebe College of Teacher Education, 1995).

Negussie Alemu, 'Addis Ababa Inter School Sports Competition: Past, Present and Future Perspective' (Unpublished BE thesis, Kotebe College of Teacher Education, 2001).

Sintayehu Tola, 'The History of St. George Sport Club' (Unpublished BA thesis, Addis Ababa University, 1986).

Zenebu Kefelew, 'The Role of the Training School & Remand Home in Correcting Juvenile Delinquents in Ethiopia' (Unpublished senior paper, School of Social Work, Haile Selassie I University, 1973).

Online Sources

Africa Scout Region, 'Scouting in Ethiopia Turns 100', SCOUTS. Creating a Better World, 12 February 2019, www.scout.org/ethiopia100 [accessed 15 September 2021].

Arada Sub-city Kebele 02 House 476/77 Dej. Jote Street, https://web.archive.org/web/20110528232845/http://130.238.24.99/library/resources/dossiers/local_history_of_ethiopia/s/ORTSOB.pdf [accessed 15 September 2021].

Breaking Away, 'The History of Legnano', 10 April 2013 https://condorino.com/2013/04/10/the-history-of-legnano [accessed 15 September 2021].

British Archives [sic], 'Leading Personalities in Eritrea (1950)', quoted by EHREA (Eritrean Human Rights Electronic Archive) 16 January 2003, www.ehrea.org/leaders.php [accessed 15 September 2021].

Chryshoheri, Irene, 'The Greeks of Alexandria', www.facebook.com/283872594957239/posts/the-greeks-of-alexandriatext-editing-irene-chryshoheri-archaeologist-art-histori/1550492204961932 [accessed 25 November 2021].

Dej. Makonnen Deste, 'Äthiopien. Kaiserreich zwischen Gestern und Morgen', BR Deutschland, www.filmothek.bundesarchiv.de/video/593861?q=Kaiser+Haile&xm=AND&xf%5B0%5D=_fulltext&xo%5B0%5D= CONTAINS&xv%5B0%5D= [accessed 15 September 2021].

'Ethiopia at the 1956 Summer Olympics', https://en.linkfang.org/wiki/Ethiopia_at_the_1956_Summer_Olympics [accessed 15 September 2021].

'Ethiopia: Cars Start Gruelling Three Thousand Mile Rally. Despite World Petrol Shortage, 1973', British Pathé www.britishpathe.com/video/VLVACVOBOHRQ371LZQB7IS89NBKKA-ETHIOPIA-CARS-START-GRUELLING-THREE-THOUSAND-MILE-RALLY-DESPITE/query/MILE [accessed 15 September 2021].

'Ethiopian Highland Rally 1965–1974', 3 January 2013, https://ulfniskanen.wordpress.com/2013/01/03/ethiopian-highland-rally-1965-1974/ [accessed 15 September 2021].

'Ethiopian Highland Rally 1967', Raw21 http://raw21.com/2017/03/02/iv-ethiopian-highland-rally-1967 [accessed 15 September 2021].

Fikreyesus Amahazion, 'Pedaling History: Eritrea's Teklehaimanot and Kudus in Tour de France', *TesfaNews*, 6 July 2015, www.tesfanews.net/eritrea-pedaling-history-at-tour-de-france/ [accessed 15 September 2021].

'History of Cameroon – YMCA', http://ymcacameroon.org/who-we-are/our-history [accessed, 15 September 2021].

'History of Football Sport in Eritrea at a Glance (Part I)', https://shabait.com/2010/08/11/history-of-football-sport-in-eritrea-at-a-glance-part-i/ [accessed 15 September 2021].

Kenya – National Council of YMCAs, 'Brief YMCA History', www.ymca.int/member/ymca-in-africa/ymca-kenya [accessed 15 September 2021].

Local history in Ethiopia, compiled by Bernhard Lindahl, https://nai.uu.se/library/resources/thematic-resources/local-history-of-ethiopia.html [accessed 15 September 2021].

Madagascar – National Council of YMCAs 'Brief YMCA History', www.ymca.int/member/ymca-in-africa/ymca-madagascar [accessed 15 September 2021].

Morgan, Sarah, 'Mussolini's Boys (and Girls): Gender and Sport in Fascist Italy', *History Australia*, 3:1 (2006), 04.1–04.12. https://doi.org/10.2104/ha060004 [accessed 15 September 2021].

Nolawi, 'Abebayoosh!' Bernos, 10 September 2006, www.bernos.com/blog/2006/09/10/abebayoosh [accessed 15 September 2021].

Old Asmara Eritrea, 'History of Cycling Races in Eritrea', Facebook, 13 July 2015, www.facebook.com/OldEritreaAsmara/posts/1513403132253616 [accessed 15 September 2021].

Pankhurst, Richard 'Educational Developments of the 1930s', www.linkethiopia.org/blog/article/educational-developments-of-the-1930s [accessed 15 September 2021].

'Royal Tour of Ethiopia (1965)', 3 April 2014, www.youtube.com/watch?v=oA3u8JzcO2Y [accessed 15 September 2021].

'Swinging Addis', BBC Radio, www.bbc.co.uk/programmes/b03ynfpl [accessed 15 September 2021].

'The Scout & Guide Spirit Flame', International Scout and Guide Fellowship, Amitié Internationale Scoute et Guide, 3 July 2008 www.isgf.org/index.php/en/publications/284-the-effects-of-the-spirit-flame [accessed 15 September 2021].

Woudstra, Rixt, 'Le Corbusier's Vision for Fascist Addis Ababa', *Failed Architecture* (9 October 2014), https://failedarchitecture.com/le-corbusiers-visions-for-fascist-addis-ababa [accessed 15 September 2021].

Yearbook of Automobile Sport http://doczz.cz/doc/66669/1---prohistoric.cz [accessed 15 September 2021].

'YMCA Arat Kilo', Y Blog, www.ymca.8m.net [accessed 15 September 2021].

Unpublished Secondary Sources

Anonymous, 'History of Olympiacos', no date, typescript provided by the Greek Club, Addis Ababa in October 2017.

Pankhurst, Richard, 'An Introduction to the History of the Ethiopian Army' (Unpublished MS., Archives of the Debre Zeit Imperial Ethiopian Air Force 101st Training Centre, 1967).

Tek'ewame Wolde Ts'adik', 'Yeītop'ya akal maselt'enyana sport tarīk' [The history of the physical education teachers' education], in Mekonnen Amdie and Tilahun Gebrekristos (eds) *Collection of research papers presented on different conferences organized by Ethiopian Physical Education and Sport Professionals' Association in 1993 & 1994* (Unpublished MS. 1995), pp. 20–25.

Index

Abebe Bikila 28, 34, 129
Aberra Jembere
  Boy Scouts 112 n.104
  YMCA 133, 145
Afewerk' Gebre Īyesus 13, 63
Akalework Haptewold 112
Alemayehu Feyisa 148 n.141
Ambo/Hagere Hiwot 93, 113, 114, 140, 183
American Peace Corps 94, 120, 130 n.57, 131 n.59, 144, 145, 151, 160, 181
Armed Forces
  Air Force 90, 97, 102, 111, 115, 184 n.3
  British Military Mission 89, 115, 181, 185
  Haile Selassie I Military Academy (Harar) 102, 185, 187
  Imperial Body Guard 90, 94, 97, 101, 102, 184
  Kagnew Station (Eritrea) 111, 141
Asfa Wossen, Crown Prince 19 n.81, 171, 174
Asmara 28, 45, 70, 72, 73, 77, 92, 110, 111, 128, 129, 131, 134, 139, 141, 143, 145, 146, 147, 162 n.39, 165, 173, 174

Boghossian, Khosroff 42

Boy Scouting
  Adventure/hiking/ trekking/camping/ mountaineering 113, 114–16, 145–6, 170
  Boy Scout School (Gulele) 26, 52, 53, 56
  Girls/women 9 n.9, 110, 115
  Greek community 51–3, 110, 115
  Militarism 110, 111, 113
  Re-establishment 98, 111
  Training 113, 114, 115
Civilization (*silt'anē*)
  Fascist 'civilizing' mission/role of sports 65–71, 76, 77, 86–7, 183
  Modern (*zemenawi-silt'anē*) 12, 24
Citizen
  Citizenship training 18, 20, 21, 104, 120
  Future Citizen School 20 n.87, 21, 117
Cold War 3, 21, 121, 126, 129, 160, 179, 185
Competitions
  Addis Ababa (Weightlifting) Championships 148
  Africa Cup of Nations 1962 and 1976 20, 147, 162 n.39, 165, 176, 20, 147, 165

Ethiopian Highland Rally
  Involvement of
    Ethiopians 173–4
  Organization and
    sponsorship 96, 155, 173
  Participation 171–3
Intercollegiate Sports
  Competitions 154, 159–60
Olympic Games 35, 56, 92, 109, 180, 185
Shoa Cycling
  Championships 75, 83–4
Shoa Football
  Championships 77, 82–3, 85
Spartakiade 9, 116, 186
University Sports Day 24, 159, 160
Constitution 14, 20, 23
Consumption of sports 7, 28, 31, 64, 65, 67, 72, 87, 182, 184
Coubertin, Pierre de 35, 162

Djibuti – Addis Ababa
  railway 38, 39, 40, 147, 169
Drill 48–9, 50, 56, 60, 61, 80, 90, 101, 156
Debre Zeit 90, 92, 93, 97, 113, 115, 159, 167, 174, 183
Dessie 47, 48, 69, 70, 95, 132, 135, 147
Dire Dawa 38, 40, 41, 48, 49, 51, 92, 106, 110, 113, 114, 115, 131, 135, 145, 147, 154, 165, 168, 169, 173, 174

Egypt 3, 4, 32, 39, 41, 47–8, 51, 52, 97, 112, 118, 120–1, 122, 149, 165, 177, 181
Emanuel Gebre Selassie 135, 136
Endalkachew Makonnen, *Lij* 135 n.78, 174
Ethiopian Modernity
  Coloniality 3, 10, 12–14, 30, 162, 180
  Grant Narrative 5
  Modern Ethiopianism 14
  Singularity 4, 10, 12
  Zemenawīnet 5, 6 n.23, 7–9, 10, 12
Ethiopian Red Cross Society 17, 95, 112, 119, 124 n.25, 146 n.132

Fascist occupation
  Fascist Youth Brigade and
    Training School for
    Boys 57
  Newspapers 63–4
  Physical education 66, 79–80, 106
  Segregation
    Racial 31 61–2, 64, 72, 82, 84, 85, 88, 180
    Religious 31, 64, 70, 81, 82, 84, 85, 86, 181
    Spatial 84, 87, 88
  Sports Bureau for the
    Natives 40, 58, 59, 68, 69, 77, 78, 86, 87, 89, 92, 156
  Wolves of Ethiopia 57, 109
Ford, Mignon Innes 110

Gigli, Henri 20, 45, 54
Gondar 79, 147, 159, 160, 166
Gustav Adolf, Swedish Crown
  Prince 14, 53, 79

Haile Mariam Guezmou 53, 55
Haile Selassie I, *Ats'ē see Ras
  Tafari*
  Athletic symbolism 30, 109
  YMCA 120, 137
Hakīm Werk'neh 25, 43, 48, 49, 52
Hanna Salib Bey 47
Harar 38, 39, 46, 47, 48, 50, 59, 95, 101, 102, 107, 147

Harrington, Sir John 43
Haylu Tekle Haymanot, *Ras* 75, 82, 84
Hermann, Edgar 173
Hirghigo 75, 111

Īyasu, *Le'ul Lij* 39–40, 43, 46

Jackson, Aron 52
Jan Mēda race court 41, 42 n.33, 43, 72, 73, 77, 81, 84, 86, 91, 156, 171, 182
Jimma 21, 28 n.117, 71, 95, 147, 160, 163, 169, 173, 174
Joginder Singh 173

Kamal, Frederick 53, 55
Kassa Fidel 73, 74 n.77
Kebede Guebret, *Ras* 75

Lakew Yigletu 101, 102, 129
Langano (lake) 93, 113, 144, 183
Lebanon 4, 48, 52, 53, 55
Le Corbusier 163
Leisure
  Leisure class 21–2, 31, 90, 93
  Rational/ useful recreation/ leisure 23, 27, 29, 36, 38, 50, 64, 67, 87, 91, 93, 96, 97, 115, 117, 120, 178

Makonnen, *Le'ul* 20, 45, 54–5, 106, 111
Makonnen, *Ras* 42, 155 n.3
Masculinity
  Bravery (*gobezinet*) 25
  Muscular Christianity 10, 25, 48–9, 114, 117
  Muscularity 24, 147, 149, 152
Mek'ele 23, 42, 92, 147, 148, 155, 158, 165–6, 169
Menelik II, *Ats'ē* 5, 38, 39, 42, 43, 46
Mengesha Seyoum, *Ras* 20, 160
Million Belete 129

Modern sports
  Acrobatics 106, 147, 148, 157, 183
  Athletics 26, 28, 34, 36, 71, 79, 80, 85, 92, 98, 99, 107, 125, 138, 157, 180, 182, 186, 187
  Badminton 128, 142, 157, 159, 169
  Basketball 17, 18, 32, 94, 95, 106, 122, 133, 136, 137, 138, 139, 141, 142, 149, 157, 159, 160, 161
  Billiards 39, 40, 94, 168 n.69
  Bodybuilding and Weightlifting 19, 24, 25, 32, 34, 136, 138, 146, 147 n.136–7, 148, 150, 152, 159, 161, 167, 181
  Bowling 19, 30, 95, 96
  Boxing 9, 18, 20, 26, 32, 34, 36, 41, 44, 45, 48, 56, 61, 92, 107, 136, 139, 139, 141–2, 146, 150, 159, 161, 167, 169, 185, 187
  Chess 36, 37, 94, 95, 100, 122, 125, 143, 169
  Cricket 36, 45, 48
  Cycling 23, 30, 34, 41, 44, 61, 64, 67, 68, 69, 70, 71, 72–6, 80, 82, 83, 85, 87, 91–2, 170, 183, 186
  Equestrian sports 14–15, 42, 48, 69, 71, 84, 95, 184
  Fencing 48, 150, 159
  Field hockey 159, 187
  Football 1, 3, 7, 17, 18, 26, 31, 34, 38, 40–3, 45, 48, 49, 61, 69, 71, 76–9, 83, 87, 91, 107, 108, 122, 125, 137, 157, 159, 161, 162, 163, 164, 168, 169, 180, 181, 184, 187
  Gymnastics/*Turnen* 18, 49, 50, 51 n.87, 60, 79–80, 87, 98, 99, 109, 113, 138, 156, 158, 161, 164, 171

Hiking   18, 113, 114, 116, 137, 143, 145
Judo   18, 94–5, 136, 138
Karate   18, 34, 136
Lawn tennis   19, 26, 42, 43, 48, 70, 94, 95, 137, 142, 157, 159, 160
Motor racing   28, 32, 96, 171, 183
Polo   37, 43
Pole vaulting   80, 157
Running   2, 26, 28, 34, 48, 69, 80–2, 126, 170, 187
Sailing   48, 92–3
Softball   106, 125, 138, 157, 159, 170
Swimming   18, 19, 48, 92, 93, 94, 98, 100, 106, 113, 136, 143, 161, 168, 170
Table tennis   9, 19, 32, 48, 94, 95, 106, 122, 125, 136, 137, 141, 142–3, 157, 161, 169
Tetherball   23, 142
Volleyball   17, 18, 23, 32, 34, 106, 107, 115, 122, 125, 136, 138, 142, 157, 159, 160–1
Wrestling (freestyle, Greco-Roman)   18, 24, 26, 36, 37, 41, 44, 50, 70, 95, 120, 139, 142, 146, 149, 149–51, 153, 159, 166, 187
Yoga   19, 113
Moraitis, Christo   53
Morality in sports
    Clothing/Dress   67, 68, 77, 83, 86, 108, 150, 151, 177, 186
    Discipline   24, 56, 74, 75, 86, 156, 177, 184
    Healthy life style   67, 104, 109, 120, 146, 152, 159, 183
    Perfection   67, 69, 80
    Sportsmanship/fair play   18, 19, 104, 107, 130, 138, 152, 181, 184
Mulugeta Kassa   73
Mulugeta Wolde Giorgis   101
Myriallis, Alexander   164
Naguib Kelada   119, 120, 121, 122
'New Men'
    'Complete Man'   18
    Etiope Nuovo/New Ethiopian   17, 64, 79, 86, 88, 90, 178, 183
    Ethiopian   20, 19, 183
    Ethiopian Student Movement   8, 174
    Fascist   16, 59–61, 64
    Homo sportivus   60
    Modern Ethiopian   20, 25, 35, 38
    Muscular Man   146, 148
    'New Emperor'   19, 116
    New Woman   23–4
    'Right type' of man   24
    Vanguard   6, 15, 17, 24, 30, 116
    Young Ethiopians   16–17, 149, 170
Norris D. Lineweaver   140, 144, 145

Onni Niskanen
    Armed forces   97, 185
    Boy Scouts   98, 112, 114
    Ethiopian Highland Rally   172
    Physical education   97, 98, 101, 102, 107
    YMCA   129
Organizations
    Confédération africaine de football   3
    Deutsche Hochschule für Sport und Körperkultur   117, 186
    Eritrean Automobile Club   171, 175
    Ethiopian Athletic Association   137
    Ethiopian Basketball Federation   94, 132, 142, 149

Ethiopian Boxing
 Federation   142
Ethiopian Cultural Sports
 Federation   151, 153
Ethiopian Cycling
 Federation   92
Ethiopian Football
 Federation   1, 89, 165, 177
Ethiopian Olympic
 Committee   1 n.2, 152
Ethiopian Swimming
 Federation   113, 168 n.70
Ethiopian Table Tennis
 Federation   142–3
Ethiopian Volleyball
 Federation   142
Ethiopian Weightlifting
 and Bodybuilding
 Federation   25, 147 n.137,
 148–9, 153
Fédération Internationale de
 Football Association   165
Imperial Ethiopian Automobile
 Club   171
International Amateur
 Athletics Federation   107
National Ethiopian Sports
 Confederation   131, 133,
 171, 175, 176, 177
Royal Gymnastics Central
 Institute (Sweden)   101
Sports Commission of the
 Ministry of Culture and
 Sports   32, 136–7, 152, 181

Quay, James K.   120, 121, 122

Pecol, Gino   94
Physical Education
 Budget   99, 105, 126
 Colleges and university   21,
  48, 52, 103, 115, 157, 159,
  160, 161, 165, 170
 Curriculum   90, 98, 99, 100, 102

Department of Physical
 Education and Boy Scouting
 (MoE)   31, 90, 97–9, 102,
 106, 107, 112, 114, 156
Ethiopian Inter-School Athletic
 Association (EISAA)   29,
 31, 90, 106–8, 157, 180
National Physical Education
 Programme   97, 122
PE teachers   31, 90, 95, 98,
 102–3, 105
Schools
 Alliance Française School
  (Addis Ababa)   49
 Amha Desta School (Addis
  Ababa)   105, 157
 Asfa Wossen School (Addis
  Ababa)   107, 158
 Atse Gelawdeos
  Comprehensive School
  (Nazareth)   106
 Atse Yohannes Preparatory
  School (Mek'ele)   166
 Beyene Merid School (Addis
  Ababa)   157
 Ecole Américaine (Addis
  Ababa)   49
 Empress Menen School
  (Addis Ababa)   49, 99,
  102, 108
 French Mission School of the
  Brothers of Saint Gabriel
  (Addis Ababa)   155
 General Wingate Secondary
  School (Addis
  Ababa)   99, 114, 158
 Greek Community School
  (Addis Ababa)   49
 Haile Selassie I School
  (Nekemte)   158
 Haile Selassie I Secondary
  School (Kotebe)   97, 99,
  102
 Indian Association School
  (Addis Ababa)   95

Kokebe Tsibah Haile Selassie I School (Addis Ababa) 49
Medhane Alem School (Addis Ababa) 53, 105
Menelik II Imperial School (Addis Ababa) 47, 101, 160
Prince Makonnen Haile Selassie Comprehensive Secondary School (Dire Dawa) 106
Seventh Day Adventists' Boys' Schools (Addis Ababa, Addis Alem) 49
Swedish Evangelical Mission Schools 49
Tafari Makonnen School (Addis Ababa) 48, 49, 52, 57, 97, 99, 113, 132, 157
Training School and Remand Home for Boys (Addis Ababa) 18, 119
Point Four Program 21, 28 n.117, 160, 181

Rece (Recreation Centre, Addis Ababa) 95, 96
Reed, Ralph 48
Regulation/sportization/standardization 29, 69, 79, 82–4, 87, 88, 105, 153, 156, 178, 180, 187

Saleh Ahmed Kekiya 75–6, 76 n.82, 84
Seyoum Mengesha, *Ras* 75, 76
Shiferaw Agonafir 101, 102, 103, 129, 159–60
Sisay Zeleke 103
Soviet Union 126, 128, 160–1, 172
Sponsorship 3, 69, 70, 75, 82, 86, 96, 103, 108, 137, 141, 172–3

Sports clubs
 Ararat 41, 94, 181, 182
 Arax Union 41, 45
 Abebe Bikila Bodybuilding Club 148
 Ethio-British (Army) Club 93, 95
 Hellenic Athletic Association 41
 Imperial Club 42
 Juventus 41, 45, 95, 96, 173
 Olympiacos 41, 94, 141 n.7, 181
 St. George Football Club 76, 78, 182
Stadiums
 Asfa Wossen Stadium (Dire Dawa) 154, 165
 Baloni/Kagnew Astadium (Mek'ele) 42, 148, 155, 158, 165, 166, 167
 Gulele Stadium/Abebe Bikila Stadium 175
 Haile Selassie I Stadium 1, 23, 29, 108, 109, 154, 158, 163–5, 166, 170, 171
 Queen of Sheba (Asmara) 154, 165
 Ras Alula Stadium (Asmara) 154, 165
Subject
 Balanced 66, 86
 Colonial 29, 59, 61, 62, 64, 166, 183
 Modern 2, 17, 38, 88
 Formation 2, 16, 20, 78, 161, 183, 187
 Sudan 38, 39, 41, 44, 94, 112, 149, 184
Swimming pools 92, 93, 94, 99–100, 113, 138, 155, 161, 168, 170

Tafari, *Ras*
 Boy Scouts 50
 Modern education 39, 48

Olympic Games 1924   35, 162
Tamrat Yegezu, Lieutenant Colonel   122, 125, 127, 174
Telahun Zerihun   122
Telios Bollolakos   51
Tewodros II, *Ats'ē*   5, 12, 37
Thompson, Robert N.   111–12
Traditional sports
  Feres gugs (polo)   37, 42, 43, 171, 180
  Feres shert (horse racing)   37, 42
  Gebeta   83, 180
  Genna (hockey)   18, 19, 36, 37, 49, 71, 87, 104, 155, 187
  Mixed martial art   45, 50, 56
  Shent'erej (chess)   37, 143
  Tigil (wrestling)   36, 37, 47, 70, 180, 187
Tsehaywork Darghie, *Weyzero*   42

Valle, Cesare   163

Wassef, Michel
  Boy Scouts   97, 112
  Physical education   47, 97
  YMCA   97, 121–4, see YMCA secretaries
Weiss, Fritz Max   44, 46
Welde-Gīyorgīs Welde-Yohannis   13
World Service workers   120, 130–1, 140, 145, 151

Yohannis I, Patriarch   66, 67

Yosēf and Bīnyam Werk'neh   45
Yohannes IV, *Ats'ē*   5
Young Men's Christian Association (YMCA) of Ethiopia and Eritrea
  All-African YMCA training centre   3, 130
  George Williams College (Wisconsin)   132, 133, 134, 151
  Leadership training, 119, 121, 126, 130, 144, 151, 183
  Operation Better Boys   139–40
  Physical education   126, 129 n.51, 130, 138, 139, 141, 145, 157
  Sahle Selassie camp   144–6
  Springfield College (Massachusetts)   132, 133, 151
  Secretaries
    Desta Girma   131–2, 134, 144
    Jarso Desta   133–4, 142
    Lee Houser   130, 133, 134, 146
    Marvin L. Ludwig   125–6, 127, 128, 130, 131, 132, 139, 141, 142, 150, 151
    Merlin Bishop   17, 123–5, 126, 127, 128, 137, 139
    Michel Wassef   47, 97, 112, 121–3, 124
    Tsegaw Ayele   134, 135, 136, 152
Yugoslavia, 96, 126, 129, 157

Eastern Africa Series

Women's Land Rights & Privatization in Eastern Africa
BIRGIT ENGLERT
& ELIZABETH DALEY (EDS)

War & the Politics of Identity in Ethiopia
KJETIL TRONVOLL

Moving People in Ethiopia
ALULA PANKHURST
& FRANÇOIS PIGUET (EDS)

Living Terraces in Ethiopia
ELIZABETH E. WATSON

Eritrea
GAIM KIBREAB

Borders & Borderlands as Resources in the Horn of Africa
DEREJE FEYISSA
& MARKUS VIRGIL HOEHNE (EDS)

After the Comprehensive Peace Agreement in Sudan
ELKE GRAWERT (ED.)

Land, Governance, Conflict & the Nuba of Sudan
GUMA KUNDA KOMEY

Ethiopia
JOHN MARKAKIS

Resurrecting Cannibals
HEIKE BEHREND

Pastoralism & Politics in Northern Kenya & Southern Ethiopia
GÜNTHER SCHLEE
& ABDULLAHI A. SHONGOLO

Islam & Ethnicity in Northern Kenya & Southern Ethiopia
GÜNTHER SCHLEE
with ABDULLAHI A. SHONGOLO

Foundations of an African Civilisation
DAVID W. PHILLIPSON

Regional Integration, Identity & Citizenship in the Greater Horn of Africa
KIDANE MENGISTEAB
& REDIE BEREKETEAB (EDS)

Dealing with Government in South Sudan
CHERRY LEONARDI

The Quest for Socialist Utopia
BAHRU ZEWDE

Disrupting Territories
JÖRG GERTEL, RICHARD ROTTENBURG
& SANDRA CALKINS (EDS)

The African Garrison State
KJETIL TRONVOLL
& DANIEL R. MEKONNEN

The State of Post-conflict Reconstruction
NASEEM BADIEY

Gender, Home & Identity
KATARZYNA GRABSKA

Women, Land & Justice in Tanzania
HELEN DANCER

Remaking Mutirikwi
JOOST FONTEIN

The Oromo & the Christian Kingdom of Ethiopia
MOHAMMED HASSEN

Lost Nationalism
ELENA VEZZADINI

Darfur
CHRIS VAUGHAN

The Eritrean National Service
GAIM KIBREAB

Ploughing New Ground
GETNET BEKELE

Hawks & Doves in Sudan's Armed Conflict
SUAD M. E. MUSA

Ethiopian Warriorhood
TSEHAI BERHANE-SELASSIE

Land, Migration & Belonging
JOSEPH MUJERE

Land Tenure Security
SVEIN EGE (ED.)

Tanzanian Development
DAVID POTTS (ED.)

Nairobi in the Making
CONSTANCE SMITH

The Mission of Apolo Kivebulaya
EMMA WILD-WOOD

*The Crisis of Democratization
in the Greater Horn of Africa*
KIDANE MENGISTEAB (ED.)

The Struggle for Land & Justice in Kenya
AMBREENA MANJI

Imperialism & Development
NICHOLAS WESTCOTT

Kamba Proverbs from Eastern Kenya
JEREMIAH M. KITUNDA

Contested Sustainability
STEFANO PONTE, CHRISTINE NOE
& DAN BROCKINGTON (EDS)

Reimagining the Gendered Nation
CHRISTINA KENNY

Decolonising State & Society in Uganda
K. BRUCE-LOCKHART, J. L. EARLE,
N. B. MUSISI & E. C. TAYLOR (EDS)

*Kenya's and Zambia's Relations with
China 1949–2019*
JODIE YUZHOU SUN

A Political Ecology of Kenya's Mau Forest
LISA ELENA FUCHS

EASTERN AFRICAN STUDIES

These titles published in the United States and Canada by Ohio University Press

Revealing Prophets
Edited by DAVID M. ANDERSON
& DOUGLAS H. JOHNSON

East African Expressions of Christianity
Edited by THOMAS SPEAR
& ISARIA N. KIMAMBO

The Poor Are Not Us
Edited by DAVID M. ANDERSON
& VIGDIS BROCH-DUE

Potent Brews
JUSTIN WILLIS

Swahili Origins
JAMES DE VERE ALLEN

Being Maasai
Edited by THOMAS SPEAR
& RICHARD WALLER

Jua Kali Kenya
KENNETH KING

Control & Crisis in Colonial Kenya
BRUCE BERMAN

Unhappy Valley
Book One: State & Class
Book Two: Violence & Ethnicity
BRUCE BERMAN
& JOHN LONSDALE

Mau Mau from Below
GREET KERSHAW

The Mau Mau War in Perspective
FRANK FUREDI

Squatters & the Roots of Mau Mau 1905–63
TABITHA KANOGO

Economic & Social Origins of Mau Mau 1945–53
DAVID W. THROUP

Multi-Party Politics in Kenya
DAVID W. THROUP
& CHARLES HORNSBY

Empire State-Building
JOANNA LEWIS

Decolonization & Independence in Kenya 1940–93
Edited by B.A. OGOT
& WILLIAM R. OCHIENG'

Eroding the Commons
DAVID ANDERSON

Penetration & Protest in Tanzania
ISARIA N. KIMAMBO

Custodians of the Land
Edited by GREGORY MADDOX,
JAMES L. GIBLIN
& ISARIA N. KIMAMBO

Education in the Development of Tanzania 1919–1990
LENE BUCHERT

The Second Economy in Tanzania
T.L. MALIYAMKONO
& M.S.D. BAGACHWA

Ecology Control & Economic Development in East African History
HELGE KJEKSHUS

Siaya
DAVID WILLIAM COHEN
& E.S. ATIENO ODHIAMBO

Uganda Now • Changing Uganda Developing Uganda • From Chaos to Order • Religion & Politics in East Africa
Edited by HOLGER BERNT
HANSEN & MICHAEL TWADDLE

Kakungulu & the Creation of Uganda 1868–1928
MICHAEL TWADDLE

Controlling Anger
SUZETTE HEALD

Kampala Women Getting By
SANDRA WALLMAN

Political Power in Pre-Colonial Buganda
RICHARD J. REID

Alice Lakwena & the Holy Spirits
HEIKE BEHREND

Slaves, Spices & Ivory in Zanzibar
ABDUL SHERIFF

Zanzibar Under Colonial Rule
Edited by ABDUL SHERIFF
& ED FERGUSON

The History & Conservation of Zanzibar Stone Town
Edited by ABDUL SHERIFF

Pastimes & Politics
LAURA FAIR

Ethnicity & Conflict in the Horn of Africa
Edited by KATSUYOSHI FUKUI
& JOHN MARKAKIS

Conflict, Age & Power in North East Africa
Edited by EISEI KURIMOTO
& SIMON SIMONSE

Property Rights & Political Development in Ethiopia & Eritrea
SANDRA FULLERTON
JOIREMAN

Revolution & Religion in Ethiopia
ØYVIND M. EIDE

Brothers at War
TEKESTE NEGASH
& KJETIL TRONVOLL

From Guerrillas to Government
DAVID POOL

Mau Mau & Nationhood
Edited by E.S. ATIENO
ODHIAMBO & JOHN LONSDALE

A History of Modern Ethiopia, 1855–1991(2nd edn)
BAHRU ZEWDE

Pioneers of Change in Ethiopia
BAHRU ZEWDE

Remapping Ethiopia
Edited by W. JAMES, D.
DONHAM, E. KURIMOTO
& A. TRIULZI

Southern Marches of Imperial Ethiopia
Edited by DONALD L. DONHAM
& WENDY JAMES

A Modern History of the Somali (4th edn)
I.M. LEWIS

Islands of Intensive Agriculture in East Africa
Edited by MATS WIDGREN
& JOHN E.G. SUTTON

Leaf of Allah
EZEKIEL GEBISSA

Dhows & the Colonial Economy of Zanzibar 1860–1970
ERIK GILBERT

African Womanhood in Colonial Kenya
TABITHA KANOGO

African Underclass
ANDREW BURTON

In Search of a Nation
Edited by GREGORY H.
MADDOX & JAMES L. GIBLIN

A History of the Excluded
JAMES L. GIBLIN

Black Poachers, White Hunters
EDWARD I. STEINHART

Ethnic Federalism
DAVID TURTON

Crisis & Decline in Bunyoro
SHANE DOYLE

Emancipation without Abolition in German East Africa
JAN-GEORG DEUTSCH

Women, Work & Domestic Virtue in Uganda 1900–2003
GRACE BANTEBYA KYOMU-
HENDO & MARJORIE
KENISTON McINTOSH

Cultivating Success in Uganda
GRACE CARSWELL

War in Pre-Colonial Eastern Africa
RICHARD REID

Slavery in the Great Lakes Region of East Africa
Edited by HENRI MÉDARD &
SHANE DOYLE

The Benefits of Famine
DAVID KEEN

www.ingramcontent.com/pod-product-compliance
Lightning Source LLC
Chambersburg PA
CBHW070802230426
43665CB00017B/2453